T0278687

COLORADO FAMILY OUTDOOR ADVENTURE

Colorado Family Outdoor Adventure

An All-Ages Guide to Hiking, Camping, and Getting Outside

HEATHER MUNDT

University of New Mexico Press • Albuquerque

© 2022 by Heather Mundt
All rights reserved. Published 2022
Printed in the United States of America

ISBN 978-0-8263-6377-0 (paperback)
ISBN 978-0-8263-6378-7 (e-book)

Library of Congress Cataloging-in-Publication
Data is on file with the Library of Congress.

Founded in 1889, the University of
New Mexico sits on the traditional homelands
of the Pueblo of Sandia. The original peoples
of New Mexico—Pueblo, Navajo, and Apache—
since time immemorial have deep connections
to the land and have made significant
contributions to the broader community state-
wide. We honor the land itself and those
who remain stewards of this land throughout
the generations and also acknowledge our
committed relationship to Indigenous peoples.
We gratefully recognize our history.

Cover photo by Michael Mundt
Maps by Mindy Basinger Hill
Composed in Minion Pro and Gotham

THANKS TO MY ADVENTURING FAMILY:

My mom, Kathy, for sending me outside as a kid
and always being my biggest fan.

My husband, Michael, for sharing
your adventuresome spirit; it's made me braver.

My mother-in-law, Linda,
for nurturing your son's love of travel.

My beloved boys, Brody and Colin,
for serving as the inspirations for every word of this book.
I'm a better writer and human for being your mom.

Contents

Preface

'm proud to be a third-generation Coloradan and was lucky enough to grow up and remain in Longmont, situated along the Front Range within view of the Rocky Mountains to the west. My parents were born and raised in the plains and farmlands of northeastern Colorado in a tiny town called Peetz—what I've nicknamed "Barely, Colorado," roughly 25 miles northeast of Sterling and 1 mile from the Nebraska border—where they learned to appreciate the outdoors.

And while we weren't an "extreme" backcountry family, my mom and dad were always taking my sister and me outside. There are lots of 1970s-era photos of us playing in the dirt and swimming or fishing in mountain reservoirs where my parents would be camping or hunting with friends.

We might not have spent every summer weekend hiking Colorado's Fourteeners (14ers)—peaks topping 14,000 feet or more in elevation—or backpacking toward remote campsites. But any time we hosted out-of-town visitors, we made sure to visit Estes Park, the eastern gateway to Rocky Mountain National Park just an hour from our home. And while we may not have spent winter weekends skiing or snowshoeing, we were most certainly out sledding and playing in the snow at every chance.

My parents provided just enough experiences as a child for me to foster a greater love for outdoor adventures as I grew older (although I have yet to develop a true love of camping, if I'm being honest). So by the time I was in high school and college, I was hiking and mountain biking in those Rocky Mountains. As I entered my twenties, I was snowshoeing to those backcountry huts with my husband, Michael, and learning to ski. And now as parents, we're getting a taste of it all as we explore Colorado with our two sons, Brody and Colin, fourth-generation Coloradans.

And that's really the whole point of this book: to inspire parents and grandparents—anyone, really—who want to travel with children in Colorado's outdoors in whatever capacity suits them. Whether that's climbing or driving to the top of a 14er, schussing the slopes or sledding them, glamping or camping, this book is for you. Young or old, American or foreign, outdoor adventurer or couch potato, a first-time visitor to the state or a resident seeking a new spot to explore in the Centennial State, I promise there's something here for you.

Acknowledgments

Thanks to my *Outdoor Families Magazine* friends Jennifer Fontaine, founder and managing editor, and Erin Kirkland, chief editor, who hired me in 2014 following several years away from freelancing. My work for you is what got me this gig; thank you for taking a chance on me. Thanks to all the convention and visitors bureaus (CVB) that helped check facts and offer area highlights—particularly Colorado Tourism and Visit Denver, which helped me create part of Denver's section—and to Lindsay Diamond from VistaWorks, who educated me on parts of my state I never knew to visit. To my friends and neighbors who love me after ignoring them for months, thanks for your encouragement. (Thanks to Annie, Becky, and Jen for reading sections.) To my husband and boys, I'm grateful for your contributions to this book (especially Michael's proofreading and photography skills!). Finally, thanks to my favorite University of Colorado at Boulder journalism professor, Doug Cosper, who told me one day in my first news-writing class in 2000, "You know, you're pretty good at this!" I feel indebted that you believed in my writing before I did.

Introduction

amily travel is equal parts adventure and education, offering a living classroom for the children who join us on vacation. I kept that in mind as I wrote, offering some historical context because kids love learning, especially when they don't know it's happening! After all, for me, the goal of family travel goes beyond making memories (although that's important too). It is also to provide context for our kids so they can appreciate their experiences and grow into good stewards of the lands they're experiencing.

The prospect of writing *Colorado Family Outdoor Adventure* was daunting with so many wonderful places to see. It's also the first Colorado title in the Southwest Adventure Series to publish and the only family-travel guide for the state. I tried to get it right. But I can't be an expert on every Colorado city, so I focused on offering the very best options for the average traveling family, like mine.

For instance, we're not a backpacking family with extensive backcountry experience, although we've gone on excursions that require both. In other words, you won't find any hardcore mountaineering advice here.

And while we love to ski, we're not skiing experts, so I've offered only the most basic information on Colorado's ski resorts, noting my family's favorites in sections throughout the book. The same goes for hiking and camping, both of which my family loves, although we wouldn't consider ourselves experts in either.

I wanted to offer readers the most distilled information that I can, focusing on those places and activities I've experienced myself or know about as an institution in Colorado. (Everything I include in this book is an activity or destination I've either experienced or would experience with my own kids.) Basically, I tried my best to give a wide variety of adventures, from soft to extreme, in an array of places to serve a range of families, including some indoor options.

Keep in mind, too, that I've probably missed a lot, both because I wrote this book during a pandemic and simply due to lack of space. I tried to see all of Colorado's lesser-known corners—between solo and family road trips, driving more than 5,600 miles in summer 2020*—but didn't come close. If I've missed a big destination or fact (I see you, Carbondale, Hotchkiss, and more!), let me know. Maybe I can include it in future editions.

*Although we've returned to some version of "normal" since the pandemic, some tourism businesses may not have survived to this book's publication. Verify all information before your visit.

How to Use This Guide

Regions of Colorado

This book divides the state into eight different regions as defined by the Colorado Tourism Office (CTO, www.colorado.com): The Great West, Mountains and Mesas, Rockies Playground, Denver and Cities of the Rockies, Pikes Peak Wonders, Mystic San Luis Valley, Pioneering Plains, and Canyons and Plains. Thank you, CTO, for allowing me to reference these regions in outlining this book's chapters.

"Other Highlights" Entries

This is an outdoor guide, but I included a handful of natural-history and Native American museums, as well as those with an outdoor element, to give context to an area or highlight. Where possible, I've also included hours open and tried to confirm them. But, again, the pandemic changed everything in travel, so double-check before visiting.

Lodging Entries

This book focuses heavily on lodges, RV spots, and campsites, with a smattering of hotels that are unique or offer extensive outdoor activities. I didn't include campsites in every location, mainly due to space issues. I've also included addresses and phone numbers for campsites without listing a web address because they're all likely searchable at www.recreation.gov or the US Department of Agriculture Forest Service, www.fs.usda.gov. If the property does not fall under one of these two domains, I've included the specific site. All Kampgrounds of America (KOAs) can be searched at www.koa.com. (I'm partial to "kamping," so several are listed.) And any properties managed by the Bureau of Land Management (BLM) can be researched at www.blm.gov.

A Guide to Costs

Instead of including prices for each activity or destination, this guidebook series indicates price ranges with the "$" icon. Following is a general guide to costs based on research and my personal experience. (Note that senior citizens, military members, and students often receive a discount on any range I list here.)

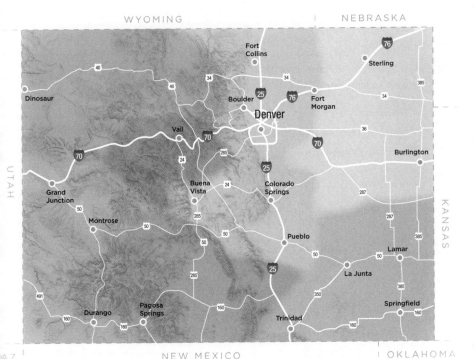

REGIONS OF COLORADO

● The Great West   ● Mountains and Mesas   ● Rockies Playground   ● Denver and Cities of the Rockies

● Pikes Peak Wonders   ● Mystic San Luis Valley   ● Pioneering Plains   ● Canyons and Plains

LODGING

A search of "average hotel room cost" per day nets answers ranging from $99 to around $180. Here's how I communicated lodging prices:

NO "$" LISTED = below $100 per night. Specifically, campgrounds and many "glamping" campgrounds need no pricing icon because they are typically understood to be the best value for travelers.

$ = an average cost per night of $100–$200

$$ = above-average cost per night, roughly $200–$300

$$$ = pricey or more than $300 to stay per night. This applies to expensive lodges and any dude ranches listed (which also tend to offer food and activities in that price).

MUSEUMS

I had to estimate museum entries because we're dealing with multigenerational travel, but the average is around $6. I also try to mention free entries. Admission ranges are as follows (child and adult):

NO "$" LISTED = average cost for entry or below $10

$ = above-average cost for entry, roughly up to $20

$$ = more than $20 for entry, of which there are few in this book

ACTIVITIES

I estimate an average activity cost around $35 for kids, $45 for adults:

NO "$" LISTED = below-average cost for entry for kids/adults

$ = roughly $50–$100 for entry per person

$$ = more than $100 for entry. This often includes animal encounters, extreme endeavors such as whitewater rafting and climbing, or full-day tours with meals.

About Hosted Trips

Journalists are often hosted at destinations—thank you to spots that hosted me for this book—which allows us to experience a wider variety of places at a minimal cost. (There are almost always fees associated with hosted trips, like tipping.) We've funded most of our family travels in Colorado, and I've never been paid to write positive opinions.

About Colorful Colorado

Named after the Spanish word "colored red" for the ruddy, red silt that 16th-century Spanish explorers noticed floating down the "Rio Colorado," Colorado's history is a mix of Native American culture and that of homesteaders, explorers, railroad builders, and outdoorsmen. The country's 8th-largest state became the 38th state on August 1, 1876, nicknamed the Centennial State for its admittance 100 years after the signing of the Declaration of Independence. Denver is roughly a mile above sea level, earning its nickname, Mile High City. The 15th step on the state capitol building marks that with the engraved words "One Mile Above Sea Level." Its lowest altitude is 3,315 feet, the Arikaree River, near Wray.

Getting Here

Colorado's largest airport is Denver International Airport (DIA), the country's fifth busiest, with about 64 million passengers traveling through annually. Featuring the iconic tented-roof structure—meant to mimic the peaks of the Rocky Mountains, Native American tepees, and other themes—it's a hub for United, Southwest, and Frontier. Located only 23 miles from downtown Denver—arrive in 30–40 minutes via airport rail line—its most recognizable resident, Luis Jiménez's "Blue Mustang" fiberglass sculpture, has been "guarding" the airport from a median on Peña Boulevard since 2008. 8500 Peña Blvd., 303.342.2000, www.flydenver.com.

WESTIN DENVER INTERNATIONAL AIRPORT

Travelers arriving late at night or departing in the early-morning hours ($) appreciate this hotel, located steps from the airport. Including more than 500 soundproofed rooms, a fitness center, an indoor heated pool and on-site dining, the 82,000-square-foot, open-air plaza between the airport and hotel offers a spot for free activities like live music and a winter ice-skating rink. 8300 Peña Blvd., 303.317.1800, www.marriott.com.

I-70 WEST AND THE EISENHOWER TUNNEL

The main route between the Denver area to nearby mountain destinations is Interstate 70 West (I-70), and anyone who's driven it knows it is often disastrously crowded. Indeed, while winter was once the main season for this road to become a veritable parking lot, it now attracts at least as much traffic in the summer. And that brings me to what we locals refer to as "the tunnel," officially known as the Eisenhower–Edwin C. Johnson Memorial Tunnel or the Eisenhower Tunnel, a 1.7-mile, four-lane passageway through the Continental Divide.

The highest vehicular tunnel in the United States (average elevation: 11,112 feet), approximately 60 miles west of Denver on I-70, the westbound portion named for President Dwight D. Eisenhower was completed in 1973. (The eastbound portion, completed in 1979, is named for Edwin C. Johnson, the former US Senator who lobbied for the interstate across Colorado.) An engineering feat that allows vehicles to drive under Loveland Pass, it's also known to Coloradans roughly as "the place where we get stuck."

Whether closed due to icy roads, a car wreck, or a semi needing to pass through it with hazardous materials, Coloradans know to plan a trip to the mountains with tunnel traffic in mind. That means on any given Friday afternoon or early evening, you're taking your chances on getting stuck for hours, particularly at said tunnel, where bad winter weather is often worse on the other side. Further, the steep grade down toward the first town, Dillon, is often icy and difficult to negotiate in winter months, even for locals. If you're not accustomed to winter roads, it's worthwhile to hire a shuttle service.

The same goes for I-70 East on a Sunday afternoon or early evening, when most Coloradans are returning to the Denver-metro area after a weekend in the high country. (Long holiday weekends are similarly nightmarish.) Basically, we Coloradans always pay attention to I-70 traffic. Beyond that, good luck!

Pro Tip: The Colorado Department of Transportation offers the Bustang, a daily west route along I-70 (with Wi-Fi, bathrooms, and bike racks) that includes eight stops, including Frisco, Vail, and Glenwood Springs. Or try the Snowstang, offering forty days of service to three ski areas: Loveland, Arapahoe Basin, and Steamboat Springs (www.ridebustang.com). Passengers can board at Denver Union Station (1701 Wynkoop St., 303.592.6712) or the Denver Federal Center (695 Kipling St., 888.999.4777).

Suggested Itineraries

Here are two itineraries that are similar to ones we've experienced as a family:

Southwest Colorado

DAY ONE

Begin in Alamosa (Mystic San Luis Valley) to sand board or sled in the Great Sand Dunes National Park and Preserve. On the way back to Alamosa, there are two fun stops just 6 miles apart: the Colorado Gators Reptile Park, followed by one of Colorado's quirkiest attractions, the UFO Watchtower.

DAY TWO

Travel 80 miles southwest for a night in Pagosa Springs at the Springs Resort and Spa. Spend the day soaking in one of its 24 pools and cool off in the San Juan River. Stop for lunch or breakfast at Pagosa Baking Company (238 Pagosa St., 970.264.9358, www.pagosabakingcompany.com).

DAY THREE

Head 60 miles due west to the historic town of Durango. Take a two-hour family rafting trip on the Animas River with Durango Rafting Company. Grab a bite in historic downtown, leaving room for Rocky Mountain Chocolate Factory treats.

DAY FOUR

The trip to Silverton will take a full day, but the journey is about as scenic as any in the state. Choose the one-way Durango and Silverton Narrow Gauge Railroad trip, about four hours. Spend as long as you can in this remote town—we loved the San Juan County Historical Society Museum and Mining Heritage Center—stopping in one of the many eateries along Blair Street. Take the 80-minute bus ride home.

DAY FIVE

Drive about 35 miles southwest of Durango to Mesa Verde National Park and stay in the park's Far View Lodge. Book ranger-led tours of Balcony House and Cliff Palace—squeeze the Long House one in if you get a chance—and stop by the Chapin Mesa Archaeological Museum.

Dinosaurs around Denver

DAY ONE

Head to the Denver Museum of Nature and Science to visit Prehistoric Journey, where an 80-foot-Diplodocus towers overhead. Watch scientists work on fossils in the Schlessman Family Laboratory of Earth Sciences, then see an IMAX® film (2000 Colorado Blvd., 303.370.6000, www.dmns.org). Drive about 30 minutes southwest for a stay in The Dino Hotel (Best Western Denver Southwest), featuring museum-quality casts, the Jurassic pit for digging, and a pool designed in the shape of the Western Interior Cretaceous Seaway. If time allows, visit the Morrison Natural History Museum, where kids can work on a real fossil specimen. Eat dinner at the hotel's Paleo Joe's Bar and Grill.

DAY TWO

Enjoy a breakfast-hour chat at the hotel's interactive fossil table before heading to Golden's 1.5-mile Triceratops Trail. Then explore both sides of Dinosaur Ridge: Golden's 3-mile, self-guided tour of the track site and Morrison's view of a 24-foot-long trackway from a duck-billed dinosaur (www.dinoridge.org). Explore Red Rocks Park and Amphitheatre, right next door. Eat dinner at the town's popular Mexican restaurant, Morrison Inn (301 Bear Creek Ave., 303.697.6650, www.morrisoninn.com).

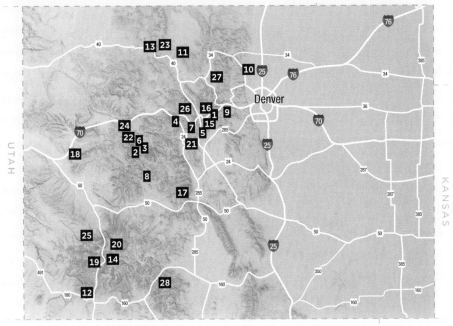

COLORADO SKI AREAS

1 Arapahoe Basin Ski Area*
28194 U.S. Hwy. 6
Keystone, CO 80435
888.ARAPAHOE or
970.468.0718
www.arapahoebasin.com

2 Aspen Highlands
199 Prospector Rd,
Aspen, CO 81611
970.923.1227
www.aspensnowmass.com

3 Aspen Mountain
601 E. Dean St.
970.923.1227
www.aspensnowmass.com

4. Beaver Creek Resort
210 Beaver Creek Plaza
Beaver Creek, CO 81620
970.754.4636
www.beavercreek.com

5 Breckenridge Ski Resort
1599 Ski Hill Rd.
Breckenridge, CO 80424
970.453.5000
www.breckenridge.com

6 Buttermilk Ski Resort
38700 CO-82
Aspen, CO 81611
970.923.1227
www.aspensnowmass.com

7 Copper Mountain Ski Resort
209 Ten Mile Cir.
866.841.2481
www.coppercolorado.com

**8 Crested Butte
Mountain Resort**
12 Snowmass Rd.
Crested Butte, CO 81225
970.349.2222
www.skicb.com

9 Echo Mountain Resort*
19285 Hwy 103, Idaho Springs,
CO 80452
720.899.2100
www.echomntn.com

10 Eldora Mountain*
2861 Eldora Ski Rd.
Nederland, CO 80466
303.440.8700
www.eldora.com

11 Granby Ranch*
1000 Village Rd.
Granby, CO 80446
888.850.4615
www.granbyranch.com

12 Hesperus Ski Area*
9848 Highway, US-160
Hesperus, CO 81326
970.385.2199
www.ski-hesperus.com

13 Howelsen Hill
Howelsen Pkwy.
Steamboat Springs, CO 80487
970.879.8499
steamboatsprings.net/131/
Howelsen-Hill-Ski-Area

Colorado's Ski Areas

What Is a Colorado Gems Resort?

These 11 lesser-known resorts throughout the state are broadly smaller and less expensive than some of the bigger names, says Chris Linsmayer, the former public affairs director of Colorado Ski Country USA (CSCUSA), a nonprofit trade association representing 23 of Colorado's 28 ski resorts.

"The Gems Resorts offer guests a different experience than they might find at a larger resort," Linsmayer says. "Many of them are more budget-conscious, and are great for families to learn and get started in skiing and snowboarding. The CSCUSA Gems Card is arguably the best deal in Colorado skiing that many people don't know about."

A $30 discount card offering two, two-for-one lift tickets or two 30-percent-off lift tickets (based on a resort's current window price for a full-day adult lift ticket), it can be used twice at each resort, or 22 times. These smaller mountains are short on crowds but big on value.

"They're especially great for families that are new to the sports of skiing and snowboarding," he says. They're also great for "those that are looking for a different experience than the larger resort experience, those that are looking for a more budget-conscious experience, and those that want to get out and explore different ski areas across Colorado, as the Gems resorts are located all over the state." www.coloradoski.com.

14 **Kendall Mountain Ski Area***
1 Kendall Place
Silverton, CO 81433
970.387.5522
www.skikendall.com

15 **Keystone Resort**
100 Dercum Square
Keystone, CO 80435
855.603.0049
www.keystoneresort.com

16 **Loveland Ski Area***
I-70
Dillon, CO 80435
303.571.5580
www.skiloveland.com

17 **Monarch Mountain***
23715 U.S. Hwy 50
Salida, CO 81201
719.530.5000
www.skimonarch.com

18 **Powderhorn Mountain Resort***
48338 Powderhorn Rd.
Mesa, CO, 81643
970.268.5700
www.powderhorn.com

19 **Purgatory Resort**
#1 Skier Place
Durango, CO 81301
970.247.9000
www.purgatoryresort.com

20. **Silverton Mountain Ski Area**
6226 State Hwy 110
Silverton, CO 81433
970.387.5706
www.silvertonmountain.com

21 **Ski Cooper***
232 CR 29
Leadville, CO 80461.
719.486.2277
www.skicooper.com

22 **Snowmass**
120 Lower Carriage Way
Snowmass Village, CO 81615
www.aspensnowmass.com

23 **Steamboat Ski and Resort Corporation**
2305 Mt. Werner Cir.
Steamboat Springs, CO 80487
970.879.6111
www.steamboat.com

24 **Sunlight Mountain Resort***
10901 CR 117
Glenwood Springs, CO 81601
970.945.7491
www.sunlightmtn.com

25 **Telluride Ski Resort**
565 Mountain Village Blvd.
Telluride, CO 81435
800.778.8581
www.tellurideskiresort.com

26 **Vail Ski Resort**
Vail, CO 81657
970.SKI.VAIL (754.8245)
www.vail.com

27 **Winter Park Resort**
85 Parsenn Rd.
Winter Park, CO 80482
877.353.1901
www.winterparkresort.com

28 **Wolf Creek Ski Area**
E. Hwy 160 E.
Pagosa Springs, CO 81147
970.264.5639
www.wolfcreekski.com

* Gems Resort

Colorado's Fourteeners

Ten Tips for Hiking Colorado's Fourteeners

We Coloradans are proud to have 58 named Fourteeners (14ers)—peaks topping 14,000 feet or higher, with Mt. Elbert near Leadville earning the highest at 14,433 feet,* more than any other state. (Alaska boasts the next-highest number at 29.) So "peak bagging" is a popular pastime, both for Coloradans and visitors alike. (They're ranked by Class I, easy hiking, to Class V, most difficult.) But given their high altitude and Colorado's often-extreme weather, it's important to follow some basic guidelines first.

1. Acclimate. Experts suggest waiting a minimum of one to three days to get used to higher elevations, where there's less oxygen than at lower altitudes.

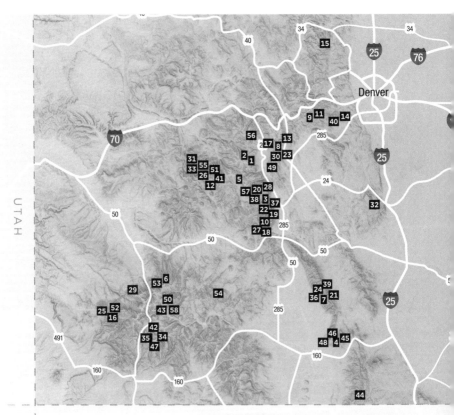

2. Start early. Weather in Colorado can be quite unpredictable. Begin early in the day to minimize exposure to storms (and hiking in the dark).

3. Go the easy route. Don't pick the most grueling hike for your first attempt, such as the journey up Longs Peak (14,255 feet).

4. Hydrate. The general rule of thumb is roughly 1 liter of water (about 32 ounces) per adult for every two hours of hiking, and more if it's hot or humid. Everyone should carry their own hydration system—adult water bladders range from 1 liter to 3, kids' versions are roughly 1.5 liters—so they get enough to drink.

5. Pack a first aid kit. Bring basic supplies such as Band-Aids, antibiotic cream, and pain relievers, since scrapes and blisters are common hiking hazards.

COMPLETE LIST OF COLORADO 14ERS AND ELEVATIONS

#	Peak	Elev.	#	Peak	Elev.	#	Peak	Elev.
1	Mt. Elbert	14,433	21	Crestone Needle	14,197	41	Conundrum Peak*	14,060
2	Mt. Massive	14,421	22	Mt. Yale	14,196	42	Sunlight Peak	14,059
3	Mt. Harvard	14,420	23	Mt. Bross	14,172	43	Handies Peak	14,048
4	Blanca Peak	14,345	24	Kit Carson Peak	14,165	44	Culebra Peak	14,047
5	La Plata Peak	14,336	25	El Diente Peak*	14,159	45	Mt. Lindsey	14,042
6	Uncompahgre Peak	14,309	26	Maroon Peak	14,156	46	Ellingwood Point	14,042
7.	Crestone Peak	14,294	27	Tabeguache Peak	14,155	47	North Eolus*	14,039
8	Mt. Lincoln	14,286	28	Mt. Oxford	14,153	48	Little Bear Peak	14,037
9	Grays Peak	14,270	29	Mt. Sneffels	14,150	49	Mt. Sherman	14,036
10	Mt. Antero	14,269	30	Mt. Democrat	14,148	50	Redcloud Peak	14,034
11	Torreys Peak	14,267	31	Capitol Peak	14,130	51	Pyramid Peak	14,018
12	Castle Peak	14,265	32	Pikes Peak	14,110	52	Wilson Peak	14,017
13	Quandary Peak	14,265	33	Snowmass Mountain	14,092	53	Wetterhorn Peak	14,015
14.	Mt. Evans	14,264	34	Windom Peak	14,087	54	San Luis Peak	14,014
15.	Longs Peak	14,255	35	Mt. Eolus	14,083	55	North Maroon Peak*	14,014
16.	Mt. Wilson	14,246	36	Challenger Point	14,081	56	Mt. of the Holy Cross	14,005
17	Mt. Cameron*	14,238	37	Mt. Columbia	14,073	57	Huron Peak	14,003
18	Mt. Shavano	14,229	38	Missouri Mountain	14,067	58	Sunshine Peak	14,001
19	Mt. Princeton	14,197	39	Humboldt Peak	14,064			
20	Mt. Belford	14,197	40	Mt. Bierstadt	14,060			

* To be ranked a 14er, a peak must rise at least 300 feet above the saddle connecting it to the nearest 14er, if there's one adjacent. These five do not meet that criterium but are recognized as 14ers on US Geological Survey maps and by Colorado Tourism.

Source: www.14ers.com, a go-to site for updated elevations, routes, trail conditions, etc.

6. Dress in layers. Temperatures and weather vary greatly, so begin with a wicking base layer that keeps moisture away from the skin. Top with a pullover or a sweatshirt, followed by a rain jacket or waterproof layer. (I swear it always rains when I don't pack the latter!) Wear comfortable hiking shoes or boots.

7. Prepare for all weather. It's common to experience a wide range of weather conditions in one Colorado day, especially at higher elevations, where it can be much colder than where you began. Make sure to bring everything from sunscreen—the chance of sunburning increases with elevation as the atmosphere decreases—to winter hats and gloves.

8. Stash snacks. Kids are *always* hungry. But it's especially important to bring extra food when undertaking several hours of physical activity, such as a lunch and plenty of snacks that travel well including bars, nuts, and fruit.

9. Understand altitude sickness. The mildest form is called acute mountain sickness (AMS), caused by rapid exposure to low oxygen at high elevations. Common symptoms include headaches, dizziness, and fatigue, even vomiting. If someone in your party starts exhibiting signs of AMS, the cure is to get to lower elevations as quickly and safely as possible—in other words, head back down the trail. There's no shame in ending a hike if AMS symptoms appear.

10. Manage expectations. Tackling a big hike may rank low on many kids' priority lists. Be sure to communicate with them so they understand the challenges ahead and that it's all right to turn around if necessary. Parents: You're not a failure if you don't complete the trek!

*According to www.14ers.com. The official Colorado Tourism Office elevation of Mt. Elbert is 14,440 feet.

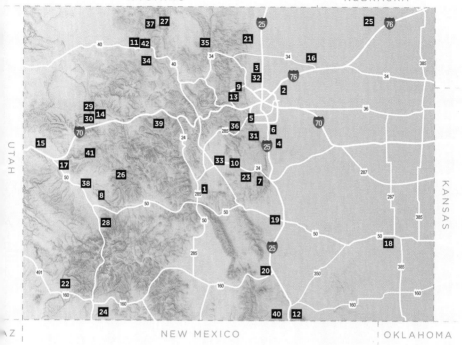

COLORADO'S STATE PARKS

1	Arkansas Headwaters Recreation Area (AHRA)	15	Highline Lake	29	Rifle Falls	
2	Barr Lake	16	Jackson Lake	30	Rifle Gap	
3	Boyd Lake	17	James M. Robb– Colorado River	31	Roxborough	
4	Castlewood Canyon	18	John Martin Reservoir	32	St. Vrain	
5	Chatfield	19	Lake Pueblo	33	Spinney Mountain	
6	Cherry Creek	20	Lathrop	34	Stagecoach	
7	Cheyenne Mountain	21	Lory	35	State Forest	
8	Crawford	22	Mancos	36	Staunton	
9	Eldorado Canyon	23	Mueller	37	Steamboat Lake	
10	Eleven Mile	24	Navajo	38	Sweitzer Lake	
11	Elkhead Reservoir	25	North Sterling	39	Sylvan Lake	
12	Fishers Peak (2020)*	26	Paonia	40	Trinidad Lake	
13	Golden Gate Canyon	27	Pearl Lake	41	Vega	
14	Harvey Gap	28	Ridgway	42	Yampa River	

* This park is not listed within this book because it is new and therefore offers few services.

THE GREAT WEST

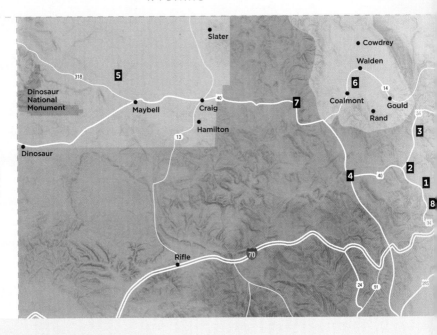

THE GREAT WEST

Fraser

Located near the western base of Berthoud Pass along US Highway 40 just 6 miles northwest of Winter Park, the Fraser Valley area drew settlers in the 1880s such as ranchers and lumbermen for its lush timber and plentiful wide-open spaces. Incorporated as Fraser in 1953, the town is often referred to in tandem with Winter Park (Winter Park/Fraser) because of their close proximity. In fact, we often rent properties in Fraser when skiing Winter Park because it's less expensive and easier to find lodging, plus there's a free shuttle bus to the ski area. www.visitgrandcounty.com.

Other Highlights

The 16.1-mile Fraser to Granby Trail, set along US Highway 40 between Fraser and Granby (easy to intermediate), is popular for biking, hiking, cross-country skiing, or snowshoeing. Surrounded by towering peaks and old mining homesteads, it passes highlights like Snow Mountain Ranch (see below) and Granby Ranch.

The High Country Stampede and Rodeo takes place every Saturday night in July and August. The junior rodeo begins at 3 p.m.; main performance at 7 p.m. Make an evening of it with a Chuck Wagon BBQ dinner. 245 Winter Park Dr., 970.449.9040, www .highcountrystampede.com.

Colorado Adventure Park

Situated next to the Fraser Tubing Hill, this spot includes areas with snow stacked high for steeper descent, and even a couple of bumps midway for extra thrills. Parents beware: You *must* watch the tubers coming down so no one gets knocked over, especially little riders. Helmets are required for tubers under age 18 and are available for rent. Ages 3 to 5 must ride with an adult.

The hill features a conveyor lift and a warming hut with bathrooms and concessions. Fat bikes, snowshoes, and mini-snowmobile rentals are available (Thurs.–Sun.). Open daily through season, 10 a.m.–10 p.m., 566 CR 721, 970.726.5779, www.coloradoadventurepark.com.

Devil's Thumb Ranch Resort and Spa

Set amid 6,500 acres of privately owned wilderness at the base of the Continental Divide in the small town of Tabernash (7 miles northeast of Fraser), Devil's Thumb Ranch is the definition of Rocky Mountain luxury. A year-round guest ranch resort, spa, and corporate retreat, it's also the go-to place for some of the world's best cross-country skiing experiences. During our stay, we took a two-hour cross-country skiing lesson, which made me feel less clumsy on the longer, narrower skis. Our boys also loved the sleigh ride, exploring the property on an open-air sled and watching the horses while keeping warm under heavy blankets. Afterward, we drank hot chocolate and met the various barn animals, including chickens, sheep, and goats.

In addition to using 75 miles of Nordic trails along the stunning Ranch Creek Valley, guests can also snowshoe, ice-skate on an outdoor ice rink, or go tubing or fat-biking. Families will especially love feeding the horses treats in the morning hours, or, at night, stargazing with the help of a guest astronomer. There's also a half-day Cowpoke Camp for kids ages 5–12 if Mom and Dad want some adults-only trail time. (Or rent a sled and pull the littles behind you!)

The resort also includes a spa with a steam room, dry sauna, outdoor hot tub, and a geothermally heated indoor-outdoor pool. (Kids 13 and older can receive spa treatments.) Year-round offerings include stables and horseback operations, yoga facilities, and 35 miles of trails for hiking and biking. Indoors features a game room and a 37-seat movie theater, in addition to free nightly s'mores at the outdoor fireplace.

The working cattle ranch means guests can also participate in cattle drives, skills training, and trail rides. Seasonal recreation offerings include ziplining, SUPing, and adventure courses in the summer and winter biathlons. Spring through fall, guests of this Orvis-designated fly-fishing lodge can take guided fly-fishing tours on private waters.

There are two main eateries on-site, Heck's Tavern and the Ranch House (in addition to more private dining options), featuring farm-to-table yields such as produce from Kendra's Garden, honey from on-property beehives, or Wagyu beef from the ranch's herd, which visitors can spot on the drive into the property.

Trail passes are available for day visits; free for kids 5 and under. Gear rental available. Sign up for e-mails under "About the Ranch" to get information on midweek discounts (Sun.–Thurs.). 3530 CR 83, 970.726.7000, www.devilsthumbranch.com.

Fraser Tubing Hill

This hill features a lift and gear rental for 60- or 90-minute time slots. (Helmets are recommended but not provided.) Kids must be at least 3 years old, and ages 3–6 must ride with an adult; ages 7–17 can ride alone with adult signature on liability waiver. Slots are 60 or 90 minutes and include tube rental. Arrive 15 minutes before start time. The main building includes a fireplace, bathrooms, and concessions. Open daily through season, 10 a.m.–10 p.m., 455 CR 72, 970.726.5954, www.frasertubinghill.com.

Winter Park Adventure Quest

Located at the Fraser Valley Sports Complex, the aerial course offers a series of 24 obstacles of varying difficulty and a two-person, 25-foot climbing wall. Roughly 90 minutes; children 10 years and younger may participate if accompanied by someone 16 or older. (Children under 5 may enjoy the 35-foot climbing tower.) Concessions available. There's also a guided rock climbing experience on a 35-foot gneiss rock wall in nearby Arapahoe National Forest (beginner and intermediate routes). Open daily, 11 a.m., 2 p.m.; climbing daily, 9 a.m., 3 p.m. Private tours available. 220 CR 522, 970.531.4143, www.wpadventurequest.com.

Meeting the horses on a chilly morning sleigh ride at Devil's Thumb Ranch. Photo by Michael Mundt.

Families seeking a vacation at a Colorado dude ranch need look no further than the Colorado Dude and Guest Ranch Association (CDGRA) member ranches, says CDGRA executive director Courtney Frazier (www.coloradoranch.com). Composed of 22 ranches throughout the state, the member network is "like the AAA of the dude-ranching world," establishing strict standards of excellence such as cleanliness, hospitality, and horse safety.

"We make sure the business is reliable and that they've got all safety measures in place," Frazier says. "We've done all the hard work for you, so all you need to do is find a ranch to meet your expectations for daily activities."

Another good resource is Gene Kilgore's *Ranch Vacations: The Leading Guide to the Best Ranch Vacations in the West* (2020).

"Children may forget what cruise ship they were on, but the amazing thing is that they will always remember the name of the ranch," Kilgore says. "It's one of the few experiences where families can really come together; I think that ranches are sanctuaries in a world that isn't always safe."

Kilgore says the biggest mistake when opting for a ranch vacation is not staying a full week.

"You really need a full six or seven days," he says. "It just takes time to get into the groove and learn the ropes, and to learn to relax and enjoy it."

It's also important to determine what kind of kids' program you want for your family. Do you want to spend the full day with your kids or allow "adult time," when kiddos can hang out with their peers? Be sure the property offers activities you're seeking, whether white-water rafting, hiking, and more.

Regardless, he says, you can't go wrong choosing a dude-ranch vacation in the Centennial State.

"The Colorado high country, the aspens, the mountain peaks," Kilgore says. "As John Denver sang, there really is a Colorado Rocky Mountain high."

Visit www.ranchvacations.com for more information.

Granby

Miles from Denver: 86

Founded in 1905, this former logging and railroad community located just 15 miles from the west entrance of Rocky Mountain National Park (RMNP) offers a ranch-town vibe that is often less hectic (and expensive) than other ski-resort destinations. As the only Designated Colorado Main Street in Grand County, a program that aims to revitalize communities through grassroots efforts, the downtown is a lively mix of restaurants and vibrant street art. Set in the Middle Park high-basin area between Fraser and Grand Lake, it's one of our favorite destinations. www.visitgrandcounty.com.

Lodging

Opened in 2020, River Run RV Resort is 2 miles northwest of town, offering lodging such as Airstream trailers, cabins, and Conestoga wagons. It includes a wellness center, general store, pool, sports complex, two restaurants, and a lake with SUP and kayak rentals. 1051 Summit Trail, 888.303.7027, www.sunrvresorts.com/river-run.

Other Highlights

Hot Sulphur Springs (est. 1860) is a small town roughly 10 miles west of Granby that features the popular resort and springs of the same name. Offering "healing waters" once used by the Ute and Arapaho tribes, it's now a funky collection of indoor and outdoor pools: 18 mineral and 1 chlorine. (Kids under 12 can soak in 9 of them.) Ute Pool is the prettiest (106 degrees); Lupe's is the hottest (109 to 112 degrees). Lodging available. 5609 Spring Rd., 970.725.3306, www.hotsulphursprings.com.

Granby Ranch

Stats: 2 mountains, 37 designated trails, nearly 406 skiable acres, 4 lifts, and a pony lift for beginner ski lessons, 1 terrain park, night skiing

Trail classification: 35 percent Beginner; 40 percent Intermediate; 25 percent Advanced

Base elevation: 8,202 feet

Designed with families in mind, this smaller resort comprises four chair lifts over two mountains: East, offering green and blue trails, and West, with more challenging blue and black ones. There's plenty of skiing for all levels, and all trails lead to the base area so it's easy to meet up with your group. In warmer months, the resort is a popular destination for mountain biking, as well as golfing at the resort's 18-hole Golf Granby Ranch course. www.granby ranch.com.

Lake Granby

Created in 1950 when the Granby Dam was built, Lake Granby is the third-largest body of water in the state. Set on the Colorado River about 5 miles outside of town, there are more than 40 miles of shoreline for fishing, boating, and camping. Camping includes Arapahoe Bay (84 nonelectric tent/ RV sites that include restrooms and potable

Trying out the summer tubing hill at YMCA's Snow Mountain Ranch. Photo by Michael Mundt.

water) and Stillwater (129 tent/RV sites with vault and flush toilets, potable water). The lake also features two marinas: Indian Peaks Marina, with a restaurant and pontoon/cat amaran rentals, open May 15–Oct. 15, 8 a.m.–5 p.m. (6 p.m. weekends) (6862 US Hwy 34, 970.887.3456, www.indianpeaks marina.com); and Beacon Landing, offering boat and canoe rentals, guided fishing trips, and the Marina Shop for snacks and bait, open May–Oct., 7 a.m.–7 p.m., 8 a.m.–5 p.m. after Labor Day (1026 CR 64, 970.627.3671, www.beaconlanding.com). The third one, Highland Marina, burned in the October 2020 East Troublesome Fire.

Snow Mountain Ranch (YMCA of the Rockies)

Officially the YMCA of the Rockies, Snow Mountain Ranch (SMR) is one of the places I most often recommend to families. (There's also a YMCA in Estes Park. See "Denver and Cities of the Rockies.") Located 8 miles south of Granby, there are several lodging options—lodge rooms, cabins, campgrounds (tent and RV), and yurts—with many on-site activities included in the price of a stay such as a mini-golf course, indoor pool, tennis courts, hiking and biking trails, reservoir fishing, lawn games, and the Kiva Recreation Center (roller skating, volleyball, basketball, badminton, tennis, pool, ping pong, etc.). The Schlessman Commons dining hall also serves three buffet-style meals daily. (No alcohol sales, but guests can bring alcohol on property.) Every other Saturday in summer, visitors can enjoy a one-hour "Lollygag with Llamas."

For additional fees, visitors can sign up for crafts, archery, mountain biking, horseback riding (even hayrides), and indoor climbing. The Nordic Center offers lessons and also rents out equipment such as snowshoes, cross-country skis, child carriers, fat bikes, and mountain bikes.

Fast Fact: Operating since 1908, SMR's Camp Chief Ouray (CCO) is the longest-running overnight camp in Colorado. www.campchiefouray.org.

One of its most unique features is the summer tubing hill, a 300-foot-long trail of "snow" made from a stiff, turf-like material that becomes slippery via 200 mist nozzles. The area includes a magic carpet, concessions, restrooms, and picnic tables.

The winter season offers one of SMR's most popular activities: dog sledding. For a fee, ride behind the musher on a 2-mile loop. (Reservations required.) Or meet the canine athletes for free (puppies if you're lucky!). A 50-minute "Long Ride" is also available Friday mornings; one adult and one child (between ages 5 and 10) not to exceed 250 pounds. Summer visitors can still meet the pups in the dog park on Mondays and Fridays for the "Hanging with the Huskies" program. Day passes available for all programming. www.snowmountain ranch.org.

Grand Lake

Miles from Denver: 102

This area is named for Colorado's largest and deepest natural body of water, Grand Lake (150 miles of shoreline), one of three major lakes in the area, including Lake Granby and Shadow Mountain Lake. Called the "Snowmobile Capital of the United States," Grand Lake is among the few places in the country where snowmobiles are allowed on the streets. Also known as the western gateway to RMNP, about 3 miles from the entrance, it may be less recognized than its eastern counterpart, Estes Park. But it's every bit as charming and historic, with shops, galleries, and bars on the historic boardwalk. I'm kinda reluctant to let the secret out! www.visitgrandcounty.com.

Grand Lake

The state's largest natural lake boasts RMNP as a backdrop (bordering it along the east side), offering some of the state's most stunning scenery. The town itself is set on its north shore, along with two marinas. Grand Lake Marina (1132 Lake Ave., 970.627.3401, www.glmarina.com) features rentals (via Boater's Choice) for pontoon/sport boats, kayaks, canoes, and SUPs, as well as the Wake Coffee Shop. Open seasonally 8 a.m.–7 p.m. Headwaters Marina (operated by the town) rents all boat types: fishing, sport, pontoon, and paddle. Scenic, one-hour tours (daily 10:30 a.m., noon, and 2 p.m.) and sunset lake tours available. Open April–Oct., 9 a.m.–5 p.m. (6 p.m. Fri. and Sat.). 1030 Lake Ave., 970.627.3435, www.townofgrandlake.com/headwaters-marina.htm.

Grand Lake Nordic Center

Offering roughly 22 miles of Nordic trails groomed for traditional classic skiing and skate skiing for all levels, as well as snowshoe trails and a tubing hill, Grand Lake Nordic Center also features gear rentals, instruction, concessions, and restrooms. Open Nov.–Mar., 9 a.m.–4 p.m., 1415 CR 48, 970.627.8008, www.grandlakerecreation.com.

Rocky Mountain Amphicar Adventures

Is it a car? Is it a boat? It's an Amphicar, aka "the sports car that swims." Officially the Amphicar Model 770, they were manufactured for civilians in Germany from 1961 to 1965. So few vehicles remain that Grand Lake is one of only three spots in the world to ride in one. (Disney Springs in Lake Buena Vista, Fla., and Branson, Mo., are the

Is it a car? A boat? It's an Amphicar, "the sports car that swims," which visitors can ride in Grand Lake. Photo by Michael Mundt.

others.) The fleet includes four Amphicars offering 30-minute rides for up to four guests. Kids and dogs welcome. Open 9 a.m.–5 p.m., summer only, closed Tues. and Wed., 900 Grand Ave., 303.868.8384, www.rockymountainamphicar.com.

Shadow Mountain Lake (Reservoir)

Bookended by Lake Granby and Grand Lake, connected to the latter by a narrow, shallow waterway (for nonmotorized and small motorized boats to pass), the reservoir was created by Shadow Mountain Dam near the headwaters of the Colorado River. Part of the Arapaho National Recreation Area and bordered on the east side by RMNP, there's plenty to do here year-round: fishing and ice fishing (rainbow and brown trout), jet skiing, boating, and more. The Green Ridge Campground (southern side) features 78 campsites and 2 boat launches. Serving both Grand Lake and Shadow Mountain, the Trail Ridge Marina offers a retail shop with snacks and rents fishing and pontoon boats, SUPs, and kayaks (12634 US Hwy 34, 970.627.3586, www.trailridgemarina.com). A popular hike is along the East Shore Trail, next to the campground and part of the Continental Divide National Scenic Trail—comprising 3,100 miles between Mexico and Canada along the spine of the Rocky Mountains (www.continentaldividetrail.org)—to the Shadow Mountain Overlook Tower (built in 1932). The 9.6-mile roundtrip trek on Shadow Mountain to 9,923 feet (1,533 elevation gain) offers gorgeous views of the lakes and RMNP.

Kremmling

Miles from Denver: 104

This town along Highway 40 roughly 50 miles southeast of Steamboat Springs is called "The Sportsman's Paradise" for its Gold Medal waters on the Colorado and Blue Rivers, as well as the Gore Canyon Whitewater Park that's perfect for rafting and kayaking. Wildlife outnumbers the humans in this town that started in the late 19th century as a general-merchandise store owned by Rudolph Kremmling, and it's said to have some of the best elk hunting in Colorado. It's also considered the "Motorsport Capital of Grand County," offering miles of ATV and OHV trails. www.kremmlingchamber.com.

Lodging

Set at the base of the iconic Kremmling Cliffs, the Muddy Creek Cabins ($) offers 10 structures with kitchenettes (sleep up to 4). 3rd St. and Kinsey Ave., 970.724.9559, www.muddycreekcabins.com.

Bluebird Backcountry

Located at Bear Mountain on the Continental Divide between Steamboat Springs and Kremmling, this "human-powered ski area" debuted in spring 2020. Offering the basic amenities of a traditional ski area—gear rentals and lessons, a lodge and warming hut, and professional ski patrol—just for the backcountry skier and boarder, there are no chairlifts. Only preset skin tracks for heading uphill, called "skinning," then skiing or riding back down to the base. Avalanche courses available. Open Thurs.–Mon., base open 8 a.m.–4:30 p.m., skiing 8:30 a.m.–4 p.m. 12210 CO-14, www.bluebirdbackcountry.com.

Fossil Ridge

Travel back 70 million years to this site featuring preserved fossils of giant ammonites and other groups of marine invertebrate fossils—nautiloids, bivalves, and gastropods—the highest concentration of this Cretaceous group of known sites in North America. From Kremmling, travel north on US Hwy 40 for approximately 11 miles to CR 25. At 0.4 miles, turn right and cross the bridge over Muddy Creek. Turn left at intersection onto CR 26 for about 3 miles. Turn left onto a two-track dirt road for about 1 mile. Park at gate and walk roughly five minutes to the top of the hill. High-clearance, four-wheel-drive vehicle recommended. Visit the BLM Kremmling Field Office for information and a map to the site. 2103 E. Park Ave., 970.724.3000.

Gore Canyon

Known for its Class V whitewater rapids, this isolated, 3-mile canyon created by the Colorado River is located just 14 miles southwest of Kremmling. Featuring dramatic, 1,000-foot canyon walls, there is no road through it, but there is a unique train adventure through it via Amtrak's California Zephyr (runs daily from Chicago to San Francisco). The new Gore Canyon Whitewater Park at Pumphouse is the perfect spot for kayaking, SUPing, boating, and fishing. The BLM maintains river access, bathrooms, parking, and the Pumphouse Campground, adjacent to the boat launches. The area also offers 20 standard campsites (up to 10 people) with tables and fire grills, 2 group campsites (up to 30 people), 1 picnic shelter with 4 tables, 3 boat launches, and 4 vault toilets. 2103 E. Park Ave., 970.724.3000.

Green Mountain Reservoir

Located 17 miles southeast of Kremmling, this reservoir is popular for waterskiing, jet skiing, fishing (ice fishing in winter), boating, and camping. There are several relatively primitive campgrounds around the lake, each with vault toilets, including Cataract Creek (5 sites with tables, first-come, first-served) and Cow Creek South (40 reservable sites). The Heeney Marina also features rentals—fishing and pontoon boats and SUPs—and a marina store. Open seasonally, 7 a.m.–7 p.m. (151 CR 1798, Silverthorne, 970.724.9441, www.heeneymarina.com). www.greenmountainreservoir.com.

Rafting Companies

Several rafting companies are located in Kremmling, including Mad Adventures, offering a half-day Upper Colorado rafting trip (Class I–III) that's good for families. 1421 E. Park Ave., 800.451.4844, www.mad adventures.com.

Williams Fork Reservoir

Set a little off the beaten path (16 miles southeast of Kremmling in Parshall), this year-round reservoir is managed by Denver Water. Includes two boat ramps: east, to launch motorized boats (must be inspected for aquatic nuisance species before entering the water); and west, for launching car-top-carried boats, including kayaks and canoes. Filled with trophy-sized northern pike for fishing, it also gets a lot of wind, making it ideal for windsurfers. But beware: its snowmelt waters are frigid, which means you'll

want a wetsuit. Dispersed camping only, vault toilets; no reservations. From I-70 West, take Hwy 40 past Empire over Berthoud Pass, continuing from Winter Park to Hot Sulphur Springs until you reach the town of Parshall; at Parshall, turn left (south) on Route 3; follow the road to the Williams Fork entrance. Note: The website includes the typo "resevoir." www.denver water.org/recreation/williams-fork-resevoir.

Wolford Mountain Reservoir

Set in the Wolford Mountain Recreation Area about 7 miles north of Kremmling on Muddy Creek, this BLM area features Wolford Campground with 70 sites, some tent-only (open year-round, Nov.–April, first-come, first-served). Perfect for fishing and waterskiing, there's also a marina (open May–Sept., 7 a.m.–7 p.m. in summer months) with pontoon and fishing boat rentals. In winter, its exceptional ice fishing makes it the perfect spot for a tournament each February. 27219 US Hwy 40, 970.724. 1266, www.wolfordcampground.com.

Moffat County

Miles from Denver: 251 (95 miles northwest of Steamboat Springs)

The northernmost county of Colorado's 64 comprises only 5 towns: Slater, Maybell, Hamilton, Dinosaur, and the largest, Craig, where more than two-thirds of residents live. A bastion of Old West history and home to one of Colorado's most remote treasures, Dinosaur National Monument, it's filled with fossil discoveries and the culture of the Fremont people, Native Americans who thrived in the area for some 300 years (more than 1,000 years ago). Definitely worth the trek to this desolate outpost straddling the Colorado-Utah border. www.visitmoffatcounty.com.

Browns Park National Wildlife Refuge

Located along the Green River about 95 miles northwest of Craig—it shares its southern border with Dinosaur National Monument—the area was once a wintering spot for Ute and Shoshone Indians, as well as a hideout for Butch Cassidy's band of outlaws known as the Wild Bunch (called Brown's Hole). Today it's a refuge for wildlife, including more than 200 bird species, and a popular recreation site for fishing, hiking, mountain biking, floating, and camping. Highlights include Irish Canyon, which contains petroglyphs and a homestead. There are two primitive campgrounds, open year-round: Crook and Swinging Bridge, both offering vault toilets, fire rings, and a boat ramp. Free sites are first-come, first-served. Pack in, pack out. 1318 CO-318, Maybell, 970.365.3613, www.fws.gov/refuge/browns_park.

Craig

Set along US Highway 40 roughly 90 miles from the Moffat County entrance to the Dinosaur National Monument, this high-desert town was incorporated in 1908 and drew cattlemen in the late 1800s for its mild winters and open lands. Its remoteness and proximity to three state borders—Colorado, Utah, and Wyoming—also attracted outlaws like Butch Cassidy and the Sundance Kid.

LODGING

We camped one night at the Craig KOA Journey, located just a couple of miles from the historic downtown. Open Mar. 15–Dec. 1, 2800 E. US Hwy 40, 970.824.5105.

Another spot, set 14 miles east of Craig in Hayden, Yampa River State Park stretches for 134 miles along the river, perfect for boating, camping, and fishing. Anglers have access to miles of flat water,

while rafters and canoeists can also experience miles of Class I–IV rapids. (There are 13 access points from Hayden to the national monument.) The state park includes a visitor/nature center and the Headquarters Campground, offering 49 sites: 35 RV, 14 tent-only. There are also 2 tepees available. Four primitive camping areas are located along the river, each with up to 10 sites; vault toilets, picnic tables, and more. 6185 US Hwy 40, Hayden, 970.276.2061.

Just 10 miles northeast of Craig lies Elkhead Reservoir State Park, the county's only water-recreation site. Featuring 900 acres and two boat ramps for boating, waterskiing, and jet skiing, there's also swimming, fishing, hiking, and biking opportunities. There are two campgrounds: Bear's Ears, with 16 tent campsites, and Pronghorn, with 30 RV/tent campsites; both campgrounds offer firepits, picnic tables, shelters, and restrooms. 135 CR 28, Craig, 970.276.2061.

For a unique stay, visit Villard Ranch, where guests can spend the night in a sheep wagon on the working sheep ranch. 679 Haughey Rd., Craig, 970.824.9302, www.villardranch.com.

Dinosaur

Renamed in 1966 from Artesia to Dinosaur for its close location to Dinosaur National Monument, this is a good final pitstop before heading into the monument. Home to a handful of services, including a convenience store and the Canyon Visitor Center (2 miles east of town), it's the last glimpse of civilization before entering the monument.

Dinosaur National Monument (DNM)

Established in 1915 by President Woodrow Wilson to protect the original 80-acre excavation site, DNM preserves one of the world's largest collections of Jurassic-age dinosaur fossils in its famous Quarry Exhibit Hall (on the "Utah side"). Housed adjacent to the Quarry Visitor Center (QVC), the exhibit hall protects the 149-million-year-old fossils "in situ," where the fossils were originally deposited, including bones from an allosaurus and a stegosaurus. Guests can walk or take a shuttle to the quarry, located 0.25 miles from the QVC. (Cars may be allowed to park at the exhibit hall, depending on season and special accommodations.) There's also an easy-to-moderate, 1.5-mile roundtrip Fossil Discovery Trail (no shade) that starts from either of the two buildings and includes stops at the Mowry Shale and the Morrison and Stump Formations. 11625 E. 1500 S., Jensen, Utah, 84035, 435.781.7700.

The second visitor center, Canyon Visitor Center (CVC) near Dinosaur, is located on the "Colorado side" and is the gateway to the monument's river canyons, including Echo Park (see "Lodging" at right). Located at the base of Harpers Corner Road, the CVC offers a bookstore, restrooms, and water. 4545 US Hwy 40, Dinosaur, 970.374.3000. www.nps.gov/dino/index.htm.

ROCK ART

In addition to its famous fossils and stunning scenery, the area features petroglyphs (carvings) and pictographs (paintings) left by the Fremont people from about AD 200 to 1300. Created in the "desert varnish," a natural combination of iron and manganese in the rock that forms perfect "canvases," designs include animal-like and human-like figures. Be sure not to touch them! A popular spot to see them is the Swelter Shelter, 0.5 miles from the QVC along the Tour of the Tilted Rocks Scenic Drive, a 10-mile (one-way) auto tour route along Cub Creek Road.

LODGING

To stay inside DNM, there are 6 campgrounds with varying amenities: Green River and Split Mountain are both 4 miles east of the quarry; and 4 first-come, first-served options include Rainbow Park (28 miles from QVC), Echo Park (38 miles north of CVC), Deerlodge Park (53 miles east of CVC, eastern border of monument, a put-in for Yampa River rafting trips), and Gates of Lodore (northern tip of monument, 106 miles north of CVC, a put-in for Green River rafting trips).

We stayed one night at Green River, a picturesque but busy site filled with families (read: loud) offering bathrooms and water. We also stayed a night in Echo Park, home of the iconic Steamboat Rock, roughly a three-hour drive from Craig, including about 45 minutes down a steep, bumpy dirt road about 1.5-cars wide. (The first 25 miles are on paved Harpers Corner Road followed by 13 miles on unpaved that can be

Petroglyphs like these are carved in "desert varnish" throughout Dinosaur National Monument. Photo by Michael Mundt.

Rafters float along the Green River past Echo Park Campground, tucked behind the trees. Photo by Michael Mundt.

unpassable when wet.) High-clearance vehicles recommended; RVs and trailers discouraged. It's remote, but the scenic drive into the canyon provides glimpses of the dilapidated Chew homestead remains (circa 1911), the dotted-pattern Pool Creek petroglyphs (less than 1 mile from campground), and a small cave just outside the campgrounds that's so cool, it feels like it's air conditioned. DNM is also designated International Dark Sky Park, so stargazing is phenomenal.

Set at the base of towering walls of granite near the confluence of the Green and Yampa Rivers—making it a popular put-in or resting spot for rafters—the 22 Echo Park sites (suitable for tents, 1 handicapped-accessible) offer picnic tables and firepits. Vault toilets and potable water are available (the latter seasonally). You can also see petroglyphs, including rock art on a cliff above Campsite 10, or along the Mitten Park Trail (all trails are unmarked) leading from that site along the river, about a 15-minute walk.

If you stay here with kids, I offer two caveats: (1) Although the river is shallow in most places and looks calm, it does have a strong current, so I'd recommend life vests. (2) The mosquitoes were murderous in early July, so the DEET bug spray I typically avoid was a necessity.

Sand Wash Basin

Located 18.5 miles northwest of Maybell, the BLM's Sand Wash Basin is a popular

Catching glimpses of the wild Sand Wash Basin herd is a popular pursuit around Maybell. Photo by Michael Mundt.

recreation spot for camping and OHV riding. But the draw of these parched scrublands are some 250 wild horses (culled in September 2021 from nearly 900), one of the country's few remaining herds. Take State Hwy 318 north for about 15 miles, then turn on Moffat County Road 67, where the Herd Management Area (HMA) begins. The roads are unpaved and unmarked, and the horses can be anywhere, but we spotted 6 after about 30 minutes. (Stay at least 100 feet away from the animals.) Wild Horse Warrior Tours led by Cindy Wright can accommodate up to 6 visitors (no age limit but no car seats available). Daily, eight-hour, custom tours include water, snacks, and a light lunch. (You may want to pack your own food too.) www.wildhorsewar riorsforsandwashbasin.com/whw-tours.

The boys and their dad cooling off in the Green River within view of the iconic Steamboat Rock. Photo by the author.

North Park

Miles from Denver: 142 (Walden)

Featuring the town of Walden (about an hour's drive northeast of Steamboat Springs)—along with smaller hamlets Cowdrey, Coalmont, Rand, and Gould—this area is the northernmost of the state's three large mountain valleys or "parks" on the western side of the Front Range. (Middle Park includes most towns in this region, including Grand Lake, Kremmling, and Winter Park; South Park comprises areas in the "Rockies Playground" regions such as Fairplay and Alma.) Boasting 1 million acres covering more than 1,600 square miles, 65 percent public lands, North Park prides itself as an Old West outpost that's a true escape from the crowds. www.visit northparkco.com.

The scenic, 6-mile Gould Loop Trail begins and ends at the Moose Visitor Center in Walden. Photo by the author.

Arapaho National Wildlife Refuge

Established in 1967 to support the diversity of plants and wildlife that lives in this high-mountain valley, this refuge located south of Walden is the highest in the Lower 48 (8,100 to 8,700 feet in elevation). Open 30 minutes before and after sunset, the most popular activity for visitors is viewing wildlife such as birds, pronghorn, and moose. (Roads are typically closed Dec.–April.) Start at the Visitors Center, open year-round, Mon.–Fri., 7 a.m.–3:30 p.m. (The access road is maintained from the Hwy 125 entrance to the headquarters building.) On a 6-mile self-guided auto tour, see habitats on the western side of the refuge, home to waterfowl, prairie dogs, and pronghorn. There's also the Moose-Goose Nature Trail, an ADA-compliant, 0.5-mile interpretive nature trail that winds along the Illinois River, providing opportunities to view songbirds and other riparian residents, as well as three ADA-compliant overlooks. 953 CR 32, Walden, 970.723.8202, www.fws.gov/refuge/arapaho.

State Forest State Park

This 71,000-acre park features alpine lakes, rugged mountains, and around 600 moose. Anglers can enjoy plenty of fishing destinations, from the Canadian and Michigan Rivers to the Ranger Lakes. There are also 158 reservable campsites, as well as 6 rustic cabins (large ones accommodate 16 to 22; small ones accommodate 6) with grills, firepits, picnic tables, propane heating stoves with propane, potable water (summer), and vault toilets (nearby). An on-site maintenance shop provides water year-round. Never Summer Nordic also offers a gift shop with snacks, wine, beer, and more, and owns and manages 11 yurts, 2 huts, and 2 large cabins ($) (247 CR 41, Walden, 970.723.4070, www.neversummernordic.com). There are also three attended entrance stations at Ranger Lakes, North Park, and North Michigan (summer season

Fast Fact: Walden is known as the Moose Viewing Capital of Colorado.

only), two corrals, a fishing pier, and the Moose Visitor Center, located about 20 miles southeast of Walden. The 6-mile Gould Loop Trail begins and ends at the visitor center, offering stunning scenery and opportunity for moose viewing. Visitor center open 9 a.m.–5 p.m., summer; closes 4:30 p.m., winter, 56750 Hwy 14, Walden, 970.723.8366.

Steamboat Springs

Miles from Denver: 156

Named by 19th-century French fur trappers who thought one of the natural springs along the Yampa River sounded like a steamboat engine, these former Ute hunting grounds drew settlers to their springs and idyllic ranch land. Nicknamed "The 'Boat," set far from the bustle of the Denver Metro area, Steamboat Springs is also known as Ski Town, U.S.A.® (or also Bike Town USA), home to light, dry snow known as Champagne Powder.® But we also love it for its laid-back vibe and Old West charm. www.steamboatchamber.com.

Lodging

We've typically stayed in rental properties on the ski mountain. But families wanting a quieter setting will enjoy Glen Eden Resort ($–$$$), located about 18 miles north of town. Rent one of 28 cabins (sleep 4–6). Amenities include year-round hot tub, seasonal heated pool, and private fishing along the Elk River (bring poles). On-property restaurant open daily for dinner (increased service seasonally). 54737 CR 129, Clark, 970.879.3907, www.glenedenresort.com.

Other Highlights

Operating since 1905, launched by Frank M. Light and two sons, the legendary F. M. Light and Sons welcomes visitors with its iconic yellow-and-black signs for miles

along US Highway 40 as they drive into town. Kids will want a "ride" on Lightning, the statue quarter horse that's been located outside the store since 1949. Open daily 9 a.m.–8 p.m., 830 Lincoln Ave., 970.879.1822, www.fmlight.com.

Fish Creek Falls

A mild 0.25-mile trek to the 280-foot-high waterfall, this is always a busy tourist destination in summer. For a more difficult adventure, head 2.5 miles one way to the waterfall's base to a second waterfall or the 6.5-mile one-way hike to Long Lake. Directions: From US Hwy 40, head north on 3rd St., then take a right on Fish Creek Falls Rd. Drive 4 miles to the parking lot and trailhead; $5 per vehicle. Open daily 6 a.m.–10 p.m.

Grizzle-T Dog and Sled Works

Located about 11 miles west of Steamboat Springs, the property is owned and operated by Iditarod Musher Kris Hoffman and his wife, Sara. For a true "call of the wild," opt for the "Mush Your Own Dog Team" half-day excursion ($$), which includes a 12.5-mile loop on private trails with a chance to drive the sled for up to two hours (or one hour if there are two riders taking turns driving). Kids 2 years and up can ride; must be at least 80 pounds to drive. HC 66 Box 39, 970.870.1782, www.steam boatdogsledding.com.

Howelsen Hill Ski Area

Stats: 18 alpine trails and 9 Nordic (13 miles), 50 skiable acres, 3 lifts, 1 terrain park, night skiing

Base elevation: 6,696 feet

Open since 1915, Howelsen Hill is the oldest operating ski area in North America and features the continent's largest natural ski-jumping complex. (It's the training ground for nearly 90 Olympians making more than 150 Winter Olympic appearances!) Fat-biking and snowshoeing are allowed on Nordic trails (with lift ticket). The Howelsen Lodge includes Olympian Hall and the Out Run Snack Bar. Snow tubing is planned to be available by the 2022–2023 season (www.steamboatsprings .net/131/Howelsen-Hill-Ski-Area).

Part of the Howelsen Park complex, in addition to the ski mountain and Nordic center, the area also includes baseball/softball fields, 3 sand-volleyball courts, tennis/pickleball courts, a skate park, a BMX track, and 55 miles of Emerald Mountain mountain-biking and hiking trails. It's also home to the Howelsen Ice Complex, featuring an Olympic-size sheet of ice and offering an array of programming, from public skating and rentals to bumper cars on ice. Open year-round. Hours vary seasonally. 285 Howelsen Pkwy., 970.871.7033.

In summertime, the park also offers the Howler Alpine Slide, one of our family's favorite activities (645 Howelsen Pkwy., 970.439.0863, www.steamboatalpineslide .com). It's also home to the rodeo grounds, site of the popular Steamboat Springs Pro Rodeo. Running every Friday and Saturday from mid-June to mid-August, the 100-year tradition includes an F. M. Light & Sons–sponsored Calf Scramble, where kids ages 6–12 run like mad through Brent Romick Arena in pursuit of a ribbon-adorned calf. (Kids 5 and under run the Ram Scramble.) 401 Howelsen Pkwy., 970.879.1818, www .steamboatprorodeo.com.

Nordic Skiing

In addition to offerings at Howelsen Hill, the Haymaker Nordic Center and Clubhouse offers roughly 6 miles of groomed trails for classic skiing, skate skiing, and snowshoeing. Rentals and lessons available for all skill levels. Lift ticket required. Open daily during the season, 9 a.m.–4 p.m. Lunch served at the clubhouse Wed.–Sun., 10:30 a.m.–2:30 p.m. 34855 E. US Hwy 40, 970.879.9444.

The Steamboat Ski Touring Center features nearly 10 miles of trails groomed for classic and skate skiing for all skills ranges, plus 6 miles of snowshoe trails. Classic and skate ski lessons for all abilities are offered daily with rental equipment. Lift ticket required. Lunch and snacks are available all day at The Picnic Basket in the Nordic Clubhouse. Open daily during the season, 9 a.m.–5 p.m., 1230 Steamboat Blvd., 970.879.8180. www.nordicski.net.

Old Town Hot Springs

Whether winter or summer, our kids won't let us leave town until we visit these hot springs, located in the heart of downtown across from the historic Rabbit Ears Motel. (Named after the town's Rabbit Ears Pass, you can't miss the neon sign from its 1952 opening. www.rabbitearsmotel.com.) Comprising eight pools—one featuring my boys' favorite climbing wall—it also includes two 230-foot water slides, eight lap lanes, a kids' play area, and an obstacle course (summer only). Open weekdays, 6 a.m.–8 p.m.; open weekends at 7 a.m., 136 S. Lincoln Ave., 970.879.1828, www.oldtownhotsprings.org.

Pearl Lake State Park

This picturesque gem situated roughly 26 miles north of town offers a peaceful, motor-free setting for endless water activities such as SUPing. (Swimming is not allowed.) On-site vendor Steamboat Paddleboard Adventure rents out boards right from the shore (www.paddleboardadven turecompany.com). The 35 RV-tent sites and 2 yurts (sleep 6, bring bedding and cookware) are available year-round (two-night minimum May–Nov.) Includes vault toilets, one flush toilet, potable water. Campers can use Steamboat Lake shower/

The "Mush Your Own Dog Team" Grizzle-T tour includes driving a dog sled for up to two hours. Photo by Michael Mundt.

laundry facilities, roughly 5 miles apart. 61105 RCR 129, Clark, 970.879.3922.

Saddleback Ranch

This working cattle ranch about 17 miles west of the ski resort offers visitors plenty of outdoor activities, from horseback rides to dinner wagon rides and cattle drives. In the winter, there is also snowmobiling and sleigh rides. But the only activity we've tried is the Yee-Haw Tubing Hill, with 90 minutes of thrilling, adrenaline-filled rides. (A helmet is recommended.) The ranch also provides free transportation from the Gondola Transit Center (2305 Mt. Werner Cir.). 36975 CR 179, 970.879.3711, www .saddlebackranch.net.

The no-wake Pearl Lake north of Steamboat Springs is a peaceful SUP destination. Photo by Michael Mundt.

Fast Fact: There are three lakes in Colorado boasting Gold Medal waters: Steamboat Lake (a reservoir), Spinney Mountain Reservoir (see "Cripple Creek" entry), and North Delaney Lake (near Walden).

Stagecoach State Park

Located 17 miles south of Steamboat, the main draw here is the 3-mile Stagecoach Reservoir. Featuring wakeless and nonwakeless areas, there are two boat ramps and the full-service Stagecoach Marina at the north end of the park offering rentals for boats, SUPs, and canoes, as well as guided fishing/ ice fishing and sunset fishing cruises (970.736.8342, www.steamboatspringsboat rentals.com). The area also includes a sandy swim beach, picnic tables, a volleyball court, and coin-operated showers. It boasts 200 bird species, waters filled with rainbow trout and northern pike, and 8 miles of

trails for hiking, biking, and horseback riding. Includes 50 picnic sites and 92 RV/tent sites in 4 campgrounds. The park offers free use of fat bikes, lake and fly-fishing rods, and activity backpacks with binoculars, field guides, and more. Call for reservations. Open Memorial Weekend–Labor Day Weekend, 8 a.m.–7 p.m., 25500 CR 14, Oak Creek, 970.736.2436.

Steamboat Lake State Park

About 5 miles northwest of Pearl Lake State Park, this is a popular summer spot for boating, fishing, and hiking and mountain biking on more than 7 miles of trails (some connecting to Routt National Forest trails). Winter features snowmobiling, ice fishing, and snowshoeing, plus a Nordic touring center with groomed trails. Set within view of Hahns Peak, the scenic spot offers 188 RV tent sites with restrooms, showers, and a laundry facility. The Steamboat Lake Marina rents pontoons, kayaks, and SUPs, as well as 10 year-round cabins with electric heater, beds for 4, a small refrigerator, showers, and restrooms (61450 CR 62, 970.879.7019, www.steamboatlakemarina.com). 61105 RCR 129, Clark, 80428, 970.879.3922.

Steamboat Ski Resort

Stats: 6 mountains, 169 designated trails, nearly 3,000 skiable acres, 18 lifts, 3 terrain parks, night skiing

Trail classification: 16 percent Beginner; 38 percent Intermediate; 46 percent Advanced

Base elevation: 6,900 feet

Set in the Park Range, the resort includes six peaks: Mt. Werner, Sunshine Peak, Storm Peak, Thunderhead Peak, Christie Peak, and Pioneer Ridge. Skiers begin from Gondola Square, which used to be slow during busy mornings, remedied in 2019 by updating the Steamboat Gondola. (A base-

The beach at Stagecoach State Park is perfect for a day of canoeing, SUPing, and playing sand volleyball. Photo by the author.

improvement project will be completed in 2023.) I'd still recommend getting an early start!

For a winter treat, enjoy a dinner with Scandinavian flair on a Ragnar's Sleigh Ride Dinner ($–$$), riding the gondola, followed by a 20-minute snowcat-drawn sleigh ride under cozy blankets to a five-course dinner (970.871.5150). Or book a horse-drawn sleigh ride before settling into a three-course dinner at the Haymaker Clubhouse. (See "Nordic Skiing" entry.) Thurs.–Sun. through the season (970.879.1265). A free shuttle leaves from the Steamboat Grand Hotel (2300 Mt. Werner Cir., 970.871.5500, www.steamboatgrand.com) every 30 minutes, 4:45 p.m.–7:15 p.m.

In the summer, visitors can take the gondola up to Thunderhead Lodge toward endless hiking trails, such as the Vista Nature Trail, a 0.86-mile loop. Or hike up along the Thunderhead Hiking Trail, a 3.8-mile trail of windy switchbacks from Mt. Werner's base Gondola Square to Thunderhead Lodge. With a 2,180-foot elevation gain, I recall lots of whining from our kids when we hiked years ago, so be sure to wear good hiking shoes and bring lots of water (and sunscreen!). For mountain bikers, check out the Steamboat Bike Park, which offers an extensive, 40-mile trail network.

The Outlaw Mountain Coaster debuted in 2017 as the longest coaster in North America at more than 6,280 linear feet (adjacent to the Christie Peak Express chairlift). Minimum 3 years old and 38 inches to ride with an adult; 54 inches to drive. Open year-round. Hours subject to weather. www.steamboat.com.

Steamboat Zipline Adventures

Featuring six ziplines ranging from 600 to 1,300 feet, the two-hour tour offers fabulous views of the Yampa Valley and Flat Top Mountain Range ($–$$). Includes a 10-minute ATV ride between ziplines five and six. Must weigh 50–250 pounds. Open May–Oct. Follow directions in lieu of inputting address to GPS: Head east on Hwy 40 toward Rabbit Ears Pass; located just past Mile Marker 140 on the right as you climb up the pass. 32075 E. US Hwy 40, 970.879.6500, www.steamboatziplineadventures.com.

Strawberry Park Hot Springs

Situated along Hot Springs Creek about 7 miles north of town, these springs comprise five pools bordered by natural stone. (One is basically creek water.) Facilities are limited: a tepee and heated cabin for changing, picnic areas, two massage rooms, and basic concessions. Lodging ranges from tent

campsites to lodges—even covered wagons and a caboose—and the facility is powered by solar energy. Parking is also limited, so shuttle services are available. Or hike 2.7 miles along the National Forest Service's Hot Springs Trail, which deposits visitors right at the springs. No pets allowed. Kids under 18 not permitted in the pools after dark, when it's clothing-optional. Open daily 10 a.m.–10 p.m., 44200 CR 36, 970.879.0342, www.strawberryhotsprings.com.

Vista Verde Ranch

Set roughly 25 miles north of Steamboat Springs, the property offers a variety of mountain activities away from the crowds ($$). Summer season runs from June through late October, featuring activities such as fishing, mountain biking, SUPing, horseback riding, and ranch activities. Winter season brings cross-country and backcountry skiing, fat-biking, and tubing; indoor activities include cooking classes and leather working. All activities include gear, guiding, and meals prepared by world-class chefs. Kids program available (ages 6–12); 12 cabins. 58000 Cowboy Way, Clark, 970.879.3858, www.vistaverde.com.

Yampa River

Coursing parallel to the city's main thoroughfare (Lincoln Avenue/US Hwy 40), the river is lined with restaurants, tour operators, and the Yampa River Core Trail, a 7.5-mile, paved trail that's ideal for walking or riding bikes. The only free-flowing river in the state—more than 250 miles unobstructed by dams or diversions—it is also perfect for tubing (roughly June–Aug.). It's an easy, 2-mile tube ride that

Tubing along the Yampa River is a must for kids during a summer visit to Steamboat. Photo by Michael Mundt.

takes about 90 minutes, depending on the time of year; my family rented tubes, life-jackets, and river shoes from Backdoor Sports, where we also stored our belongings. At the end, a shuttle returns guests from the put-out site to the shop. Tubing hours: 10:30 a.m.–4 p.m. 841 Yampa St., 970.879.6249, www.backdoorsports.com.

Winter Park

Miles from Denver: 66

Originally a 10-cabin enclave for hunters and fishermen named Hideaway, construction of the Moffat railroad tunnel began in 1923, linking the Denver area to these mountains. Passing under the Continental Divide via the Moffat Tunnel, trains were shuttling skiers to the area's ski jump and few ski trails by 1938. Becoming Winter Park Resort in January 1940, the town was renamed Winter Park in 1978. (The city of Denver currently owns the resort.) With some 600 miles of trails in the area, the town is also known as Mountain Bike Capital USA™. www.visitwinterpark.com.

Tour Operator

Ride a snowmobile along the Continental Divide for sweeping views of Winter Park and Fraser Valley ($–$$). One- and two-hour family tours and unguided rentals available. In warmer months, go off-roading on a journey that includes views of the historic train trestle that once operated as a 23-mile railroad route over Rollins Pass. Minimum 4 years old. 970.726.9247, www.grandadventures.com.

Winter Park Resort

Stats: 7 territories—Winter Park, Eagle Wind, Parsenn Bowl, Terrain Park, Vasquez Ridge, Cirque, Mary Jane—166 designated trails, 3,081 skiable acres, 1,212 acres of off-piste terrain, 23 lifts, 7 terrain parks

Trail classification: 8 percent Beginner; 18 percent Intermediate; 74 percent Advanced

Base elevation: 9,000 feet

Debuting in the 1939–1940 ski season, Winter Park Resort is the state's longest continually operated ski resort and the closest major one to Denver International Airport (DIA). It's also one of our family's most beloved spots in all of Colorado, particularly skiing the long, wide-open runs of Mary Jane and the high-alpine Parsenn Bowl, topping out at 12,060 feet. Bonus? While Winter Park still requires access on the high-traffic I-70 west corridor, it doesn't require driving through the Eisenhower Tunnel. Or skip driving altogether via the Winter Park Express Ski Train, which transports guests straight from DIA to the resort. (The airport rail takes visitors to downtown's Denver Union Station for $10.50 each way; the 23-mile ride takes about 27 minutes.) From Denver Union Station, board the 7 a.m. Amtrak "Superliner Sightseer" train and arrive just 100 feet from a ski lift at 9 a.m. ($). Kids ages 2–12 ride for half-price with a ticketed adult.

The Coca-Cola® Tube Park, located next to the village, includes four lanes, a covered conveyor-lift, and a warming lodge with restrooms and snacks. Or skate for free on the Village Ice Rink, open 10 a.m.–8 p.m. daily through ski season; free ice-skating lessons on Sunday, 12 p.m.–1 p.m. Rentals available. New in 2020, the resort's frozen ice pond is home to ice bumper cars (15-minute slots). Minimum 48 inches.

The ski area is also known for its adaptive skiing program—a wing of the National Sports Center for the Disabled is located in a building at the base—designed to get disabled adults and children safely onto the slopes. Offering lessons and assistance to individuals and groups, the facility uses equipment to accommodate a variety of disabilities, including blind skiers and amputees.

In summertime, check out Colorado's longest alpine slide, 3,000 feet of track winding from the top of the Arrow Chairlift to the base. Mountain bikers can also enjoy the resort's Trestle Bike Park, featuring more than 40 miles of trails for all ages and abilities. Lessons and camps available (www.trestlebikepark.com). www.winterparkresort.com.

Taking a ski break on a bluebird day at Winter Park Resort. Photo by the author.

The spectacular view from the top of Parsenn Bowl, one of our favorite Winter Park Resort ski spots. Photo by Michael Mundt.

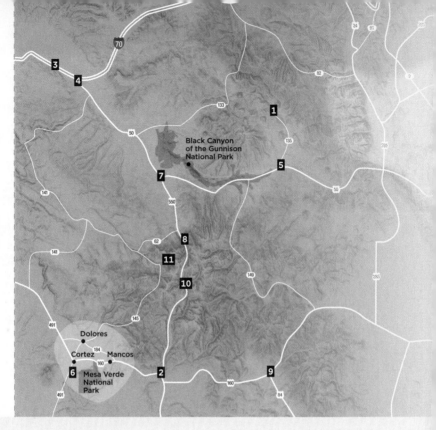

MOUNTAINS AND MESAS

Crested Butte

Best known as the Wildflower Capital of Colorado, celebrated annually during the Crested Butte Wildflower Festival in July, this former mining-camp supply hub and coal-mining spot is also nicknamed "the last great Colorado ski town." Founded in 1880, its main drag, Elk Avenue, is also one of the most colorful and charming of all the state's Victorian mountain towns—roughly 85 percent of the buildings date back to the late 19th and early 20th centuries—and is both a designated National Historic District and Certified Colorado Creative District. www.visitcrestedbutte.com

Other Highlights

It's more than 270 miles to drive from Crested Butte to Aspen, but the hike between them is less than 11 miles (6–10 hours). The Nordic Inn at Mt. Crested Butte can help coordinate the trek between the

My older son, Brody, came up with the idea in 2014 to bring our Lego likenesses on adventures. Here Michael is photobombing us in front of Mt. Crested Butte. Photo by the author.

two towns, including arranging Aspen lodging. 14 Treasury Rd., 970.349.5542, www.nordicinncb.com.

Tour Operators

Colorado Backcountry Guide Services offers year-round guiding services around Crested Butte, from hiking to biking, snowshoeing, and more. 970.349.0800, www.coloradobc.com.

For extreme skiers and riders, head up 12,000 feet toward Colorado's steepest cat-serviced terrain with Irwin Guides (about 12 miles west of town) ($$). 866.479.4677, www.irwinguides.com.

Try fly-fishing tours with Dragonfly Anglers, who have guided throughout Gunnison and Crested Butte since 1983. 307 Elk Ave., 800.491.3079, www.dragonfly anglers.com.

Crested Butte Mountain Resort

Stats: 121 designated trails, 1,547 skiable acres, 15 lifts, 4 terrain parks

Trail classification: 18 percent Beginner; 29 percent Intermediate; 53 percent Advanced

Base elevation: 9,375 feet

Opened in 1961 just 3 miles from downtown, it was Colorado's second resort to open a gondola (after Vail). Considered the birthplace of freeskiing (tricks, jumps, and terrain parks), this resort is known for offering extreme terrain.

Away from slopes, take a dog-sled tour via Cosmic Cruisers, which leaves just minutes from the resort on a one-hour tour, where you can ride or drive your own team ($$). All ages. Full-day tour available. 970.641.0529, www.gunnisonsleddogs.com.

There's also the base-area Adventure Park, located next to the Treasury Building and the Red Lady Express, offering many activities in winter and summer, including the Crested Butte Zipline Tour ($), 6 ziplines ranging from 120- to 400-feet long,

The Crested Butte Mountain Bike Park features 29 trails for all skill levels. Photo by Michael Mundt.

Crested Butte Nordic Center

Maintaining over 30 miles of trail, some just steps from downtown, the center also rents gear and offers clinics, lessons, and back-country tours for all ages. The Skate Ski 4 Free introduction takes place the first Thursday of every month. Youth (ages 5–16) and family lessons (minimum 5 years old) are offered daily through the season, 9:30 a.m. and 11 a.m. Reservations required ($). There are also ski/snowshoe moonlight dinners at the Magic Meadows Yurt (roughly 45 minutes each way). Cost includes trail pass and equipment rental; dinner at 6:30 p.m. Kids welcome. 620 2nd St., 970.349.1707, www.cbnordic.org.

The town also owns and operates the Big Mine Ice Arena, adjacent to the center, featuring a warming house and skate rentals. Open daily Dec.–Mar., 10 a.m.–9 p.m. Free if you have skates. 970.349.5616.

There's also a small tubing hill at Big Mine Park next to the center.

about two hours. (Minimum 70 pounds.) There's also miniature golf, a bungy-jump trampoline, and a climbing wall (970.349. 2211). Summer's highlight is the Crested Butte Mountain Bike Park, offering 29 trails traversing more than 30 miles of terrain. (Lift-served biking via the Red Lady Express.) The park features trails for all skill levels, from the beginner Hotdogger (green circle) to the expert Psycho Rocks (double-black-diamond).

My boys also enjoyed a full day of camp via the resort's Mountain Adventures, offering activities such as rafting, fly-fishing, swimming, and biking. They chose a full day of rock climbing at Hartman Rocks (see "Gunnison" entry) while we parents hiked. Everyone wins! There's also free transportation from the mountain to town via the Mountain Express Town Shuttle, which operates every 15 minutes (970.349.5616). www.skicb.com.

Durango

Miles from Denver: 337

A Nationally Registered Historic District, the welcoming downtown takes visitors back to circa 1880, when it was founded by the Denver and Rio Grande Western Railroad. Located 55 miles east of Mesa Verde National Park, it's a great base camp for exploring Colorado's Southwest. www .durango.org.

The Durango-La Plata Airport, roughly 19 miles southeast of downtown, is a regional airport with service from American Airlines and United Airlines. 1000 Airport Rd., 970.375.6050, www.flydurango .com.

Other Highlights

The Southern Ute Museum offers education, exhibits, and cultural events, giving meaning to the phrase "Numi Nuuchiyu, We Are the Ute People." Free. About a 35-minute drive from Durango. Open daily 10 a.m.–5 p.m., 503 Ouray Dr., Ignacio, 970.563.9583, www.southernutemuseum.org.

Animas River

Referred to as "The River of Lost Souls" for the Spanish explorers who died here and whose bodies were never recovered, the Animas River runs right through Durango. Comprising 126 miles, the river offers Gold Medal waters and plenty of whitewater rapids for rafting and kayaking enthusiasts. For the nature lover who prefers to stay out of the water, head to the Animas River Trail (ART), a 7-mile, shared-use, riverside path that offers access to a variety of parks, open spaces, and more. We opted for a two-hour trip with Durango Rafting Company, which also offers four-hour and kayak trips. Kids 8 years and under raft for free! 305 S. Camino Del Rio, Suite V, 970.259.8313, www.durangoraft.com. Mild to Wild Rafting and Jeep Tours offers trips from two hours to four days for ages 4 and up; the half-day Lower Animas trip is a good introduction to rafting. (Jeep tours also available in Durango, Silverton, Mesa Verde, and more. All ages.) 50 Animas View Dr., 970.247.4789, www.mild2wildrafting.com.

At 4 Corners Riversports, located near the town's Whitewater Park, you can rent SUPs, kayaks, and more. 360 S. Camino del Rio, Ste. 100, 970.259.3893, www.riversports.com.

Bar D Chuckwagon

This Old West Cowboy Music show and supper—which comprises the restaurant, stage show, shops, train, and activities—includes a short-line railroad and a playground, as well as gold panning, wagon rides, and more. Meal begins at 7 p.m. sharp. Ticket booth opens at 5 p.m. Reservations recommended. Season runs

approximately June–Sept., 8080 CR 250, 970.749.2572, www.bardchuckwagon.com.

Blue Lake Ranch

Located 15 minutes from downtown Durango in Hesperus, this secluded, 200-acre estate offers family-friendly options, including suites, casitas, and cabins ($–$$). Walk the lakeside paths to view wildlife or fish for trout in the lake. Enjoy complimentary, Southwest-inspired breakfast featuring tamales, enchiladas, pozole, chorizo, and quiches with fresh produce from the garden. Order a picnic lunch for activities you can book from the hotel, such as fishing and mountain biking. Visit alpacas at nearby Pleasant Journey Alpacas (4128 CR 129, Hesperus, 970.259.3384, www.pleasant journeyalpacas.com). 16919 CO-140, Hesperus, 970.385.4537, www.bluelakeranch.com.

Durango Adventures

Just 1 mile west of downtown Durango, the three-hour course features 12 ziplines and a choice between one that ends on a rooftop patio or offers a jump off a 45-foot-tall tower. Snacks and water included ($$). A 6-zipline option is also available ($). Other adventures include axe throwing, whitewater rafting, mountain biking, and the popular half-day, guided adventure ride ($$). Minimum 5 years old for most adventures. 20673 US-160, 970.759.9880, www.durango adventures.com.

Durango and Silverton Narrow Gauge Railroad (D&SNGRR)

Once a lifeline for Silverton mines, this historic train has continued operating since 1881 ($). Even if you don't have time to ride the train to Silverton ($–$$), a 45-mile, four-hour (one way), cliff-hugging journey, be sure to check out the free museum located in the railyard just outside the Durango depot. (There's a second museum in Silverton's depot.)

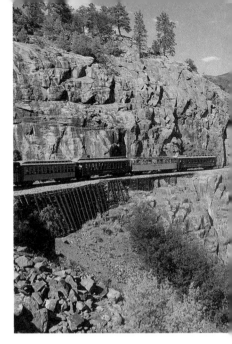

The Durango and Silverton Narrow Gauge Railroad is one of the most scenic train rides in Colorado. Photo by Michael Mundt.

For an authentic experience, choose an open-air gondola, complete with stunning views of the Animas River and sooty skin. (Traditional cars are also available, as well as bathrooms and concessions.) Reduce travel time with an 80-minute bus ride to Silverton and the four-hour ride to Durango (or reverse). There are also adventure packages available, combining the train ride with an afternoon rafting trip or a winter snowmobile tour. Soaring Tree Top Adventures offers a full-day tour that combines the train ride with a 5.5-hour zipline adventure and a gourmet lunch ($$). All ages. 964 CR 200, 970.769.2357, www.soaringcolorado .com.

Some travelers use the train to access the San Juan National Forest and the Weminuche Wilderness for backpacking, day hikes, rafting, and fishing trips at two main access locations: Needleton, the entrance to Chicago Basin; and Elk Park, the access point to the Colorado Trail (www.colorado trail.org), the 567-mile path from Durango to Denver. (For information on trail conditions, maps, or backcountry insurance, contact the US Forest Service, 970.247.4874.) During the holidays, families can also enjoy the Polar Express™ roundtrip excursion to the North Pole that reenacts the holiday classic (60 minutes). Open daily 8 a.m.– 5 p.m., 479 Main Ave., 877.872.4607, www .durangotrain.com.

Durango Hot Springs Resort and Spa

Formerly Trimble Hot Springs, this resort is set 8 miles north of downtown Durango and 15 miles south of Purgatory Resort. The only natural hot spring in the world to infuse nanometer and micrometer oxygen bubbles, which are said to increase the health benefits and purity of the waters, the property includes 26 mineral-water features, including 16 natural mineral hot springs soaking pools; 8 private Japanese-inspired cedar soaking tubs; a reflexology walking path; a swimming pool; dry saunas; a cold-plunge pool; and more. Open daily from 9 a.m.–10 p.m. Reservations are required. 6475 CR 203, 970.247.0111, www.durango hotspringsresortandspa.com.

Hesperus Ski Area

Stats: 26 designated trails, 60 skiable acres, 1 lift, 1 terrain park, night skiing
Trail classification: 19 percent Beginner; 31 percent Intermediate; 50 percent Advanced
Base elevation: 8,100 feet

Just 11 miles west of Durango in the small town of Hesperus, this ski area is an affordable family option, providing beginners (7 and older) up to three free lessons with the purchase of a full-day, full-price lift ticket. Every child age 10 and under also receives a free season pass to Hesperus, Purgatory Resort, and several other area resorts.

Includes a day lodge, rental shop, ski and ride school, and the Marmot Hill tubing hill, located on the west side of the lower mountain. (Minimum 3 years old, 36 inches tall; 2-year-old kids may ride with an adult.) www.ski-hesperus.com.

Purgatory Resort

Stats: 105 designated trails, 1,605 skiable acres, 11 lifts, 4 terrain parks

Trail classification: 20 percent Beginner; 45 percent Intermediate; 35 percent Advanced

Base elevation: 8,793 feet

This resort just 25 miles north of Durango opened in 1965, offering a blend of steep tree-skiing trails and wide-open cruisers with stunning views, including the kid-friendly run, Animas City, and the Animas City Adventure Park. (It offers the same lessons and free pass for kids 10 and younger as does Hesperus, above.) It also boasts Colorado's largest snowcat skiing operation, featuring more than 35,000 acres of expansive terrain. (Expect up to 10 runs and 10,000 feet of vertical, depending on skill and terrain.) 970.385.2115.

There are also Snowcat Scenic Tours and Dinners on select dates, offering sunset views, as well as guided group or private tours on 75 miles of trails. The Skier Shuttle, operated by Purgatory's Transportation Services, provides roundtrips to and from the Durango Transit Center on weekends and select holidays. 970.259.5438.

The Village Plaza base area features a variety of activities such as the Snow Coaster Tubing Hill's three lanes of high-speed fun. (Hourly rentals.) Children 3–5 years must ride with an adult. (970.385.2168). Take a sled-dog tour with Durango Dog Ranch along a scenic snowy trail with breathtaking views of Engineer Mountain ($) (2 people per tour). Hourly tours depart from the kennel near the Purgatory base area Fri.–Mon., 10 a.m.–3 p.m. (970.259.0694). The Inferno Mountain Coaster is also open year-round. (Driver minimum 9 years, 52 inches; passengers minimum 36 inches with a driver 16 years or older.) www.purgatoryresort.com

Located 0.3 miles north of the base of Purgatory on the east side of Hwy 550 is the Durango Nordic Center at Purgatory, owned and operated by the nonprofit Durango Nordic Ski Club. Featuring more than 12 miles of forest trails groomed for classic cross-country and skate skiing, and nearly 4 miles of snowshoe trails, the area includes a new community center, ski and rental equipment, and group and private ski lessons. Open daily, 9 a.m.–4 p.m., through ski season, 49786 Hwy 550 N., 970.385.2114, www.durangonordic.org.

In summer, try out the tubing slope, racing more than 900 feet down multiple lanes of slippery material. (Ride the Columbine Lift 9 back up.) There's also an alpine slide, bungee trampoline, treasure panning, and guided hikes (all weather permitting). Try the Mountain Bike Uplift (Lifts 1 and 4) up from the base, then bike down the mountain on any number of trails. Check out the Divinity Flow Trail, a 1.5-mile intermediate trail and Durango's longest downhill flow trail. Or try the resort's newest trail, Shangri-La (completed summer 2020), a 6.4-mile green trail for all skill levels that starts at the top of Lift 1.

Spend the day at Twilight Lake—directly across from the entrance to Purgatory—with SUPs, canoes, and kayaks from Durango Board and Boat (www.floatdurango.com). 49786 N. US Hwy 550, 970.903.3962.

Take a horseback adventure with Buck's Livery, one- and two-hour rides. Pony and sunset dinner rides available. Open daily 8 a.m.–5 p.m., Memorial Day to Labor Day. In winter, 35-minute sleigh rides depart hourly 1 p.m.–5 p.m. daily. Children 5 and under ride free. 49786 Hwy 550 N., 970.385.2110, www.buckslivery.com.

Vallecito Reservoir

Set in a secluded mountain valley just 18 miles from Durango (in Bayfield), the reservoir offers about 12 miles of shoreline. Summer months feature horseback riding, mountain biking, fishing, or hiking one of seven different hiking trails. Winter activities include snowmobiling, Nordic skiing, snowshoeing, and ice fishing. (Check out unique carvings of lakeside trees that were damaged by a 2002 fire, created by artist Chad Haspels.) The full-service Vallecito Marina rents fishing/pontoons, kayaks, SUPs, canoes, and more. Open daily 7 a.m.–7 p.m., May–Sept., 14772 CR 501, 970.884.7000, www.vallecitolakemarina.net.

Stay at the Pine River Lodge ($), featuring vacation cabins for 2–11 guests (1–3 bedrooms with full kitchens, TV, WiFi, and more). Winter hours only during holiday season; snowshoes for rent. 4443 CR 501, 970.884.2563, www.pineriverlodge.com.

Fruita

Miles from Denver: 254

Established in 1884 as a fruit-producing region, agriculture remains an important industry in Fruita. Best known as a mountain-biking paradise, this town located 10 miles from Grand Junction offers the perfect combination of terrain to challenge riders of all skill levels with beautiful scenery. www.fruita.org.

Lodging

Combine camping with mountain biking at the North Fruita Desert campground, featuring 35 campsites with fire rings and picnic tables (including 2 group sites) and miles of well-maintained biking trails. Vault toilets, no potable water. 18 Road Trailhead, 970.244.3000.

Imondi Wake Zone

This unique spot offers a safe and exciting experience for visitors to learn and progress in their watersports abilities using a cable system (instead of a boat). Includes wakeboarding, kneeboarding, and SUPing, plus an inflatable floating playground. Recommended minimum age 6; kids 10 and under are required to take a lesson. Open seasonally, Thurs.–Sat., 10 a.m.–7 p.m., Sun., 10 a.m.–5 p.m., 1583 Cipolla Rd., 970.639.0327, www.imondiwakezone.com.

McInnis Canyons National Conservation Area

This high-desert area adjacent to Colorado National Monument comprises more than 120,000 acres of BLM-administered land, encompassing the Black Ridge Canyons Wilderness that boasts the second-largest concentration of natural arches in North America (behind Utah's Arches National Park) with more than 35, as well as 25 miles of the Colorado River that are perfect for

The Colorado National Monument offers two entrances, one in Fruita. The monument's Rim Rock Drive includes several lookouts such as this one at the Coke Ovens. Photo by Michael Mundt.

rafting. For mountain bikers, there's Koko-pelli Loops, 142 miles of trails (easy to very difficult) stretching from Loma to Moab, Utah, that include singletrack, pavement, and old jeep roads. (No e-bikes.) No pota-ble water. Begins at Loma Boat Launch, located right off I-70. As a state wildlife area, access rules and fees may apply. Con-tact the Colorado Parks and Wildlife Grand Junction office before visiting, 970.255.6100.

Another popular spot for bikers and hik-ers is Rabbit Valley, a pinyon-juniper desert landscape bordering the Colorado River that includes the Western Rim Trail, a favor-ite for mountain bikers with more than 6 miles of fast singletrack winding around the

rim above the Colorado River. Budding paleontologists will enjoy hiking the Trail Through Time (approximately 1.5-mile loop, right off I-70 at Mile Marker 2), where visi-tors can see 140-million-year-old dinosaur bones in place (and maybe Museum of Western Colorado volunteers excavating fossils). There's also Dinosaur Hill, an easy

1.5-mile hike featuring 10 points of interest and views of Colorado National Monument and the Colorado River. (Located 1.5 miles south of downtown Fruita on Hwy 340. Restrooms, picnic area, RV parking.) To see the area's famous arches, take Rattlesnake Arches Trail, about 5 miles roundtrip (add a mile if you include the overlook trail) if you can access the Upper Black Ridge Wilderness Parking Lot, which requires a high-clearance, four-wheel-drive vehicle. (It's 16 miles if you start at the Pollock Bench Trailhead!) Contact the BLM for more information, 970.244.3000.

Grand Junction

Miles from Denver: 243

For centuries, the Ute, Fremont, and other tribes inhabited the Grand Valley—Grand Junction (GJ), Fruita, and Palisade—leaving their history etched in cave paintings and petroglyphs before white settlers came to farm its fertile lands. Set at the "junction" of the Gunnison River and Colorado River (formerly the Grand River), Colorado's largest Western Slope town is one of the state's largest food producers. Also known as Colorado's Wine Country, where 28 wineries flourish in this temperate climate, the Grand Valley is the state's second designated grape-growing region or American Viticultural Area (AVA) (along with West Elks AVA around Paonia). The Grand Junction Regional Airport, the state's fourth largest, services several airlines (2828 Walker Field Dr., 970.244.9100, www.gjairport.com). www.visitgrandjunction.com.

Other Highlights

The Colorado Riverfront Trail features a 24.5-mile paved trail from Loma (6 miles northwest of Fruita) through Fruita, GJ, and Palisade, connecting several parks, lakes, and recreational amenities. A good access point is the Las Colonias Amphitheater (655 Struthers Ave.), next to the Western Colorado Botanical Gardens. 641 Struthers Ave., 970.245.3288, www.westerncoloradobotanicalgardens.org.

The world-famous Enstrom almond toffee was born in GJ in 1960, after Chester K. "Chet" Enstrom began developing candy as a hobby for his ice cream business. Watch toffee being made and shop for treats. Open Mon.–Fri., 7 a.m.–7 p.m., Sat., 8 a.m.–7 p.m., Sun., 10 a.m.–4 p.m., 701 Colorado Ave., 970.242.1655, www.enstrom.com.

The 36,000-acre Little Book Cliffs Wild Horse Area, 8 miles northeast of GJ, is home to as many as 150 wild horses, whose lineage stretches back more than a century. It's easiest to see them during early morning and evening, and a good access point is Coal Canyon Road, which begins at the Cameo exit from I-70, about 15 miles east of GJ. (The road is closed Dec. 1 to May 30 to protect foaling areas.) Roads require high-clearance vehicles. For more information, call the BLM office, 970.244.3000, or visit www.friendsofthemustangs.org.

Just 12 miles northeast of GJ lies Palisade, an agricultural hub filled with fruit orchards and wineries that's known to most to Coloradans for its delicious peaches. Stop at SunCrest Orchard Alpacas and Fiber Works, where visitors can walk an

Take a Drive: Drive southbound along Colorado's Unaweep Tabeguache scenic and historic byway (about 133 miles, three hours), offering views of the Dominguez-Escalante National Conservation Area and Uncompahgre National Forest. Highlights range from the red canyons of Gateway (home to Gateway Canyons Resort, a 58-room luxury destination, 43200 CO-141, 970.931.2458, www.gatewaycanyons.com) to the remains of the 1890s Hanging Flume aqueduct system.

Walking through a peach orchard in Palisade is more fun with an alpaca in tow. Photo by Michael Mundt.

Fast Fact: The GJ area is the only spot in Colorado to experience New Zealand–style jet boating, where you fishtail and power slide along the Colorado River in Jet Boat Colorado's Wild Mustang (in De Beque, about 33 miles northeast of GJ). A scenic river tour is available for guests who prefer to stay dry. Reserve early because summer tours get booked up fast ($$). Open mid-May–mid-Sept. Minimum 40 inches and 50 pounds. 2237 Roan Creek Rd., 970.644.1121, www.jetboatcolorado.com.

alpaca through a peach orchard. 3608 E. 1/4 Rd., Palisade, 970.464.4862, www.suncrest orchardalpacas.net.

For lavender lovers, visit Sage Creations Organic Farm to pick some and shop. Open April–May, Thurs.–Sun., 9 a.m.–4 p.m. By appointment June through mid-Sept. 3555 E Rd., Palisade, 970.623.9556, www.sagecrea tionsorganicfarm.com.

Lodging

The Hotel Maverick ($), opened in 2020, is both a hotel and a hospitality teaching facility located on the Colorado Mesa University campus. It's also home to the only king-sized bunkbed we've ever seen, great for families. 840 Kennedy Ave., 970.822.4888, www.thehotelmaverick.com.

Colorado National Monument

Home to the area's iconic red-rock cliffs and sandstone spires, the 31-square-mile Colorado National Monument (National Park System) features two entrances: the East Entrance in GJ and the West Entrance in Fruita, which includes the Saddlehorn Visitor Center (open 9 a.m.–4:30 p.m.; summer, 8 a.m.–6 p.m. 1750 Rim Rock Dr., 970.858.2800) and the only established campground, Saddlehorn Campground (4 miles from the entrance near the visitor center). Surrounded by pinyon pine and juniper trees, the campsite includes an amphitheater and 80 RV/tent sites in three loops—A Loop sites are first-come, first-served, B Loop sites can be reserved (both good for RVs up to 40 feet and trailers), C Loop sites are first-come, first-served (tents, smaller trailers)—each with restrooms, flush toilets, and water (seasonal). Sites offer picnic tables and charcoal-only grills. The campground also features amazing viewpoints of the monument such as Sentinel Spire and Independence Monument, climbed every July Fourth by locals, who plant an American flag at the top. The easiest way to see the highlights is on the 23-mile, paved Rim Rock Drive, offering 19 overlooks.

Featuring a 45-mile trail system, the monument offers two short hikes near the GJ entrance, including the Devil's Kitchen Trail, a 1.5-mile roundtrip hike to a natural rock "room" formed by upright boulders, and the Serpents Trail, part of the main

The boys taking in the vistas around Book Cliffs View near the Colorado National Monument Saddlehorn Campground. Photo by Michael Mundt.

road until 1950, a 3.5-mile hike along "The Crookedest Road in the World." For climbers, the tall (500+ feet), skinny Independence Monument is a popular spot. Park-approved, guided tours ($$) include Summit Ridge Guides (970.216.2953, www .summitridgeguides.com) and Glenwood Climbing Guides (341 Park Dr., Glenwood Springs, 970.319.0656, www.glenwood climbingguides.com). www.nps.gov/colm /index.htm.

Dominguez-Escalante National Conservation Area

A BLM-managed national conservation area situated southeast of GJ (northwest of Delta and Montrose), this land of red-rock canyons and bluffs is part of the Uncompahgre Plateau. (See "Montrose" entry.)

Named for the two Spanish friars who in 1776 traveled through the region in search of a passageway from the missions in New Mexico to those in California, there are 115 miles of streams and rivers in the area, including 30 miles of the Gunnison River. Home to more than 50 protected species of plants and animals, the 19th-century Old Spanish National Historic Trail (the shortest trade route between New Mexico and Los Angeles) also passes through it.

The Big Dominguez Campground features 10 sites with fire rings and picnic tables, as well as the Big Dominguez Creek, a popular fishing spot. Vault toilets, no potable water. Due to road conditions, RVs and travel trailers are not recommended. The campground can be accessed either from Hwy 141 or from Hwy 50. Big

---

Fast Fact: Completed in July 2021, the Palisade Plunge features 32 miles and more than 5,000 feet of relief connecting the Grand Mesa to Palisade, making it one of the country's longest singletrack downhill mountain-bike trails.

Dominguez Canyon is a good spot to see bighorn sheep, petroglyphs, and archaic rock shelters. (Located about 20 miles south of town on Hwy 50; turn west on Bridgeport Rd. and follow about 3 miles to the Bridgeport Trailhead. Restroom available. At the 2.5-mile point, take the sharp right into Big Dominguez. Little Dominguez is straight ahead. Look for the large rock-art panel on the left side of the trail at mile 4, plus about 100 yards farther. More rock art continues on remaining 3 miles.)

In Escalante Canyon, you can also camp in the Potholes Recreation Site (12 miles into the canyon), offering 10 designated campsites with picnic tables and shade shelters, as well as natural swimming pools carved into the rock. Vault toilets, no potable water. The Escalante Canyon petroglyphs are located about 1 mile into the canyon, some depicting the bighorn sheep that still inhabit the area. 5524 650 Rd., Delta, 970.244.3000.

Grand Mesa

Encompassing more than 500 square miles perched around 11,000 feet, this is the largest flat-top mountain in the world. Located about a 45-minute drive from downtown GJ, it's a giant expanse of 300+ lakes traversed by the Grand Mesa Scenic Byway (63 miles through national forest, about 90 minutes via the Land's End route), a drive that felt as if we were heading through long, beautiful alpine meadow. Surrounded by several towns, including Mesa, Collbran, and Skyway to the north, and Cedaredge to the south—as well as Powderhorn

Mountain Resort (see entry)—the Grand Mesa is a city unto itself.

A good place to start is at the Grand Mesa Visitor Center in Cedaredge (along the byway). Open Memorial Day weekend through Sept., 9 a.m.–5 p.m., GPS address: 20090 Baron Lake Dr., 970.856.4153.

If you only have a little bit of time to explore, drive to the historic Land's End Observatory (12 miles off Hwy 65 on a road that is half-paved, half-dirt, but easily accessible even for smaller vehicles). Although the observatory is no longer in use, its surrounding views include the La Sal Mountains in Utah (more than 120 miles away) and the Colorado National Monument. Beware the begging chipmunks!

LODGING

Cobbett Lake Campground, near Cedaredge, is the only reservation campsite in Grand Mesa with 20 sites, vault toilets. Open June–mid-Sept. From Cedaredge, travel north on Hwy 65; at 15.7 miles, turn right at north end of Cobbett Lake to campground.

The Black Bear Cabin, Mesa Lakes Lodge, and Moose Manor at Mesa Lakes ($), located on the north side of the Grand Mesa National Forest, are part of the Mesa Lakes Ranger Station Complex. Cabins include a shower/flush toilet, refrigerator, electric cooking stove, cookware/utensils, electricity (light and heat), and beds for up to 8 adults (with air-mattress cots). Open July–Sept. Must reserve at least three days in advance. The Mesa Lakes Recreation area features seven lakes within walking distance and includes a hand-carry boat launch for canoes and nonmotorized boating. It also offers access to one of the area's most popular hikes, the Lost Lake Trail (#502), about a 2.5-mile roundtrip hike to a narrow, emerald-green lake. 50710 SW 60 Rd., 970.242. 8211.

The stunning scenery around Land's End Observatory on Grand Mesa. Photo by the author.

Also in Cedaredge, Thunder Mountain Lodge offers 10 cabin rentals, sleep 4–7 ($), as well as guided snowmobile tours and canoe/SUP rentals. 20703 Baron Lake Dr., 970.856.6240, www.thundermountainlodge .net.

In Mesa, there's the Grand Mesa RV Park, which offers 29 RV sites and 9 rustic cabins (sleep 2–3). Shower/restrooms, laundry, grocery store, and more. CO-65, Mesa, 970.268.5651, www.grandmesarv.com.

Located in Collbran, Vega State Park is set at 8,000 feet on the edge of the mesa. Offering easy access to Grand Mesa National Forest, this year-round spot features a 900-acre reservoir, great for trout fishing, sailing, canoeing, and waterskiing. Features 113 campsites (10 walk-in tent sites), a visitor center, boat ramps, 5 cabins (sleep 6), showers, and more. 15247 N. 6/10 Rd., Collbran, 970.487.3407.

Highline Lake

Located roughly 25 miles northwest of GJ, Highline Lake is popular for jet- and water-skiers, paddleboarders, and boaters. (The smaller Mack Mesa Lake allows boating for hand-propelled and electric craft.) Offering warmwater fishing for largemouth bass and crappie, the lake is also stocked in fall and spring with rainbow trout. There are more than 9 miles of trails for hiking and biking—the Highline Lake Trail is a 3.5-mile loop—and some 200 bird species. The year-round campground features 36 RV/tent sites, visitor center, 2 boat ramps, laundry, showers, and picnic sites. 1800 11.8 Rd., Loma, 970.858.7208.

James M. Robb-Colorado River State Park

A string of five "pearls" describes this five-section, 35-mile park along the Colorado River. Three of them are day-use only:

Connected Lakes, Corn Lake, and the Colorado River State Wildlife Area and Pear Park, offering varying water sports and recreation opportunities. The Island Acres section features four lakes for swimming, fishing, and hiking (hand-propelled, sail watercraft, and electric-motor boats), as well as 80 RV campsites with laundry, showers, and group sites. Exit 47 off I-70 (east of Palisade), 970.464.0548.

The Fruita Section offers spectacular views of the Colorado National Monument and Book Cliffs. There are 63 RV/tent sites, a boat ramp, a visitor center, picnic areas, showers, and laundry. Good for fishing, boating, hiking, and biking. 595 Hwy 240, Fruita, 970.858.9188.

Powderhorn Mountain Resort

Stats: 63 designated trails, 1,600 skiable acres, 4 lifts, 2 terrain parks

Trail classification: 20 percent Beginner; 50 percent Intermediate; 30 percent Advanced

Base elevation: 8,200 feet

Located along the northern edge of Grand Mesa about 40 miles east of GJ, roughly 70 percent of the trails are "beginner" or "intermediate." First-time skiers or riders receive three free lessons, rentals and lift tickets throughout the season, plus special offers after completing the program. (Sundays, 8 years and older). There's also a multiuse trail system on the land below the ski resort that's open to fat-biking, Nordic skiing, and snowshoeing. Odin Recreation rents gear and offers lessons (adult, kids, private) at the resort. Full- and half-day snowshoe tours available Saturdays through the season. In summer, enjoy 11 miles of downhill mountain-biking trails and 5 miles of hiking trails. Then stay in a Tiny Home, located at the base (4–8 guests); kitchens and microwave plus firepit. 48338 Powderhorn Rd., 970.268.5700, www.powderhorn.com.

Gunnison

Miles from Denver: 201

Inhabited by the Ute tribe before Spanish explorers and white prospectors flooded the area, this town established in 1880 was named for the US Army officer John W. Gunnison who surveyed for the transcontinental railroad in 1853. A bustling college town, "Gunny" is home to Western Colorado University (the first college on the Western Slope, opened in 1901 as Colorado State Normal College) and the Gunnison-Crested Butte Regional Airport, located just five minutes from downtown (711 W. Rio Grande Ave., 970.641.2304, www.flygunnisonairport.com).

Other Highlights

Home to the state's largest research-quality telescope available to the public, the Gunnison Valley Observatory is open to visitors on Friday and Saturday nights (mid-June–mid-September) for viewing on the 30-inch scope, as well as lectures and special events. Located off Gold Basin Road at the base of "W" Mountain, just southwest of Gunnison on US Hwy 50. 970.641.0634, www.gunnisonobservatory.org.

The Pioneer Museum grounds feature more than 25 historic buildings, including a log-cabin chapel, a narrow-gauge train, and more. Open daily, mid-May–Sept., 9 a.m.–5 p.m., 803 E. Tomichi Ave., 970.641.0155, www.gunnisonpioneermuseum.com.

Experience some of the most pristine areas of Gunnison County via dog sled ($$) on tours with Lucky Cat Dog Farm, 900 CR 13, 970.641.1636, www.luckycatdogfarm.com.

Fast Fact: The CBGTrails is the free trail map app that includes every mile of trail in Gunnison and Crested Butte. www.cbgtrails.com/app.

Located about 1 mile from downtown Hwy 50, the Gunnison River Whitewater Park is built for canoeing, kayaking, and rafting (and tubing, when the water is low enough). Kids 13 years and younger must wear a life jacket. There are also picnic areas and plenty of parking.

The Signal Peak trail system (BLM-managed) features a couple-dozen miles of singletrack for mountain bikers. www.gunni sontrails.org.

Tour Operators

Want a luxury glamping experience in the backcountry? Dog Daze Outfitters will set up an entire camp for visitors in the Gunnison National Forest, just a short hike or drive from Taylor Park Reservoir (motorized) or Spring Creek Reservoir (nonmotorized), perfect for fishing, kayaking, or SUPing. Camp includes luxury canvas ($) or traditional tents (sleep 2) with queen beds or air mattresses, plus a wood-burning stove, firewood, a full-size grill with cookware and utensils, coolers, a private bathhouse, and more. Bring the food you want to cook, and you're set for a backcountry adventure (2-day minimum). Camping-equipment rentals available. 970.208.5851, www.dogdazeoutfitters.com.

Almont

Almost equidistant between Gunnison (about 17 miles northeast) and Crested Butte, this small town at the confluence of the Taylor and East Rivers (forming the Gunnison) is a fishing haven. Anglers will enjoy Three Rivers Resort, a year-round, full-service property on a private stretch of the Taylor River, offering RV sites, cabins ranging from basic to upscale (up to five bedrooms), a restaurant (seasonal), a fly-fishing shop, daily raft trips (roughly May–Sept.), guide service, and more. 130 CR 742, 970.641.1303, www.3rivers resort.com.

The town also boasts the Roaring Judy Fish Hatchery and Rearing Unit, a cold-water facility and home to the largest kokanee salmon run in the country. Self-guided tours and stream/pond fishing available. Call ahead. 14131 N. Hwy 135, 970.641.0190.

Or check out Campfire Ranch, a new, privately owned campground along the Taylor River that offers 10 tent sites, vault toilets, potable water, and activities such as campfire-building clinics and sunset hikes. Includes camping-gear rentals and an adventure concierge to help plan activities. 900 CR 742, 833.CAM.PACR, www.camp fireranch.co.

Finally, drive from Almont to Buena Vista along the highest paved mountain route over the Continental Divide, Cottonwood Pass (12,126 feet).

Curecanti National Recreation Area

A former summer destination for the Ute tribe named for the Ute Indian subchief who roamed through eastern and southern Colorado from the 1860s to 1870s, Curecanti (kur-uh-KAHN-tee) includes three reservoirs: Crystal, Morrow Point, and Blue Mesa, with corresponding dams on the Gunnison River (www.nps.gov/cure). There are 10 campsites (970.641.2337), 8 on Blue Mesa, which I've broken down by reservoir:

CRYSTAL

The westernmost and smallest reservoir of the three, connected on the north border to the Black Canyon of the Gunnison National Park (closest to Montrose), Crystal Reservoir is limited for boating to hand-carried craft.

The East Portal Campground includes 15 shaded RV/tent sites along the Gunnison River. Adjacent to and only accessible from Black Canyon of the Gunnison National Park, it includes vault toilets and potable water (seasonal), first-come, first-served. No vehicles exceeding 22 feet. For hiking,

The Bay of Chickens is a popular swimming area along Blue Mesa Reservoir. Photo by Michael Mundt.

the 5-mile roundtrip Crystal Creek Trail (moderately strenuous) ends at an overlook above the Crystal River. Check for ticks in summer. Located 24 miles from Hwy 50 and Hwy 92 junction.

MORROW POINT

Despite negative reports by Captain John W. Gunnison, who surveyed the area in 1853 for the Pacific Railroad, the Denver and Rio Grande Western Railroad was carrying ore, cattle, and more through Curecanti by 1882. The railroad bore the iconic 700-foot granite spire Curecanti Needle (set on the southern bank of the reservoir) on its "Scenic Line of the World" logo. Now most of the old railroad bed is submerged beneath Morrow Point. (*The Jungle Book* author Rudyard Kipling famously rode the train in 1889.)

Learn about railroad history and see the Needle (a popular climbing spot) on a 90-minute, ranger-led boat tour through the Black Canyon of the Gunnison (early June–Sept.), departing Wed.–Mon., 10 a.m., 12 p.m. Reservations required via www.recreation.gov or in person at the Elk Creek Visitor Center a day before. Tours begin at the Pine Creek boat dock, accessed from the Pine Creek Trail at US Hwy 50, Mile Marker 130 (35 miles east of Montrose and 25 miles west of Gunnison). Leave no later than 45 minutes before departure for the walk down 232 stairs followed by an easy, 1-mile walk along the old railroad bed toward the boat dock. Preboarding begins 15 minutes prior to start time. Contact Black Canyon of the Gunnison National Park service with questions: 970.641.2337.

Guided fishing tours on Morrow Point available via Fishing Guide Ryan Van-Lanen, 970.596.4946, www.fishbluemesa.com/morrow-point.

The Cimarron Campground offers 21 RV/tent sites, located near the dam at the site of the historic railroad. Potable water, flush toilets (seasonal), and vault toilets. First-come, first-served. Hikes include Pine Creek, 2 miles roundtrip, which passes the old railroad bed into the Black Canyon (moderately strenuous), located 1 mile west of the Hwy 50 and Hwy 92 junction. Limited parking. On the 4-mile roundtrip Curecanti Creek hike (strenuous), the Curecanti Needle towers above the trail's end. Trailhead begins at the Pioneer Point overlook, 5.7 miles from Hwy 50 and Hwy 92 junction.

BLUE MESA

Twenty miles long with some 96 miles of shoreline, Blue Mesa is Colorado's largest body of water within Colorado. (Navajo Reservoir, partially in New Mexico, is the largest.) It's one of the top kokanee salmon fisheries in the United States, stocked with brown, rainbow, and mackinaw trout, and a favorite water-sports spot. The farthest east of the three reservoirs (closest to Gunnison), there are two marinas:

Elk Creek Marina (open May–Sept., 7 a.m.–5 p.m., 970.641.0707) offers boat launching, boat rentals, tackle, gasoline, kayaks, SUPs, and canoes and includes Pappy's Restaurant (open May 21, 11 a.m.–

8 p.m., 970.641.0403), a campground, and a National Park Service visitor center. (The latter two are open year-round.) Located 16 miles west of Gunnison on Hwy 50. The Elk Creek Campground features 160 sites, 27 electric hookups, 14 tent-only. Flush and vault toilets (seasonal), potable water, coin-operated showers (seasonal). In summer, visitors can rent one of five Blue Mesa Adventure Pods, cabin-like structures accommodating 2–3 people (dogs allowed in some), which come with 2 paddleboards, 2 Pappy's drink tokens, a bundle of firewood, picnic table, and firepit. Summer only ($). Contact marina for pod reservations.

Lake Fork Marina (open May 15–Sept., 7 a.m.–5 p.m., 970.641.3048), set on the reservoir's west end near the dam, offers boat launching, a store, gasoline, boat slips (970.596.4946), and a campground with paved spots for RVs and trailers. Located 29 miles west of Gunnison on Hwy 50. Lake Fork Campground offers 90 sites, 4 tent-only. Flush and vault toilets, potable water, coin-operated showers (seasonal).

Both marinas offer guided fishing tours via Elevation Angling in Gunnison, 970.691.1582, www.elevationangling.com.

Hiking includes the Neversink Trail, 1.5 miles roundtrip (easy), set on the north bank of the river by a great blue heron rookery, 5 miles west of Gunnison on Hwy 50 (wheelchair accessible). Dillon Pinnacles, 4 miles roundtrip (strenuous), offers good views of the reservoir and mountains, 6 miles west of Elk Creek Visitor Center on Hwy 50.

OTHER PUBLIC CAMPGROUNDS

Stevens Creek: 53 RV/tent sites are surrounded by sage and rabbitbrush but no natural shade, vault toilets, potable water (seasonal).

Ponderosa: 28 RV/tent sites, located at the northwest end of the Soap Creek Arm,

vault toilets, and potable water (seasonal). First-come, first-served.

Dry Gulch: 9 RV/tent sites, shaded by large cottonwood trees, vault toilets, and potable water (seasonal), first-come, first-served.

The East Elk Creek, Red Creek, and Gateview campgrounds are all small (1–6 sites, some group) with potable water (seasonal) and vault toilets. First-come, first-served.

OTHER PRIVATE CAMPGROUNDS

A nine-minute walk to the reservoir, Gunnison Lakeside Cabins and RV Park offers tent/RV sites plus cabins (sleep 4–6) with restrooms, refrigerators, and more. 28357 US-50, 970.641.0477, www.gunnisonlakeside.com.

Ferro's Blue Mesa Ranch features cabins with full kitchens/TV and more, as well as a full-service store (tackle, groceries, liquor), plus fishing trips and horseback rides. 3200 CR 721 (Soap Creek Road), 970.641.4671, www.ferrosbluemesaranch.com.

Blue Mesa Recreational Ranch features RV/tent sites, cabins, and cottages, as well as pools–miniature golf, and activities. (May–Oct.) 27601 W. Hwy 50, 970.642.4150, www.bluemesarvcamping.com.

Hartman Rocks Recreation Area

Set in the high desert about 5 miles south of town, these 8,000 acres of public land offer 45 miles of singletrack trails for mountain biking and 45 miles of road for biking (fat-biking and Nordic skiing in winter). Also a good motorcycling and climbing area. There are 50 dispersed-camping sites. Guided climbing tours for all levels ($$) are offered through Scenic River Tours Inc., 703 W. Tomichi Ave., 970.641.3131, www.scenicrivertours.com, or Irwin Guides (Crested Butte), with half-day climbs (9 a.m., 1 p.m.) for beginners and families,

970.349.5430, www.irwinguides.com. (The Mountain Adventures kids' program, noted under the Crested Butte Mountain Resort entry, guides there as well.)

Visit a local bike shop for trail advice, including Rock 'n' Roll Sports (608 W. Tomichi Ave., 970.641.9150), or Double Shot Cyclery (yes—they sell coffee too!). Open 7 a.m.–6 p.m., 222 N. Main St., 970.642.5411, www.rockandrollsports.com.

All Sports Replay is a bike shop and used-gear store. Open Mon.-Sat., 9 a.m.–6 p.m., Sun., 10 a.m.–4 p.m., 115 W. Georgia, 970.641.1893, www.asrgunnison.com.

In winter, there's plenty of snowmobiling, plus Nordic skiers have access to 16 miles of trails maintained by Gunnison Nordic Club (www.gunnisonnordic.com). Contact the Gunnison BLM field office for more information, 970.642.4940.

Lake City

About 55 miles southwest of Gunnison, this remote town is known as an ice-climbing destination. Featuring the free Lake City Ice Park just one block south of downtown (970.944.2333), there's also ice-skating on the state's second-largest natural lake, Lake San Cristobal, or the Lake City Ski Hill (opened in 1966), with one lift and seven runs.

The town is famously known as the former home of the Colorado's cannibal, Alferd Packer, who was jailed for killing and eating five fellow gold prospectors in 1874 when their group became trapped in a blizzard on nearby Slumgullion Pass. The massacre site is just a five-minute drive south of the town's miniature golf course, identified with signage. The Hinsdale County Museum boasts the most extensive collection of Packer memorabilia known. Open Memorial Day–Labor Day. Hours vary. (130 N. Silver St., 970.944.2050, www.lakecitymuseum.com). www.lakecity.com.

Mesa Verde Country

Miles from Denver: 371 (Mesa Verde National Park)

Comprising renowned Mesa Verde National Park, the area boasts 2,000 years of history throughout several significant historic sites. Featuring the towns of Cortez, Dolores, and Mancos (and Towaoc, Colorado's most southwestern town and the headquarters of the Ute Mountain Indian Reservation), it also offers plenty of rugged canyons, scenic mountain trails, and water for year-round recreation. I've outlined the three main towns first (with highlights), followed by other area destinations and activities. www.mesaverdecountry.com.

Cortez

The largest of the cities in this region, this spot nestled between the La Plata Mountains and Sleeping Ute Mountain is often called the archaeological center of America (just 10 miles from the Mesa Verde entrance). www.cityofcortez.com.

LODGING

The Cortez / Mesa Verde KOA Journey offers RV/tent sites and cabins, as well as access to Denny Lake, where you can fish, kayak, or hike the 1.5-mile trail around it. Includes a dog park, pool, and camp store. Open April 15–Oct. 15, 27432 US-160, 970.565.9301.

OTHER HIGHLIGHTS

Located in a historic 1909 building in downtown, the Cortez Cultural Center includes a gift/book shop, art gallery, and outdoor amphitheater, featuring a lifelike mural depicting a traditional pueblo. It serves as a backdrop for the summer Native American dances, one of the highlights of our Cortez visit. Open Memorial Day to Labor Day, Mon.–Sat., 7 p.m. Donations recommended. The Center also owns the Hawkins Preserve (1490 S. Cedar St.), a 122-acre natural and cultural preserve with hiking trails and climbing spots. (Permits required; download from site.) 25 N. Market St., 970.565.1151, www.cortezcultural center.org.

The Yucca House National Monument is an unexcavated Ancestral Puebloan archaeological site located between Cortez and Towaoc (estimated to house around 100 buildings). Visitors can poke around looking for above-ground ruins, but there are no signs or trails. If you want to visit, I'd suggest checking in first with the Colorado Welcome Center at Cortez (928 E. Main St., 970.565.8227). 19751 Rd. B (off CR 20.5). www.nps.gov/yuho/index.htm.

CROW CANYON ARCHAEOLOGICAL CENTER

This 170-acre archaeologic research facility and "living classroom" offers hands-on archaeology programs and small-group tours led by American Indian scholars and archaeologists. The free, 0.5-mile (one-hour) walking tour features behind-the-scenes views of a working archaeology lab (Wed., Thurs., June–September. Arrive 8:45 a.m.). Full-day tours available 9 a.m.–4 p.m., Aug.–Sept. Minimum age 10. Includes a visit to excavation site and lunch ($). Open Mon.–Fri., 9 a.m.–5 p.m., 23390 Rd. K, 970.565.8975, www.crowcanyon.org.

SAN JUAN MOUNTAINS LLAMA TREKS

Includes full-day picnic hikes and two-day hiking trips or longer. Custom trips available. A family-friendly trip is the two-night, three-day itinerary to the High Camp Hut in San Juan Mountains backcountry. (See "Telluride" entry.) 12626 Rd. 25, 970.565.2177, www.sanjuanmountainsllamatreks .com.

Dolores

Named after the river on which it is located, the Ancestral Puebloans lived here until roughly AD 1300, followed by the Ute tribe. Established as a major stop along the route between Durango and Ridgway with the 1891 Rio Grande Southern Railway, it was incorporated as Dolores in 1900. https://sennasocialmediaco.wixsite.com/dolores chamber.

LODGING

The Dolores River Campground and Cabins range from RV/tent sites to yurts, vintage travel trailers, Conestoga wagons, and full-service cabins ($). 18680 CO-145, 970.882.7761, www.doloresrivercamp ground.com.

The Cozy Comfort R.V. Park features RV/tent sites, laundry, and restrooms/showers. 1501 Central Ave., 970.882.2483, www.cozycomfortrvpark.com.

The summer-evening Native American dances at the Cortez Cultural Center are a highlight of visiting Cortez. Photo by Michael Mundt.

Across from the McPhee Reservoir entrance, The Views RV Park and Campground offers RV/tent sites, glamping tents, laundry, shower/restroom facility, SUP rentals, and more. 24990 Hwy 184, 970.749.6489, www.theviewsrvpark.com.

Don't miss the town's famous Galloping Goose 5, which parks outside the free Rio Grande Southern Railroad Museum (421 Railroad Ave.). It's one of a series of seven railcars called "motors," built in the 1930s as an economic means of transporting small amounts of freight, passengers, and mail. Ride it for free during the city's summer event, the Dolores Escalante Days. 970.882.7082, www.gallopinggoose5.org.

CANYONS OF THE ANCIENTS VISITOR CENTER AND MUSEUM

Considered the area's premier archaeological museum, exhibits focus on Ancestral Puebloan, Native American, and historic cultures in the Four Corners region. Formerly named the Anasazi Heritage Center, the museum offers permanent and special exhibits, plus tours of two 12th-century archaeological sites, the Escalante and Dominguez Pueblos. Located at McPhee Reservoir, there's also a picnic area and 0.5-mile nature trail. Hours vary by season. 27501 CO-184, 970.882.5600.

Once a thriving homestead settled by miners in search of fortune, the remoteness of the area eventually drove them away by 1918 from the log houses they'd built along the West Dolores River. They're now part of one of Colorado's most upscale destinations, featuring 13 restored cabins, a spa and yoga studio, a "saloon" that serves meals, a winery, and a library ($$$). The hot springs (85 to 106 degrees) can be enjoyed several ways, including inside the restored 19th-century

bathhouse or the pool just outside it. Rates include all meals and beverages. (In addition to other properties, the Dunton River Camp, set across the mountain from Telluride, features 8 luxury, safari-style tents, open June–mid-October.) 8532 CR 38, Dolores, 970.882.4800, www.duntondestinations.com/hot-springs.

Mancos

Founded in 1894, this ranching and farmland community between the La Plata Mountains and Mesa Verde (2 miles from the entrance) describes itself as the place "where the old west meets the new." A Colorado Creative District filled with galleries and restaurants, Mancos retains its Wild West charm with cattle drives running right through the center of town.

Set within walking distance to town, the Riverwood RV Resort offers RV/tent sites, laundry, showers, restrooms, and more. 350 E. Grand Ave., 970.533.9142, www.rvparkmancos.com.

Or head a few minutes from town to Willowtail Springs Lakeside Cabins, set on a 60-acre nature preserve with private lake. Two cabins accommodate 2–4 guests; a third cabin accommodates 6 ($$). Free use of canoe and fishing gear. Guided nature tours available (for a fee). 10451 Road 39, 970.533.7592, www.willowtailsprings.com.

The Mancos Burro Fest takes place in the summer, featuring burro racing, a burro-packing demonstration, and more.

JERSEY JIM FIRE LOOKOUT TOWER

Home to US Forest Service fire lookouts from the 1940s to the 1970s, the cab (living area) includes the original furniture (table and chairs for 4; one double bed); propane heating, lighting, refrigerator, and stove

47

MOUNTAINS AND MESAS
MESA VERDE COUNTRY

with small oven; as well as dishes, cooking, and eating utensils. (Guest supplies can be hoisted up to the cab via pulley.) Rent for one or two nights, late May–mid-October, weather permitting. Located 14 miles north of Mancos on Forest Road #561, a well-graveled forest road accessible by two-wheel-drive vehicles. Water is available from a hand pump at Transfer Campground (4 miles before tower). Pack in, pack out. www.jerseyjimfoundation.org/jersey-jim -fire-lookout-tower.

MANCOS STATE PARK

Featuring Jackson Gulch Reservoir, there's plenty of year-round recreation for canoeists, kayakers, wakeless powerboaters, and anglers (perch and rainbow trout). The 5.5-miles of trails cross through town, meeting Chicken Creek Trail (good for mountain biking), which connects to trails on US Forest Service land and the famed Colorado Trail. Used for hiking, horseback riding, and biking, the trail system is perfect for Nordic skiing and snowshoeing in the winter. The 23-site main campground offers potable water and vault toilets; 9 rustic tent sites on the northwest side feature restrooms but no water; 2 yurts are available with microwave, refrigerator, dining table with 4 chairs, and mattresses (2 double futons with frame plus a single bunkbed). 42545 CR N., 970.533.7065 (970.882. 2213 off-season).

MCPHEE RECREATION AREA

Colorado's fifth-largest lake, McPhee Reservoir offers 50 miles of shoreline for year-round boating, fishing, camping, hiking, and biking. Created by damming the Dolores River, the Lower Dolores is considered prime Colorado fishing territory, particularly during fall when the area's brown trout spawn. The reservoir is also stocked with both warm- and cold-water fish, including walleye and smallmouth bass.

Adjacent to the boat ramp is the Can Do Trail, a 1.1-mile hike that climbs to a scenic overlook. April through October, the full-service Doc's Marina offers supplies and boat rentals (pontoon, fishing, ski, kayaks), SUPs, and utility task vehicles (UTVs). Visitors can also use the marina's BBQ grills. Winter snowmobile tours also available. Open May–Oct., 970.560.4801, www.docsmarinamcpheereservoir.com.

The McPhee Campground, located on a mesa 500 feet above the reservoir, offers 71 campsites (50 reservable; a dozen are walk-ins with tent pads near scenic overlooks; 2 sites offer tables and toilets accommodate wheelchairs). Flush toilets, showers, and laundry house available in summer months. The adjacent McPhee Group Area offers four group campsites (reservation only) with volleyball posts, a ball field, and horseshoe pits (bring equipment). Water, vault toilets, picnic tables, and fire grates. (No services Oct.–May.) Mountain bikers will enjoy the McPhee/House Creek Bike Route, a 16-mile trail following paved and gravel roads that starts and finishes at the campground.

RIMROCK OUTFITTERS

Experience views of the Mancos River and Mt. Hesperus via horseback on one of Rimrock's trail rides, from one-hour to full-day tours. (Minimum 6 years; younger kids can get a complimentary ride at the corral.) Offering breakfast, dinner rides, and sleigh rides (roughly mid-December to around New Year's Day), they also feature multiday pack trips ($–$$). 12175 CR 44, 970.533. 7588, www.rimrockoutfitters.com.

Canyons of the Ancients National Monument (CANM)

Containing the country's highest-known density of archaeological sites, CANM's 176,000 acres along the Utah-Colorado border (west of Cortez) became a national

Rock art and ancient sites abound in Canyons of the Ancients National Monument. Photo by Michael Mundt.

monument in 2000. Preserving more than 6,000 ancient sites as part of the BLM's National Landscape Conservation System, only a handful of them are clearly identified. (Don't disturb artifacts or structures!) I'd suggest stopping first in Dolores at the Canyons of the Ancients Visitor Center and Museum. Or consider a guided tour via the Southwest Colorado Canyons Alliance, which offers half-day "Family Time on the Monument" tours (ideal for parents and kids ages 5–13), such as a 2-mile hike to the Saddlehorn Pueblo (up to 5 guests). Multi-day tours also available. 970.560.1643, www.swcocanyons/tours.

Here are three must-see sites:

Lowry Pueblo: The only developed recreation site within CANM, it features a 40-room village with standing walls that have been stabilized, as well as 8 kivas, including a Great Kiva (defined as more than 100 square meters in area). There's also a 0.2-mile trail (wheelchair-accessible), a picnic area, and a restroom. From Cortez, head roughly 18 miles north on US Hwy 491 (666) to the "Pleasant View and Lowry" sign (Rd. CC). Turn west (left) on Rd. CC and follow the signs.

Painted Hand Pueblo: Named for the outlined hands on a boulder (pictographs), the site features a standing tower perched on a boulder. (It has never been excavated.) To get there, turn west off Hwy 491 at CR CC and go 5.5 miles west. Take CR 10 south 11.3 miles, and watch for the sign/kiosk and turn left. Continue on dirt road for 1 mile to the trailhead. The trail is about 0.4 miles, one way.

Sand Canyon: Containing several Puebloan archaeological sites, the 6.5-mile (one way) Sand Canyon Trail is used for hiking, mountain biking, and horseback riding. One of the largest prehistoric settlements in the region—420 rooms, 100 kivas, and 14 towers—the stunning Saddlehorn Pueblo, built between 1250 and 1285 in a scenic alcove beneath a rock formation resembling a saddle horn, is about 1 mile into the hike. From Cortez, take US Route 491 south and turn west on CR G. Head 12 miles and look for the parking area on the right side of the road. There are no services available at trailhead. Pro Tip: The trailhead is located in McElmo Canyon across the road from Sutcliffe Vineyards, one of our favorite stops in the area. Open daily, noon–5 p.m., 12174 Rd. G, 970.565.0825, www.sutcliffewines.com.

Canyon of the Ancients Guest Ranch

Set in scenic McElmo Canyon between the southern border of CANM and the northern edge of the Ute Mountain Reservation, this 2,000-acre working ranch once owned by local rancher Elden Zwicker is one of our all-time favorite destinations ($$). Offering 5 guesthouses (2–8 people),

The Canyon of the Ancients Guest Ranch is a fun, historic headquarters for adventure in Mesa Verde Country. Photo by Michael Mundt.

owners Garry and Ming Adams have decorated each in authentic Southwestern style. Guests are welcomed with a bowl full of fresh garden produce and eggs. (Cabins feature kitchens and grills, plus you can order ranch-raised lamb and beef. No on-site dining.) The owners also provide organic tortilla chips for guests to feed the flock of pet Navajo-churro sheep, and Garry will leave cat food for you to feed any feline visitors. He is also happy to guide you in his favorite CANM spots, including an ancient village discovered on their land. The only downside of staying here is that it's about 20 miles west of Cortez. Stock up on groceries for your stay, or drive 30 minutes into town for meals. 7950 CR G, Cortez, 970.565.4288, www.canyonofthe ancients.com.

Four Corners National Monument

About 39 miles southwest of Cortez, this Navajo Nation monument is more than just the point where four states (Arizona, Utah, Colorado, and New Mexico) meet in one place, the only quadripoint of its kind in the country; it's also a rite of passage for

Coloradoans. There's not much other than a long line for a photo op at the actual spot; an amazing craft market by local Navajo and Ute artisans; and a delicious fry-bread stand. But it's absolutely worth a stop. Yes, the location is roughly 1,800 feet off course because of a disagreement about borders and surveying techniques used in 1912, when it was established. As far as I'm concerned, however, my body was in four states at once. 597 NM-597, Teec Nos Pos, AZ, 86514, 928.206.2540, navajonation parks.org/tribal-parks/four-corners -monument.

Hovenweep National Monument

Located on Cajon Mesa spanning southwestern Colorado and southeastern Utah, Hovenweep features five sites built between AD 1200 and 1300. Displaying similarities in architecture, masonry, and pottery to inhabitants of Mesa Verde, it comprises a

The Navajo Nation's Four Corners National Monument is the only point in the country where four states meet. Photo by Michael Mundt.

A view of Sleeping Ute Mountain from Hovenweep National Monument, which features several square, circular, and D-shaped ancient dwellings. Photo by Michael Mundt.

mix of square and circular towers, D-shaped dwellings, and ceremonial kivas.

Of the five sites, the Square Tower Group is the largest and most accessible. Adjacent to the visitor center (Hovenweep Rd., Montezuma Creek, Utah, 84534), take the easy, 1.5-mile Little Ruin Trail surrounding the canyon, featuring remnants of several buildings including Stronghold House and Twin Towers. Another 4 miles northeast along the road are the Holly and Horseshoe/Hackberry sites—hike the 0.8 miles between them—followed by Cutthroat Castle, another 4.5 miles northeast. (The Cajon site is in Utah, about 9 miles southwest of the visitor center.) The 31-site Hovenweep Campground is set near the visitor center (open year-round), first-come, first-served.

Most are tent sites with a few for RVs with tent pads, fire rings, and picnic tables with shade structures. 970.562.4282, www.nps .gov/hove.

Mesa Verde National Park (MVNP)

Colorado's only UNESCO World Heritage Site and the country's largest archaeological preserve, MVNP maintains nearly 5,000 known archaeological sites of the Ancestral Pueblo people, who lived here for over 700 years. Established in 1906 as the country's first park specifically celebrating a prehistoric culture and its people, more than 600 of its sites are the renowned cliff dwellings, including Balcony House; the largest, the 150-room Cliff Palace (both on Chapin Mesa, open year-round) and Long House

The 150-room Cliff Palace is the largest Ancestral Puebloan cliff dwelling in Mesa Verde National Park. Photo by Michael Mundt.

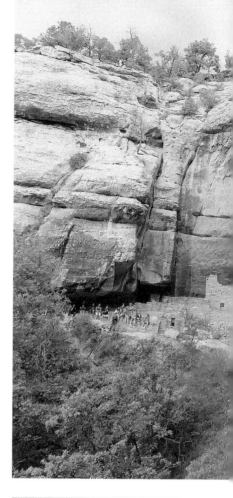

(Wetherill Mesa, open May–Sept., weather permitting). All three can only be visited via ranger-guided tour. Purchase tickets at the Visitor and Research Center, located just east of the park exit ramp off US Hwy 160. Reservations required. (Skip the four-hour bus tour if you have young kids—ours were horribly bored—and opt for the ranger tour. You're welcome.)

Another good stop is the Chapin Mesa Archaeological Museum, located 21 miles (45 minutes) from the park entrance, open year-round. From there, drive two popular routes: the 6-mile Mesa Top Loop, featuring pit houses and the Square Tower House, and the 6-mile Cliff Palace Loop, which passes Cliff Palace, Balcony House, and overlooks to other cliff dwellings. Park lodging includes Morefield Campground (services mid-May–mid-October), located just 4.5 miles from the park entrance. Offering 267 campsites, the full-service village features the Knife Edge Café, a gift shop, and grocery and camp stores—even a dog-boarding facility. There are several hiking trails nearby, such as the 7.8-mile Prater Ridge Trail (loop) or the 4.4-mile (roundtrip) Point Lookout Trail.

From late April to mid-October, visitors can also stay at the Far View Lodge ($), featuring 150 rooms and on-site dining. Mile Marker 15, 844.684.9427, www.visitmesaverde.com. MVNP, 970.529.4465, www.nps.gov/meve.

Mountain Biking the Mesas

The area boasts 600 miles of beginner, intermediate, and challenging (green, blue, and black) mountain-biking trails, plus higher elevations with cooler riding temperatures. In Cortez, Phil's World (9450 Rd.

Fast Fact: In April 2021, MVNP became the world's 100th International Dark Park.

30.1, Cortez) features plenty of loops for all skill levels, including the 10.6-mile Main Loop, the 26.8-mile Phil's World Sampling, or one of its most famous, the blue-level Rib Cage (about 1.2 miles roundtrip). The 3.5-mile Trust Loop (green) is also great for families. In the San Juan National Forest around Dolores, Boggy Draw is an 8.4-mile, smooth, primarily singletrack that is also good for families (dispersed camping

only). (To get there from Cortez, head north 10 miles on CO Hwy 145. Passing through Dolores, turn left on 11th St. and head up the hill. Turn right on CR W; the trail parking lot is just down the road.) Or try Chicken Creek in Mancos, located in Mancos State Park (see Mancos entry), which follows the creek for about 7.8 miles. (E-bikes are allowed on several trails. Check before visiting.) Bike rentals available at Kokopelli Bike and Board in Cortez (open Mon.–Sat., 9 a.m.–5 p.m., 130 W. Main St., 970.565.4408, www.kokopellibike.com).

Ute Mountain Ute Tribal Park

Designated a Historical District in 1972, this land that has been inhabited for centuries by Ancestral Puebloans, Fremonts, and Utes can only be toured with a Ute Tribal Guide. There's an easy, half-day tour (9 a.m.–noon), featuring visits to geologic highlights and surface sites (40 miles). The active, full-day tour (9 a.m.–4 p.m.) includes a 3-mile walk on unpaved trails and ladder climbs to four cliff dwellings in Lion Canyon (80 miles). Meet at the Tribal Park Visitor Center, located at highway junction 160/491 (about 20 miles south of Cortez) near the iconic

Jackson Butte, aka Chimney Rock (5,452 feet). Water and drinks available for purchase, but guests should bring their own food, snacks, and a full tank of gas. Reservations recommended ($10/person): utepark@fone.net or 970.565.9653.

The primitive campground is located 15 miles in the park boundary along the Mancos River. Camp anywhere in the campground; no running water or electricity (water tanks for drinking and washing); firewood with designated firepits. Cabins are available for $15/day but are empty, so bring your own bedding. A permit must be obtained before camping. Contact above e-mail/phone for camping permit and cabin use. www.utemountaintribalpark.info.

There's also the Sleeping Ute RV Park (next door to the Ute Mountain Casino Hotel), offering RV/tent sites, laundry and showers, convenience store, and an indoor pool. 3 Weeminuche Dr., Towaoc, 800.258.8007, www.utemountaincasino.com/sleeping-ute-rv-park.

Montrose

Miles from Denver: 265

Established in 1882 as a supply hub to nearby mining communities, Montrose then served as a transportation hub from Denver to Salt Lake City once railroads arrived in the late 19th century. With the slogan "Stay here. Play everywhere," it's now an outdoor-adventure hub known as the gateway to the Black Canyon of the Gunnison (South Rim). It's also home to the Montrose Regional Airport, with flights from several carriers (2100 Airport Rd., 970.249.3203, www.flymontrose.com). www.visitmontrose.com.

Lodging

We opted to stay close to town at the Montrose / Black Canyon National Park KOA

Journey. Set roughly 12 miles west of the South Rim entrance, the campground includes a pool and dog park. 200 N. Cedar St., 970.249.9177.

Other Highlights

The Museum of the Mountain West features a collection of historic log cabins, Western town stores, and more. Open Tues.–Sat, 9:30 a.m.–4 p.m., 68169 Miami Rd., 970.240.3400, www.museumofthemountainwest.org.

The Ute Indian Museum, situated on the original homestead site of the famous Ute leader Chief Ouray and his wife, Chipeta, features walking paths, tepees, and more. Book tours here to see the petroglyphs of Shavano Valley on the Uncompahgre Plateau (about 6 miles west of Montrose). Open Mon.–Sat., 9 a.m.–4:30 p.m., Sun., 11 a.m.–4 p.m., 17253 Chipeta Rd., 970.249.3098, www.historycolorado.org/ute-indian-museum.

The Montrose Water Sports Park on the Uncompahgre River includes six drop structures, ADA-accessible put-in and take-out ramps, and terraced spectator and beach areas. Located minutes from Main Street in Riverbottom Park, it's surrounded by picnic areas, playgrounds, ball fields, trails, a disc-golf course, and skate park. 210 Apollo Rd.

Colorado's North Fork Valley, located about an hour northeast of Montrose (near the North Rim of the Black Canyon of the Gunnison National Park), encompasses three towns worthy of their own guidebooks: Hotchkiss, Crawford, and Paonia. Home to Certified Creative Districts, wineries, and art enclaves, the area also comprises the West Elks American Viticultural Area (Cedaredge, Hotchkiss, Paonia), one of two designated wine grape-growing regions in Colorado. (Grand Valley is the second.) Seventeen miles northeast of Paonia lies Paonia State Park, home to Paonia Reservoir on the North Fork Gunnison

River. Includes 13 scenic but primitive campsites. Vault toilets, no water. 3111 CR 12, Somerset, 970.921.5721.

Built solely for recreation, Sweitzer Lake State Park is located about 21 miles northwest of Montrose near Delta. Enjoy sailing, power boating, canoeing, and swimming (swim area only), as well as 179 bird species. Catch and release catfish, bluegill, and carp. One boat ramp and several picnic sites. Day use only. 1735 E. Rd., Delta, 970.874.4258.

Black Canyon of the Gunnison National Park (BCGNP)

This national park's name says it all: 47 square miles of dramatic, black walls plummeting up to 2,700 feet into a 48-mile canyon carved by the Gunnison River. With shadowy depths so vast, sunlight only reaches the river for a few hours each day (some only for 30 minutes), making the 2-billion-year-old cliffs appear black. Comprising 14 miles of canyon within the park, the area's exceptional depth, narrowness (40 feet at its tightest, called "The Narrows"), verticality, and darkness are some of the reasons its designation changed in 1999 from a national monument to a national park. It's the least-visited one of Colorado's four national parks, likely due to lack of infrastructure, not beauty. For instance, there are just three campsites and only one year-round visitor center. But "The Black" is also home to Gold Medal waters, world-class climbing spots, and Colorado's tallest cliff, the 2,250-foot Painted Wall. It also was certified in 2015 as an International Dark Sky Park, so programming includes night-sky viewing with telescopes, as well as an annual astronomy festival. (Check park calendar for details.) www.nps.gov/blca/index.htm.

There are two main entrances, North Rim (Crawford) and South Rim (Montrose), and three campsites. (Hiking is available in both areas; check which trails allow pets.) Without any bridge between the two entrances, it takes two–three hours to drive from one to another.

NORTH RIM

The North Rim Ranger Station is open intermittently in the summer and closed in the winter. (There's a self-pay station for the park-entrance fee and a self-registration kiosk for wilderness permits.) The entrance is located 11 miles southwest of Crawford (see "Crawford State Park" entry) and offers one campground. The last 7 miles of the park access road and the entire North Rim Drive road are unpaved gravel but passable by most vehicles (closed in winter). This area provides five overlooks and the best view of "The Narrows."

There are three recommended trails in this area, but keep in mind that limited cattle grazing is permitted here, so keep cattle gates closed if you encounter them (roundtrip mileage): Chasm View Nature Trail, 0.3 miles, is located at the end of the one-way campground loop, offering views of Painted Wall and Serpent Point. North Vista Trail has two options—to Exclamation Point (moderate), 3 miles, for good views of the canyon, and to Green Mountain (strenuous), 7 miles, which begins at the ranger station toward mountain views and an aerial perspective of the canyon. Deadhorse Trail (easy to moderate), 5 miles, is a good birding spot; park at the Kneeling Camel Overlook and walk a few yards east to a spur (branch) road that leads to the old ranger station. The trail is an old service road.

The North Rim Campground offers 13 spacious spots. First-come, first-served. Vault toilets; water fill-up stations at campground; ranger station in summer. Water is trucked in, so use conservatively.

SOUTH RIM

The South Rim Visitor Center, open year-round (8 a.m.–6 p.m. in summer), is located 15 miles east of Montrose. Providing

The Black Canyon of the Gunnison National Park boasts Colorado's tallest cliff, the 2,250-foot Painted Wall. Photo by Michael Mundt.

more services, facilities, and overlooks (12) than the North Rim, as well as amazing views of the Painted Wall, this entrance includes access to two campgrounds. 10346 CO-347, 970.641.2337.

There are four established trails for visitors in this area (roundtrip mileage): Rim Rock Nature Trail, 1 mile along the canyon rim, begins near the entrance to Campground Loop C and ends at the South Rim Visitor Center. Oak Flat Loop Trail (strenuous), 2 miles, exploring the rim without hiking to the river, begins near the visitor center. Cedar Point Nature Trail (easy), 0.6 miles, is a moderately sloped trail that features two overlooks to the river below, as well as Painted Wall. Warner Point Nature Trail (moderate) is 1.5 miles. Some trails pass steep drop-offs, so hike carefully. In winter months, the unplowed South Rim Drive becomes an ideal, 6-mile (one way) Nordic-ski trail. The Rim Rock Trail and upper part of Oak Flat Loop are also great snowshoe options. (Heading into the canyon in winter is not recommended.)

The South Rim Campground is just 1 mile from the visitor center, featuring 88 sites that are fairly close together but partially shaded (56 reservable). Vault toilets, potable water.

East Portal is within the Curecanti National Recreation Area boundary but accessible from the South Rim. (Turn right onto the East Portal road at the park-entrance station.) A popular Gold Medal waters fishing destination, it includes 15 first-come, first-served spots. Vault toilets and potable water (seasonally). Not ADA accessible; no trailers. The two-way road is paved but windy and steep; vehicles over 22 feet prohibited.

GETTING TO THE RIVER

There are well-worn but unmaintained trails down the canyon, so very few opt to descend to the river (best for experienced hikers and families with older children). Additionally, the inner canyon is a designated wilderness that requires a permit to enter, both for day and overnight trips, available at the South Rim Visitor Center and North Rim Ranger Station. (No reservations. Must obtain permit the day of the trip. Limited numbers.) Did I mention the water gets up to only 50 degrees (very cold!) and 5-foot-tall poison ivy grows along the banks of the Gunnison? But if you're brave enough to trek down, chances are good you'll have the trail and a private fly-fishing spot to yourself.

The river itself features Class V rapids, so rafting isn't possible. But you can opt for a fly-fishing excursion in the Black Canyon ($$), offered by a handful of outfitters. (Only a few companies own commercial permits in the area, and they are restricted to a certain number of days and visitors per day. Advance reservations required.) One- to three-day float trips are offered via Gunnison River Expeditions (8949 Pleasure Park Rd., Hotchkiss, 970.872.3232, www .gunnisonriverexpeditions.com) and Black Canyon Anglers, which boasts the only fishing lodge on the Lower Gunnison River, a 1,400-acre property with over 2 miles of private riverfront, petroglyphs, and a hiking trail (7904 Shea Rd., Austin, 970.835. 5050, www.blackcanyonanglers.com). Nonanglers welcome!

Climbing is also a popular pursuit in the canyon, although it's recommended for those with experience ($$). Tour operators include Peak Mountain Guides (311 Main St., Ouray, 970.325.7342, www.peakguides .com) and San Juan Mountain Guides (710 Main St., Ouray, 970.325.4925, www .mtnguide.net).

Crawford State Park

Set about 11 miles northeast of the BCGNP North Rim entrance, the centerpiece is the 400-acre Crawford Reservoir (6,600-foot elevation). Located 1 mile south of the artsy Old West town of Crawford, recreation includes jet skiing and waterskiing, sailing, canoeing, and swimming. Anglers can catch rainbow trout, northern pike, and more. In winter, it's perfect for Nordic skiing and ice fishing. There are 66 tent/RV campsites between two campgrounds (with shower facilities), Iron Creek (electric and water at each site) and Clear Fork. 40468 CO-92, 970.921.5721.

Gunnison Gorge National Conservation Area

Located about 7 miles northeast of Montrose just downstream from the BCGNP, this 62,000+-acre, BLM-managed area is home to a stunning, black-granite and red-sandstone double canyon formed by the Gunnison River. There are tons of mountain-biking and hiking trails here, but the true draw is the Gold Medal angling opportunities for rainbow and brown trout, as well as rafting on Class II–IV whitewater rapids. For guided fly-fishing services, check out Montrose Anglers (309 E. Main St., 970.249.0408, www.montroseanglers.com) or RIGS Fly Shop and Guide Service (565 Sherman St., Ridgway, 970.626.4460, www.fishrigs.com). For rafting trips, try Montrose Kayak and Surf (245 W. Main St., 970.249.8730, www.montrose-kayak.com). (Also see "Getting to the River" in the BCGNP entry on the next page.)

If you want to camp along the river, the Cottonwood Grove Campground offers 6 free campsites, including one ADA accessible site with an adjacent accessible fishing pier, situated along the Gunnison. Site amenities include a boat ramp (nonmotorized watercraft only), shade structures, picnic tables, fire rings, and a vault toilet.

First-come, first-served. S. River Rd., Delta, 970.240.5300.

Ouray

Miles from Denver: 301

The nomadic Tabeguache Ute traveled here during summers for hunting and soaking in the "sacred miracle waters," also serving as guides for Spanish expeditions seeking passage through these mountains in the 1700s. Established in 1876 as Ouray, a nod to the revered Ute chief who lived in the area, this spot rich in gold and silver also served as a supply and cultural hub for surrounding mining districts. Despite the downturn in mining and Depression years, tourism allowed Ouray to thrive, drawing visitors to this historic spot nicknamed "The Switzerland of America." www.ouraycolorado.com.

Lodging

Get off-the-grid luxury at Red Mountain Alpine Lodge (accommodates 18–20), offering gourmet food, a bar, and a wood-burning sauna ($). Situated at the top of Red Mountain Pass, book backcountry ski tours from the lodge. US-550, Ridgway, 866.315.2361, www.redmountainalpinelodge.com.

Or stay at the Thelma Hut (sleeps 8, $480/night), open year-round, featuring solar energy, a full-service experience—your host cooks three meals daily—and access to backcountry terrain year-round. Located 0.6 miles north of Red Mountain Pass Summit, 970.708.0092, www.thelmahut.com.

Other Highlights

Take the Bachelor-Syracuse Mine Tour, walking 1,500 feet into Gold Hill to experience it the way miners did a century ago.

The historic hot-springs town of Ouray is nicknamed "The Switzerland of America." Photo by Michael Mundt.

Learn about ore veins and mining equipment, then pan for gold or head to a turn-of-the-century blacksmith shop. Hours vary. 1222 CR 14, 970.325.0220, www.bachelorsyracusemine.com.

Box Canyon Waterfall and Park

Accessible from the southwest corner of town, the lower trail is an easy 500-foot hike via a walkway and suspension bridge straight to the falls. See the beautiful box canyon and enjoy sheltered picnic areas throughout the park. Includes a visitor center (May–mid-October) and short but steep hike to the bridge for a better view. It's also designated an important bird-watching area by the National Audubon Society. Trails open year-round, 8 a.m.–dark, CR 316, 970.325.7080.

Hot Springs Hotspot

There are five hot-springs options around Ouray (free of the stinky sulfur smell of many hot springs), starting with the Ouray Hot Springs Pool. Opened in 1927 and renovated in 2017, it features five geothermal heated pools (with an adult-only section),

two water slides, an obstacle course, a climbing wall, eight lap lanes, and two all-ages pools. Open Mon.–Fri., noon–8 p.m., weekends open 11 a.m., 1220 Main St., 970.325.7073, www.ourayhotsprings.com.

Ranging in temperature from 102 degrees to 108 degrees, the Wiesbaden Hot Springs Spa and Lodgings offers a vapor cave with soaking pool, outdoor hot springs swimming pool, and a private, hot springs soaking pool with waterfall. Lodging ranges from small rooms with two twin beds to cottages and more ($–$$). Spa treatments, massages available. 625 Fifth St., 970.325. 4347, www.wiesbadenhotsprings.com.

Located in downtown Ouray, the Twin Peaks Lodge and Hot Springs features three pools (9 a.m.–9 p.m.), lodge rooms, an on-site restaurant and spa—even jeep rentals. 125 3rd Ave., 970.519.2084, www.twin peakslodging.com.

Recognized as one of Ouray's most popular lodging spots, the Box Canyon Lodge and Hot Springs features four redwood spas terraced on the mountainside behind the lodge (guests only) and standard rooms to suites and more ($). 45 Third Ave., 970.325. 4981, www.boxcanyonouray.com.

In nearby Ridgway, the Orvis Hot Springs Massage and Lodge offers eight unique pools (24-hour access for guests) and restorative massage treatments. Heads up, families: it's clothing-optional! Includes RV/tent campsites and traditional lodging

Take a Drive: The 25-mile stretch of US Highway 550 from Ouray to Silverton along southwest Colorado's San Juan Skyway Scenic and Historic Byway is known as the Million Dollar Highway. Reaching an elevation of more than 11,000 feet at Red Mountain Pass, its name, some say, came from costing $1 million per mile to build; others say it's for the million-dollar views. I vote for the latter.

($). 585 CR 3, Ridgway 970.626.5324, www
.orvishotsprings.com.

Ouray Ice Park

Considered the premier climbing destination in Colorado, the Ouray Ice Park is so
famous worldwide, one of our guides in
Iceland knew about it. Nestled in the
Uncompahgre Gorge just a few-minute
walk from downtown, the man-made park
is home to more than 100 named ice and
mixed climbs, from beginner to advanced,
located just 15 minutes from the entrance.
Open from mid-December through mid-
March, the park is free to visitors (100 percent donor-funded), although beginners
should take a lesson ($$). Several outfitters
are permitted to work in the park, includ-
ing San Juan Mountain Guides (725 Main
St., 970.325.4925, www.mtnguide.net) and
Peak Mountain Guides (280 7th Ave.,
970.325.7342, www.peakguides.com). Visit
in January for the annual Ouray Ice Festi-
val, offering more than 100 clinics and sem-
inars for all skill levels. Open Mon.–Fri., 8
a.m.–4 p.m., weekends, 7:30 a.m.–4 p.m.,
280 CR 361, 970.325.4288, www.ourayice
park.com.

Ouray Via Ferrata

Opened in May 2020, the route is located
on city-owned land within the Uncompah-
gre Gorge. Created by nonprofit Friends of
the Ouray Via Ferrata, the route is free to
the public. Visitors can rent gear or sched-
ule lessons with San Juan Mountain Guides.
(See "Ouray Ice Park" entry.) Check site for
more guiding options. Open daily, 8 a.m.–
4 p.m., 735 Main St., 970.325.4925, www
.ourayviaferrata.org.

Ridgway State Park

Located 11 miles northwest of Ouray in
beautiful Ridgway—a Certified Creative
District and International Dark Sky Com-
munity filled with galleries and

restaurants—the area encompasses a 1,000-
acre reservoir off the Uncompahgre River.
Anglers can catch rainbow and brown trout
in the reservoir, or fly-fish in the river; hik-
ers and bikers can explore 15 miles of trails,
as well as 3 geocache sites. During high sea-
son (April–Oct.), there are 258 RV/trailer
sites and 25 walk-in tent sites (20 RV sites
and 15 walk-in tent sites are available year-
round); or stay in one of 3 yurts. 28555 Hwy
550, 970.626.5822.

Pagosa Springs

Miles from Denver: 277

Home to the world's deepest geothermal
hot spring, according to Guinness World
Records, the town was named "Pagosah" or
"healing waters" by the Ute tribe that dis-
covered their therapeutic qualities. Located
just 35 miles from the New Mexico border,
Pagosa Springs is surrounded by more than
2.5 million acres of wilderness and national
forest areas, including the Weminuche
Wilderness, the San Juan and Rio Grande
national forests, and Southern Ute Indian
lands. With the San Juan River running
right through it, plus some 650 miles of
recreation trails, there's plenty of outdoor-
recreation opportunities. www.visitpagosa
springs.com.

Lodging

The Pagosa Riverside Campground, located
along the San Juan River just 1.5 miles from
town, features 86 RV/tent sites plus 3 cab-
ins, as well as restrooms, showers, laundry,
grocery, fishing supplies, and more. 2270 E.
Hwy 160, 970.264.5874, www.pagosariver
side.com.

Pagosa Pines RV Park, located 1 mile
from town, offers 23 RV/tent sites and 2
cabins (up to 6 people). 1501 W. Hwy 160 #3,
970.264.9130, www.pagosapinesrvpark.com.

Other Highlights

Located just 15 miles east of town on Hwy 160, Treasure Falls is a 105-foot waterfall tumbling over cliffs that visitors can see from the road.

Chimney Rock National Monument

Just 23 miles southwest of Pagosa Springs, this spot is believed to be one of the most sacred sites of the Ancestral Puebloans of the Chaco Canyon (New Mexico), serving as a celestial observatory and seasonal calendar for the tribe over 1,000 years ago. All tours begin at the visitor cabin, where fees are collected. (Only tours may drive to the mesa top.) With a 2.5-mile drive up a steep, winding gravel road to the upper parking lot (7,400 feet), the site preserves 200 ancient homes and ceremonial buildings (some excavated), including a kiva and a multifamily dwelling. Guided and audio tours May 15–September 30. The Visitor Cabin is open 9 a.m.–4:30 p.m., 970.883. 5359, www.chimneyrockco.org.

Cooling off in the San Juan River during a stay at the Springs Resort & Spa in Pagosa Springs. Photo by Michael Mundt.

Healing Waters Resort and Spa

Just across the street from the Springs Resort and Spa, soaking options include an outdoor swimming pool, an outdoor hot tub, and separate men's and women's indoor hot baths and saunas. Features rooms, suites, and cabins. Massages available. Open daily 8 a.m.–10 p.m., 317 Hot Springs Blvd., 970.264.5910, www.pshotsprings .com.

Navajo State Park

Home to Colorado's largest lake *not* fully within the state, Navajo Reservoir is set on the San Juan River, offering the perfect spot for sailors, houseboaters, and motorboat enthusiasts. Nicknamed Colorado's Lake Powell, it's located 36 miles southwest of Pagosa Springs, running 20 miles into New Mexico (two-thirds is in the latter). On the Colorado side, the full-service Two Rivers Marina offers boat rentals (pontoon, fishing, ski), gasoline, tackle, food, and more (open daily 9 a.m.–5 p.m., 970.883.2628). The park offers 119 tent/campsites with camper services, buildings with showers and flush toilets, and 3 (2-bedroom) log cabins. 1526 CR 982, Arboles, 970.883.2208.

Overlook Hot Springs Spa

This Victorian-era property offers rooftop soaking in two pools, a sauna, and a hot tub. A popular après-ski spot for locals, there are also five indoor pools, spa treatments, and massage. A private soaking room is available by the hour. Open 10 a.m.–10 p.m., 432 Pagosa St., 970.264.4040, www.overlookhotsprings.com.

Springs Resort and Spa

The town's largest hot springs property, the Springs Resort and Spa features 24 pools ranging from 83 degrees to 114 degrees terraced alongside the San Juan River (includes a mineral-water swimming pool and 5 age 23+ pools). Features 79 rooms

The drive into Pagosa Springs features stunning views along Wolf Creek Pass from Lobo Overlook. Photo by Michael Mundt.

and suites, as well as 24-hour soaking access for guests. Home to the world's deepest measured geothermal hot spring, the Mother Spring (on property but controlled by the town), and the most geothermal hot-spring-fed pools in Colorado, this is one of our favorite soaking spots. There are also several on-site dining options, spa services, and aqua and traditional yoga classes. Day passes available. In summer months, family movies are featured nightly at the kid-friendly geothermal swimming pool. The resort also helps book extra adventures via Wilderness Journeys Pagosa (fly-fishing, wildlife, hiking tours, and more) and Pagosa Rafting Outfitters. Or try a hot-air balloon ride ($$). Day-pass hours

are 9 a.m.–10 p.m. 323 Hot Springs Blvd., 800.225.0934, www.pagosahotsprings.com.

Wolf Creek Ski Area

Stats: 133 designated trails, 1,600 skiable acres, 10 lifts
Trail classification: 20 percent Beginner; 35 percent Intermediate; 45 percent Advanced
Base elevation: 10,300 feet

Perched at 10,000 feet on the top of Wolf Creek Pass (on Hwy 160 between Pagosa Springs and South Fork), Wolf Creek boasts "The Most Snow in Colorado," averaging 430 inches per year. A favorite family resort just 30 minutes from Pagosa Springs, the parking and shuttles to the base are free,

Visiting Silverton is like stepping into a Gunsmoke episode, circa 1880. Photo by Michael Mundt.

The Durango and Silverton Narrow Gauge Railroad deposits visitors into the heart of historic Silverton. Photo by Michael Mundt.

Silverton

Miles from Denver: 356

Set at 9,318 feet in the San Juans, this "gem" of a find for history buffs is a National Historic Landmark District that Hollywood discovered midcentury as an ideal backdrop for Western films such as *Butch Cassidy and the Sundance Kid* (1969). By 1882, Silverton was the center of commerce in the region with the completion of the Denver and Rio Grande Western Railroad line. Today, visiting this spot where miners pulled "silver by the ton" is like stepping into 1880, with its original jail and saloons, historic hotels, and former bordellos. Tucked between two rugged mountain passes, Red Mountain and Molas, it's also an outdoor-lovers paradise. www.silverton colorado.com.

Lodging

The Molas Lake Park and Campground offers 58 RV/tent campsites, a fishing lake, campground store, onsite SUP and kayak rentals, water, and hot showers. US Hwy 550, 970.403.4145, www.molaslake.com.

The South Mineral Campground, located along South Mineral Creek, features 26 RV/tent first-come, first-served sites. Vault toilets, potable water. Its most renowned feature is the Ice Lake Trail, a steep trail adjacent to the campground (roundtrip 4.5 miles to lower lake, 7 to upper.)

There are also several campsites in town, including the Silverton Lakes RV Resort (and another location, Silverton Lakes South, about four blocks away nearer town), offering RV/tent camping and cabins, a general store, laundry, restrooms, showers, and more. 2100 Kendall St., 970.387.9888, www.silvertonlakes.com.

and there are several amenities, including ski and snowboard rentals, retail shops, a ski school, and 7 eateries including an espresso bar. Featuring 55 percent beginner and intermediate trails, there's also plenty of tree skiing and advanced/expert ski runs. Known as a no-frills resort (opened in 1939), families will pay less for a day on the slopes here than at other spots. There's a fee-based ski shuttle from Pagosa Springs via Wilderness Journeys (daily 7:30 a.m./4:15 p.m.); the office is inside the Best Western Pagosa Lodge (3505 US Hwy 160, 970.731. 4081, www.wildernessjourneyspagosa.com). www.wolfcreekski.com.

Experience Silverton's "rich" mining history with a tour at the Old Hundred Gold Mine. Photo by Michael Mundt.

Other Highlights

Experience the "rich" mining history first-hand with a tour at the Old Hundred Gold Mine, riding a vintage, electric-powered mine train through a hand-blasted tunnel into the heart of Galena Mountain. Watch equipment demonstrations on machines dating back to the 1930s, search for tommy-knockers (the miner equivalent of a leprechaun), and pan for copper, silver, and gold. (Keep what you find!) Tour times vary by season. 721 CR 4A, 970.387.5444, www.minetour.com.

Kendall Mountain Ski Area

Stats: 7 designated trails, 16 skiable acres, 1 lift, 1 terrain park

Trail classification: 50 percent Beginner; 40 percent Intermediate; 10 percent Advanced

Base elevation: 9,313 feet

Kids ages 5 and under ski here for free! The area includes four groomed trails, multiple tree runs, and a small terrain park. Concessions offered when the lift is running, and the ice-skating rink is open as conditions permit. Skating, sledding, cross-country skiing, and snowshoeing are free and allowed any time. Ski, snowboard, ice-skate, and tube rentals are available in the base lodge. For Nordic enthusiasts, Ski Kendall Nordic is open Fri.–Sun. (and holidays) 11 a.m.–4 p.m. The 2.5-mile of Silverton Town Loop offers picturesque views, and the town maintains a network of mixed-use winter trails: Nordic skiing, fat-biking, snowshoeing, snowmobiling, and more. www.skikendall.com.

Silverton Mountain

Stats: 1,819 skiable acres, 22,000-plus additional acres of heli-skiing and hike-to access, 1 lift

Trail classification: 100 percent Advanced

Base elevation: 10,400 feet

The most expert ski area in Colorado and the highest ski area in North America (13,487 feet), this spot that opened in 2002 offers one chairlift that leads to a high-alpine environment with zero clear-cut runs or groomers (advanced and expert only). Aside from avalanche mitigation, the mountain is as nature leaves it, and the "easiest" is a 35-degree slope. (Typical "steep" slopes are 30 degrees.) Guided-only season (group or private): late Dec.–mid-Mar., Thurs.–Sun. Or opt for the "6-Run Heli Day" ($1,190). Includes rental and retail store. www.silvertonmountain.com.

Redwood Llamas

Offering 11 multiday summer itineraries that comprise four wilderness areas and a National Recreational Trail system, as well as the Colorado Trail and the Continental Divide Trail, custom trips are available. Or lease llamas for an unguided expedition (minimum of 2 required because they travel best in pairs). Includes gear, saddlebags, halters, and a three-hour tutorial. 1708 Greene St., 970.560.2926, www.redwoodllamas.com.

Telluride

Miles from Denver: 362

By 1878, this rowdy mining camp first known as Columbia was established as Telluride, a boomtown that continued to prosper with the arrival of the 1890 Rio Grande Southern Railroad (RGS). Today it's a National Historic Landmark District (since 1964), Certified Creative District, and renowned vacation spot. The Telluride Regional Airport—located 6 miles from town at 9,078 feet above sea level, the highest commercial airport in North America—offers direct flights from Denver via United Airlines partner Denver Air Connection (1500 Last Dollar Rd., 970.728.8603, www.tellurideairport.com). www.telluride.com.

Lodging

The Hotel Telluride ($$) gets an entry because of its unique outdoor-adventure packages, including a Ropes and Rungs rock climbing and via ferrata tour, as well as a Wings Over Telluride bird-watching adventure. I experienced the Two Picks and a Prayer ice-climbing experience, a half-day beginner ice climb at Lower Ames Falls, with San Juan Outdoor Adventures (www.tellurideadventures.com). (Minimum requirement for ice climbing is being able to climb a ladder.) Or opt for a half-day snowmobiling excursion with Telluride Outside, which also offers four-wheel-drive tours to Tomboy Ghost Town, one of the continent's highest ghost towns (11,509 feet), rafting on the San Miguel River, and fly-fishing trips (121 W. Colorado Ave., 800.831.6230, www.tellurideoutside.com).

The author looking the part on a half-day beginner ice climb at Lower Ames Falls.
Photo by Pam LeBlanc.

199 Cornet Ln., 970.369.1188, www.the hoteltelluride.com.

For a backcountry experience, stay at The High Camp Hut, set at over 11,000 feet (about 15 miles from town). Equipped with a kitchen, wood-fire hot tub, outhouse, sauna, and sleeping amenities for 12. Meet up at designated location and load gear into a snowcat or jeep. The hike—2.5 miles, 1,000-foot climb—takes about two hours. 970.708.3786, www.highcamphut.com.

Other Highlights

The popular, multiuse Valley Floor Trail is a scenic, accessible area that's perfect for biking in the summer and Nordic skiing or fat-biking in the winter. We rented fat bikes from Box Canyon Bicycles (open daily, 10 a.m.–5 p.m., 300 W. Colorado Ave., 970.728.2946, www.boxcanyonbicycles .com), riding about 3 miles to a beer-tasting at the Telluride Brewing Company (156 Society Dr., 970.728.5094, www.telluride brewingco.com).

Accessible from town is the San Miguel River Trail offering 4.25 miles one way, following the river along the length of town. Great for walking, running, and getting good views of the box canyon.

Imogene Pass, which connects Telluride to Ouray, is one of the highest-paved passes in Colorado and a popular four-wheel-drive destination to the ghost town of Tomboy, set at more than 11,000 feet. Check out a tour with Telluride Outside (see "Lodging," opposite page), Telluride Offroad Adventures (970.708.5190, www.tellurideoff road.com), or Dave's Mountain Tours (970.728.9749, www.telluridetours.com).

Telluride's via ferrata, located at the east

end and south-facing wall of the box canyon (accessed via Bridal Veil Falls Road), is available for public use. Inexperienced climbers should try guided tours via Mountain Trip, located in downtown Telluride. 135 W. Colorado, 2A, 970.369.1153, www .mountaintrip.com.

Additionally, Telluride's free Galloping Goose bus service runs loops through the town and ski resort every 10–15 minutes. www.telluride-co.gov.

Finally, the Town of Mountain Village is set nearly 1,000 feet above the town of Telluride, linked by a free, 13-minute-ride gondola (pet-friendly, ADA accessible) that's nicknamed the "G." There are three primary stations: Station Telluride, Oak Street, access to Telluride; Station St. Sophia, mid-mountain stop, access to Allred's Restaurant and Bar, The Ridge Club, and ski resort trails and runs; Station Mountain Village, access to Mountain Village. (Across from this last station, a shorter gondola stretch connects to Station Village Parking, offering access to a free parking garage, and to grocery and liquor stores.)

Tour Operators

Experience snow-covered trails throughout the San Juan and Uncompahgre national forests via Alaskan-husky power with Wintermoon Sled Dog Adventures. Kids welcome. Half-day tour leaves from meeting locations in Telluride and Mountain Village at 8:10 a.m. 970.729-0058, www.telluride dogsledding.com.

Telluride Horseback Adventures, about 33 miles northwest of Telluride, offers wagon rides (up to 12 people) and sleigh rides (up to 10), as well as one- or two-hour (or private) trail rides. Call Roudy at the barn! 4019 CR 43ZS, Norwood, 970.728. 9611, www.ridewithroudy.com. For an evening sleigh ride to dinner in a heated tent ($$), contact Telluride Sleighs and Wagons. 220 E. Colorado, Suite 214, 833.753.4447, www.telluridesleighs.com.

Fast Fact: Similar to the Galloping Goose No. 5 in Dolores, one of seven "motors" built in the 1930s, Telluride is home to Galloping Goose No. 4, on display at the San Miguel County Courthouse (305 W. Colorado Ave.).

Several companies offer fly-fishing guiding services, including Telluride Outside (see p. 65, "Lodging"), Telluride Angler (121 W. Colorado Ave., 800.831.6230, www.tellu rideangler.com), and Telluride Fly Fishers (970.728.4440, www.tellurideflyfishers.com).

For year-round tour options, from snowmobiling to the ghost town of Alta, razor tours and SUP rentals to whitewater rafting, check out Telluride Outfitters. Open daily 9 a.m.–5 p.m., 456 Mountain Village Blvd., 970.728.4475, www.tellurideoutfitters.com.

The concierge ski and snowboard rental/delivery service Ski Butlers is available in Mountain Village (Aspen as well), offering in-room fitting services and on-call equipment support (618 Mountain Village Blvd., Unit E, 877.754.7754, www.skibutlers.com). Black Tie Ski Rentals also offers free delivery and in-room fittings (866.360.6433, www.blacktieskis.com).

San Juan Outdoor Adventures guides ice climbing (see p. 65, "Lodging"), hiking to backcountry huts, climbing the via ferrata, and more. In wintertime, kids ages 5 and up will especially enjoy a private Kids' Snowshoe Adventure ($), featuring sledding, snowman-building, and hot-cocoa drinking. 9 a.m.–2 p.m., 223 E. Colorado Ave., 970.728.4101, www.tellurideadventures .com.

Bridal Veil Falls

The tallest free-falling falls in Colorado (365 feet), they include a 1907 power station perched atop them, creating a scenic spot for bikers and hikers (also considered one of the country's most difficult ice climbs). Includes a 3.6-mile roundtrip trek to the top of the falls (1,650-foot elevation gain). To get there, drive east through town along Colorado Ave. toward the east side of the box canyon and continue past the Pandora Mill site on your left. Park in the area to the right, and hike up the new Bridal Veil Trail at the bottom of the falls. Continue on the road to the top.

The centerpiece of artsy Camp V is Burning Man artist Robert Hoehn's interactive Prairie Wind Chapel. Photo by the author.

Naturita

A former mining town located roughly 53 miles northwest of Telluride, Naturita (pronounced "NAT-uh-REE-tuh") might be little known outside of Southwest Colorado. But locals know it as a quieter spot for recreation such as hiking, biking, and camping. Set along the Unaweep Tabeguache scenic and historic byway that follows the Dolores and San Miguel rivers (see "Grand Junction" entry), it was jointly designated with the town of Nucla (5 miles north) as an International Dark Sky Community in June 2021. Naturita is also home to one of *the* coolest glampsites I've ever visited: Camp V, a former mining camp built in 1942 by the Vanadium Corporation to house its uranium engineers and their families. Offering 12 renovated cabins—6 studios and 6 two-bedroom options, both with kitchenettes—all are restored with original flooring, hardware, and more. There are also 3 fully furnished Airstream trailers, 3 Lotus Belle Onion canvas tents with shade areas, and 6 RV sites with full hookups (plus a bathhouse). There's yet more across the street along the San Miguel: a refurbished school bus with Wi-Fi and seating area; Lake V, which offers an SUP, a canoe, and a floating dock; and 20 primitive camp-sites (with outdoor shower). Camp V also boasts WEarts, a nonprofit with a goal to provide this rural community with access to art, featuring a variety of pieces through-out, including "found" art like an old water-tank and interactive works such as Burning Man artist Robert Hoehn's Prairie Wind Chapel; there's even a buried bus visitors can search for during their visit. Food boxes available. No on-site dining. Ee 26 Rd., Vancorum, 970.369.9520, www.campv .com.

Telluride Nordic Center

Located in Town Park in the historic Unruh House, the center offers lessons for classic or skate skiing with certified instructors in 90-minute lessons (10:30 a.m. or 1 p.m. daily). Group or private lessons available ($). Enjoy roughly 2 miles of groomed trails in Town Park, or set off for the wide-open spaces of the Valley Floor Trail. The center offers rentals for classic or skate skis, as well as snowshoes, sleds, and ice skates. The free

Firecracker Sledding Hill is located on the south side of Town Park, and the park's free outdoor ice rink (warming hut and restrooms) is open December through March. The fully enclosed, NHL-sized indoor rink, the Hanley Pavilion (late Oct.–mid-Mar.), also offers open skate hours. In summer, the Town Park features a skate park, swimming pool, kids' fishing pond, basketball courts and more. Nordic center open daily, 10 a.m.–4 p.m., mid-Nov.–Mar., 500 E. Colorado Ave., 970.728.1144, www .telluridenordic.com.

Telluride Ski Resort

Stats: 148 designated trails, 2,000 skiable acres, 19 lifts, 2 terrain parks

Trail classification: 23 percent Beginner; 36 percent Intermediate; 41 percent Advanced

Base elevation: 8,725 feet

Famous for uncrowded slopes, lack of lift lines, and accessibility—Lifts 7 and 8 are based right in Telluride—there are four hike-to areas for more advanced skiers and

The Telluride Ski Resort is known for uncrowded slopes, lack of lift lines, and easy accessibility. Photo by Michael Mundt.

two terrain parks, plus more than 6 miles of Nordic trails. Featuring the Town of Mountain Village, the ski-in/ski-out destination perched nearly 1,000 feet above Telluride offers plenty of lodging and activity. For extreme skiers and riders, Telluride Helitrax (970.728.8377, www.helitrax.com) is located in and flies out of the Peaks Resort and Spa ($$+), a ski-in/ski-out *and* golf-in/golf-out spot (136 Country Club Dr., 888.696.6734, www.thepeaksresort.com). Ice-skating and rentals available at the Madeline Hotel and Residences (568 Mountain Village Blvd., 970.369.0880, www.aubergeresorts.com/madeline).

In warmer months, try the free, 18-hole Double Cabin Disc Golf Course, open summers from sunrise to sunset (located across the street from Market Plaza, formerly Town Hall Plaza, and the Market at Mountain Village). There's also an Adventure Center from mid-June through Labor Day (9 a.m.–6 p.m., weather dependent), where kids can enjoy a ropes course or bungee trampoline, then try to strike gold at the mining sluice.

Open since July 2019, Telluride Ski and Golf Resort's new bike-park trails meander through meadows and aspen glades before finishing in Mountain Village. Served by both the gondola and Lift 4 for all skill levels, a favorite beginners' trail is the 5.8-mile Tommyknocker. Purchase tickets at Oak Street and Mountain Village ticket windows (open June–Sept., 10 a.m.–6 p.m., 970.728.7517, 697 Mountain Village Blvd.). For adrenaline junkies, experience tandem paragliding ($$) via Telluride Paragliding, ages 5 and above. (As long as you can run for a few seconds to take off, you can paraglide.) Morning tours offer the calmest air and friendliest skies. 651 W. Pacific Ave., 970.708.4247. www.tellurideskiresort.com.

Trout Lake

Roughly a 15-minute drive west of town, Trout Lake is one of the most pristine high-altitude lakes in Colorado (offering fantastic Nordic-skiing terrain). Stocked by the Hotchkiss National Fish Hatchery, anglers can reel in some rainbow or brown trout. Summer activities include kayaking, canoeing, SUPing, and swimming. (Remember, mountain lakes are *cold*!) There are also occasional SUP yoga classes offered via Bootdoctors. (There are two retail locations, one at 650 Mountain Village Blvd., and another in town at the base of the gondola, 970.728.8954, www.boot doctors.com. In addition to boot fitting and gear rentals, they offer year-round guided adventures in rafting, hiking, biking, and more.)

There are two campgrounds near Trout Lake. The closest one is Priest Lake Campground, a dispersed-camping area with nine designated sites, vault toilets. (No trailers due to lack of parking.) Limited fishing available. The nearby Galloping Goose Trail—a 19-mile trail flowing along the old narrow-gauge rail line from Lizard Head Pass (10,222 feet) to Telluride—is popular for hiking, mountain biking, and horseback riding. The other site, Matterhorn Campground, offers 28 campsites (4 with RV hookups), with picnic tables, fire rings, or grills. Flush and vault toilets, drinking water, showers. Firewood for purchase. To reach the campground from Telluride, travel west 3 miles to Hwy 145; turn left and travel south for 8 miles. Campground is on the left side of the highway.

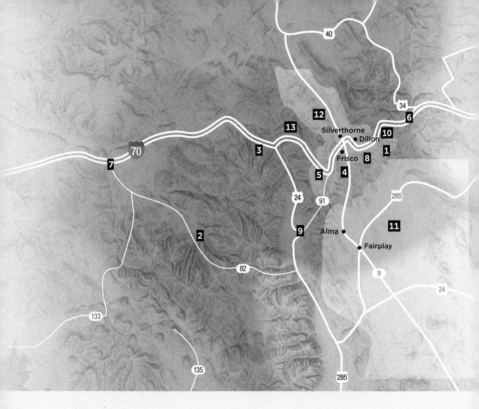

ROCKIES PLAYGROUND

Arapahoe Basin

Stats: 147 designated trails, 1,428 skiable acres, 9 lifts, 3 terrain parks

Trail classification: 7 percent Beginner; 20 percent Intermediate; 73 percent Advanced

Base elevation: 10,780 feet

Opening in 1946 with one tow rope and a $1.25 lift ticket, Arapahoe Basin or "A-Basin" is known as "The Legend" for the longest season in Colorado: typically October through June. Park for free at the resort's famous lodge, a former NASA rocket-tester known as "the A-Frame," and be on a lift in minutes. Hang out at "The Beach," a swath of flattened snow bordering the Early Riser, the country's highest parking lot (13,050 feet), which is walking distance to both base-area lifts. There's no lodging here, but it offers a kids' center, three freestyle terrain parks, and the highest lift-served restaurant in North America, European bistro Il Rifugio at Snowplume (12,500 feet).

Summer season (late June through early Sept.) includes on-mountain dining and scenic chairlift rides (daily 9 a.m.–3 p.m.) to mountain-biking/hiking trails, such as the 1-mile roundtrip Half Moon Vista Trail toward views of the Continental Divide. There's also a free, 20-hole disc-golf course. New in 2020, the Aerial Adventure Park offers the Lil' Kids Adventure Park (ages 4–7) and High Alpine Adventure (ages 7+, minimum 50 pounds). Up to two hours ($). New in 2021, North America's highest-elevation via ferrata (13,000 feet) features half- or full-day guided tours ($$) (minimum 12 years old). www.arapahoebasin.com.

Aspen

Miles from Denver: 198

Once a summer hunting spot for the Ute tribe, this charming hamlet along the Roaring Fork River became a mining boomtown in the 1880s. Skiing brought it back from the 1893 silver-market crash, starting in 1947 with Aspen Mountain; three more resorts developed over the next two decades. As John Denver best described Aspen, it's a town of cathedral mountains and clear-blue mountain lakes that inspire a "Rocky Mountain High." Visitors can fly into Aspen-Pitkin County Airport, 4 miles from town, served by United Airlines, American Airlines, and Delta Air Lines (233 E. Airport Rd., 970.920.5380, www.aspen airport.com). www.aspenchamber.org.

Lodging

The Aspen Meadows resort ($+) is home to the world-renowned Aspen Institute, staffing its own curator to oversee the resort's hundreds of works of art and indoor galleries/exhibitions (complimentary guest tours available). The summer Aspen Music Festival and School performs on the campus, a favorite for families. (Arrange for a packed picnic/wine for the occasion.) 845 Meadows Rd., 970.925.4240, www.aspenmeadows .com.

Other Highlights

Roughly 9 miles east of Aspen along Independence Pass, the 1-mile Grottos Trail hike is a popular one leading to unique ice caves featuring otherworldly rock formations. 26692 CO-82.

Aspen Center for Environmental Studies (ACES)

This nonprofit environmental-science education organization (ACES) offers two-hour, daily snowshoe tours (10 a.m., 1 p.m.) and 45-minute downhill ski tours (11 a.m., 1 p.m.) on Aspen and Snowmass Mountains ($). In the summer, there are free, 45-minute hikes on both. On Aspen Mountain, winter and summer activities start at the top of the Silver Queen Gondola. Hikes on

Aspen Mountain are hourly each day, 11 a.m.–3 p.m. (45 minutes one-way, return on your own in 15–20 minutes).

Daily ski tours are offered from the Wapiti Wildlife Center at the top of the Elk Camp lift on Snowmass; hiking tours begin in the Snowmass Village Mall (105 Daly Ln.). The two-hour hikes from Snowmass village are daily, 10 a.m., 1 p.m.

The organization also offers daily nature hikes at Maroon Bells (10:15 a.m., 1:15 p.m.; 45-minute and 2-hour options, one-way). Meet outside of the Maroon Bells Information Center near the bus drop-off. First-come, first-served, 9-person maximum. Visitors can also hire a guide for a private tour to places like the historic ghost town of Ashcroft or for a 2,000-foot climb, 6.4-mile trek to Cathedral Lake ($). 970.925.5756, www.aspennature.org.

Four Mountains

One lift ticket for all. www.aspensnow mass.com.

ASPEN HIGHLANDS

Stats: 144 designated trails, 1,040 skiable acres, 5 lifts

Trail classification: 0 percent Beginner; 23 percent Intermediate; 77 percent Advanced

Base elevation: 8,040 feet

Opened in 1958, this resort offers plenty of midmountain intermediate terrain for less experienced skiers and riders (no beginner runs). But the resort's crown jewel (since 2002) is the Highland Bowl, considered some of the best big-mountain skiing in the state. Earn the turns by hiking a nearly 800-foot ascent from the top of Loge Peak lift (to 12,392 feet), or take the free snowcat (weather permitting).

ASPEN MOUNTAIN

Stats: 76 designated trails, 675 skiable acres, 8 lifts

Trail classification: 0 percent Beginner; 48 percent Intermediate; 52 percent Advanced

Base elevation: 7,945 feet

Opened in December 1946 after installation of a single-seat chairlift, Lift-1, then the longest chairlift in the world, Aspen Mountain is famous for its black-diamond terrain (no beginner slopes). Often called by its original name, Ajax, here visitors can ski or ride the same runs that have hosted the World Cup races for decades. (The resort hosted its first FIS World Alpine Championships in 1950.) A luxury snowcat can take visitors to untracked areas on the mountain's backside via Aspen Mountain Powder Tours. (For reservations, call 970.920.0720 or visit the desk in the Silver Queen Gondola Building). Enjoy the view at the Sundeck Restaurant, worth the 20-minute, 3,000-foot ascent, even in nonskiing months. At the base, head to *the* après-ski spot, The Little Nell's Ajax Tavern.

BUTTERMILK

Stats: 44 designated trails, 470 skiable acres, 8 lifts, 8 terrain parks

Trail classification: 35 percent Beginner; 39 percent Intermediate; 26 percent Advanced

Base elevation: 7,870 feet

Originally developed in 1958, "the Milk" is a great resort for beginners. Offering plenty of easy green and blue cruisers, start at West Buttermilk for easier terrain, then increase difficulty at Main Buttermilk and end in Tiehack (difficult). Daredevils can check out the legendary X Park, consisting of approximately 25 advanced and expert features, plus a 22-foot superpipe. Kids will especially love Fort Frog, a wooden structure that includes a "post office" tower with a spiral slide, a swinging rope bridge, climbing areas, and more. (Anyone can explore the fort, but the warming hut serves the ski school.)

SNOWMASS

Stats: 98 designated trails, 3,342 skiable acres, 20 lifts, 3 terrain parks

Trail classification: 5 percent Beginner; 48 percent Intermediate; 47 percent Advanced

Base elevation: 8,604 feet

Set roughly 9 miles northwest of Aspen (in the small town of Snowmass Village) and the largest of the four mountains, the area's youngest mountain (1967) boasts the country's longest lift-served vertical (4,406 feet). It's also one of the state's most family-friendly resorts with its wide-open cruisers and kids' programming. The free Snowmass S'mores takes place daily at 3:30 (starting late Nov.–April). And the skating rink in Snowmass Base Village is free—even free skate rentals! There's also the Breathtaker Alpine Coaster, winding 1 mile through forest on an elevated track at up to 28 miles per hour (minimum 54 inches, 16 years to drive), in addition to a tubing hill and snowbikes. And the Treehouse Kids' Adventure Center offers Colorado-themed playrooms and supervised activities for kids (8 weeks to 4 years old). In winter, take a backcountry dog-sledding adventure with Krabloonik Dog Sled Tours, one of the best ways to explore Colorado's backcountry ($$$). The hour-long ride carries two adults and a small child, led by an experienced musher. Try a twilight ride at 4 p.m. 4250 Divide Rd., 970.923.3953, www.krabloonik .com.

In summer, the Lost Forest features biking trails, ropes challenges, and a climbing wall—even fishing ponds (in addition to the coaster). The Canopy Run Zipline Tour offers 7 ziplines; rappel from 30- to 90-foot-high towers and experience the nation's only diagonal rappel. There's also the

Snowmass Bike Park, with lift-served mountain biking for all skill levels. www .gosnowmass.com.

The Snowmass Base Village was completed in 2018 and includes an ice rink, shops, restaurants, the Collective Snowmass (a hub for community events), and condos. It also includes the new Limelight Hotel Snowmass and Colorado's tallest indoor climbing wall: 54 feet. Open to the public. 65 Wood Rd., 970.924.5100, www .limelighthotels.com/snowmass.

Maroon Bells Scenic Area

Alleged to be the state's most photographed peaks, the two, red-hued "bells" are located about 12 miles southwest of Aspen. Featuring 14ers Maroon and North Maroon Peaks, anchored by stunning Maroon Lake, the area offers several popular hikes: a 1-mile route on the Maroon Lake Scenic Trail, beginning at the parking lot and following along the lake; the 3.8 roundtrip hike to Crater Lake (difficult and crowded); or the Maroon Creek Trail, roughly 6.4 miles roundtrip, an easier trek that's less trafficked.

Since 2020, reservations have been required to park at Maroon Lake. Or ride the Roaring Fork Transportation Authority (RFTA) bus ($15.95 fare), which operates 8 a.m.–5 p.m., mid-June–mid-October. (Check updated information with www .aspenchamber.org or call the Maroon Bells Information number, 970.945.3319.) Park your car for a fee at the Aspen Highlands parking structure, located at the base of Aspen Highlands Ski Resort, 199 Prospector Rd.

There are three campgrounds in the Maroon Bells Scenic Area: Silver Bar Campground, with 4 primitive sites, vault toilets; Silver Bell Campground, with 14 sites along Maroon Creek, vault toilets, both reserved and first-come, first-served;

Fall is the most beautiful season to visit the iconic Maroon Bells Scenic Area.
Photo by Michael Mundt.

and Silver Queen Campground, with 5 campsites (tents, trailers, and RVs) with reservation, vault toilets, and potable water. Five-day stay limit on all three.

Rafting the Fork

The upper section of the river, just 15 minutes from downtown, offers rapid names like Toothache, the Abscess, and Catcher's Mitt. A half-day trip with Elk Mountain Expeditions features moderate (Class III) rapids ($), starting 9 a.m. and 2 p.m. daily. Minimum age depends on water levels. 100 Smuggler Mountain Rd., 970.456.6287, www.raftinginaspen.com.

Take a Lower Roaring Fork rafting trip with Blazing Adventures, a mellow introduction for younger guests ($$). 8:30 a.m. and 1 p.m. Minimum 5 years old. The company offers several other tours: hiking, SUPing, and biking, as well as a sunset BBQ dinner, where guests ride in jeeps up Snowmass Mountain ($$). 555 E. Durant Ave., Aspen, or 1 Village Mall, Snowmass Village, 970.923.4544, www.blazingadventures.com.

The Rio Grande Trail

A combination of asphalt, concrete, and gravel spanning 42 miles from Aspen to Glenwood Springs along the former route of the Denver and Rio Grande Western Railroad, it's ideal for a walk or bike ride, even in parts. Bike Butlers delivered bikes right to our hotel (209 Aspen Airport Business Ctr., Unit D, 970.300.4912, www.ski butlers.com). (There's also a ski version, Ski Butlers.) Everyone is welcome on the trail system: dogs, horses, and Nordic skiers in winter. Endpoints are Herron Park, 108 Neale Ave., Aspen, and Two Rivers Park, 740 Devereux Rd., Glenwood Springs, www.rfta.com/trail-information.

Fast Fact: The Ritz-Carlton, Bachelor Gulch, offers guests a free guided hike (snowshoeing in winter) that's likely to include one of the two dogs-in-residence: Scout, the Bernese Mountain Dog, or Bachelor, the St. Bernard. Thurs.–Sun. mornings. Reservations recommended. Family programs include family hike/snowshoe adventures with an on-site naturalist and a ski nanny, who gets kids to and from ski school. (The hotel provides slope-side access with their own chairlift.) There's also a Ritz Kids program for ages 5–12 ($). Call 970.343.1138 for reservations. (Half-day, full-day, and evening options available.) 0130 Daybreak Ridge Rd., Avon, 970.748.6200, www.ritzcarlton.com/en/hotels/colorado/bachelor-gulch.

The guided hikes at the Ritz-Carlton, Bachelor Gulch, in Beaver Creek Resort typically include one of two dogs-in-residence, including Scout the Bernese mountain dog. Photo by the author.

Beaver Creek Resort

Stats: 3 base areas, 150 designated trails, 1,832 skiable acres, 24 lifts, 2 terrain parks
Trail classification: 19 percent Beginner; 42 percent Intermediate; 39 percent Advanced
Base elevation: 8,100 feet

Located adjacent to the town of Avon, the resort opened in 1980, comprising three village base areas: Beaver Creek, Bachelor Gulch, and Arrowhead. It offers a variety of terrain, including some extreme enough to host the Birds of Prey Men's World Cup in December. There are also areas for beginner and intermediate skiers: Red Buffalo Park, with 13 trails designated as a family-adventure zone and snow sculptures, and Haymeadow Park, featuring a beginner gondola and lift. The 2021–2022 season added McCoy Park, a family-friendly zone featuring 17 groomers. Kids will most love meeting Willy the Mountain Safety Dog, who educates visitors *and* shakes paws! In summer, enjoy hiking on the 62 miles of trails linking the three villages. www.beavercreek.com.

Breckenridge

Miles from Denver: 80

This spot along the Blue River was inhabited for hundreds of years by the Ute tribe until white settlers arrived in 1859 for Colorado's Gold Rush. After several "booms," Breckenridge was at risk of becoming a ghost town by the 1940s during World War II. Saved in 1961 with the opening of Peak 8 Ski Area, "Breck" is Colorado's largest historic district and a family favorite destination—particularly in September, during the largest Oktoberfest street party in Colorado's Rockies. Prost! www.gobreck.com.

Other Highlights

Breckenridge Heritage Alliance offers history and ghost tours, as well as a 2.5-mile guided hike through the Golden Horseshoe, one of Colorado's most fertile mining regions (can be booked as a private tour). www.breckheritage.com.

In January, Breckenridge hosts the International Snow Sculpture Championships, where teams of artists from around the world carve sculptures using only hand tools. The masterpieces are located near 150 W. Adams Ave., around the Riverwalk Center.

Breckenridge Nordic Center

Located just 1 minute from downtown, visitors can take the Free Ski and Ride Shuttle right to the lodge's front door. Offering Nordic equipment and snowshoe rentals, all ages and abilities can get a lift ticket. Lessons and guided tours available. (Nonwalking kiddos can be pulled via sport-specific sleds.) Warm up afterward with food and drinks in the lounge. Open daily, 9 a.m.–4 p.m., 9 Grandview Dr., 970.453.6855, www.breckenridgenordic .com.

Breckenridge Troll

Created in 2018 by Danish artist Thomas Dambo, Isak Heartstone, aka "The Breckenridge Troll," is a 15-foot sculpture made from recycled wood. Located on the Trollstigen Trail in the southeast corner of the Stephen C. West Ice Arena parking lot (189 Boreas Pass Rd.), next to Illinois Gulch Trailhead, it's a popular photo opportunity. Please don't climb him! The trail isn't maintained in winter, so be extra careful when it's icy.

Breckenridge Ski Resort

Stats: Five mountains, 187 designated trails, 2,908 skiable acres, 34 lifts, 4 terrain parks
Trail classification: 11 percent Beginner; 31 percent Intermediate; 58 percent Advanced
Base elevation: 9,600 feet

Opened in December 1961, today's resort comprises Peaks 6–10 spanning the southern half of the Tenmile Range. Known for decades as a family destination, there's plenty of wide, gentle terrain for beginners (mostly Peaks 8 and 9) and blue groomers (on Peak 7). More experienced skiers and riders can head to Peak 6 (added in 2013) for intermediate bowls and hike-to chutes for experts.

Take a break from skiing on the Gold Runner Alpine Coaster (minimum 3 years, 38 inches; minimum 54 inches to ride alone). In summer, the mountain's Epic Discovery at Breckenridge (sister to Vail's) is the spot for summertime fun. In addition to the coaster, there's the alpine slide; Gold Summit Climbing Wall, 40-feet-tall with 16 routes for all skill levels (minimum 22 pounds); Alpineer Challenge Course; and a 15-feature aerial course (minimum 75 pounds). There are also three ziplining options: the Little Flyer (30–100 pounds), Breck Flyer (minimum 55 pounds, 45–80 inches), and Expedition Zipline Tour (minimum 10 years, 75 pounds), featuring eight lines and an aerial-bridge walk (Independence Outpost on Peak 7). Or take a trail ride on horseback with Breckenridge Stables, featuring a 90-minute tour between Peaks 9 and 10 with views of the Continental Divide. All ages; minimum 6 years to ride alone. Sleigh rides available in winter. Peak 9, 970.389.1777, or Gold Run Nordic Center, 970.453.4438, www.breckstables .com.

Ride the free BreckConnect Gondola (daily, 9 a.m.–4 p.m.) to a free tour of the

Cucumber Gulch Wildlife Preserve, home to wetlands, critters, and mining history. Mon.–Sat., 9:30–11 a.m., www.breckenridge recreation.com. www.breckenridge.com.

Gold Run Nordic Center

Located at Breckenridge Golf Club, the center offers nearly 19 miles of groomed ski and 9 miles of snowshoe trails, as well as equipment rentals and group and private lessons. Group ski lessons, either skate or classic cross-country, offered daily 10 a.m. (minimum age 10). Youth under 13 must be accompanied by an adult. Evening snowshoe tours, 5p.m.–7 p.m., include a full-moon excursion (minimum 6 years old). Fee includes snowshoes and headlamp (\$). There's also a full-moon fat-bike tour with snack, 6 p.m.–8 p.m. (minimum 16 years old). Bring your own fat bike or rent one of the Borealis fleet bikes. Register in advance. Open daily, 9 a.m.–4 p.m., Dec.–Mar., 200 Clubhouse Dr., 970.547.7889, www.brecken ridgerecreation.com.

Quandary Peak

Colorado's 13th-highest peak (14,265 feet) is relatively easy for most fitness levels to hike the 7.5 miles roundtrip. But it gets crowded! Trailhead is located on McCullough Gulch Rd., roughly 20 minutes south of town. A pilot program launched from July to October 2021 requiring parking reservations for Quandary Peak and McCullough Gulch (with access to a free shuttle system). For up-to-date information, visit www.summit countyco.gov/1446/Quandary.

Summer Dog-Sled Tour

Just a 10-minute drive outside of Breckenridge, Good Times Adventures offers guests a 2-mile tour in a golf cart via dog power. Get a scenic ride through Swan River Valley (90 minutes), starting with a tour of the yard to meet some of the 150 huskies (\$). In winter, enjoy a 6-mile cruise through a snowy wonderland (up to 6 people), switching between mushing and riding in the sled or a passenger sleigh (\$\$). Arrive early to cuddle with the pups! (All activities, minimum age 4). Snowmobile tours also available. 6061 Tiger Rd., 970.453.7855, www.goodtimesadventures.com.

Copper Mountain

Stats: 3 mountains, 148 designated trails, 2,527 skiable acres, 24 lifts, 10 terrain parks
Trail classification: 21 percent Beginner; 25 percent Intermediate; 54 percent Advanced
Base elevation: 9,712 feet

Located about 75 miles from Denver (8 miles west of Frisco, roughly 20 miles east of Vail), this resort that opened in 1972 is known for its naturally divided terrain that progresses in difficulty from west to east. If you go by looker's right (instead of skier's right), most of the West Village area is for beginners, progressing toward the Center Village and East Village areas (from Union Peak to Copper Peak and Tucker Mountain). Three lively, pedestrian-only villages are filled with restaurants, bars, shops and lodging. Other winter activities include an ice-skating rink (on West Lake) and tubing hill (the latter in East Village, near Super Bee chairlift, minimum 36 inches)—even guided introductions to uphill skiing. The Rocky Mountain Coaster is open year-round (minimum 9 years, 52 inches for single riders), as well as the Woodward Copper Barn, an indoor, action-sports training facility. Filled with foam pits, jumps, and trampolines, it's perfect for practicing tricks.

Summer fun includes a climbing wall and go-karts on Summit County's only track. There's also a zipline over West Lake, as well as bumper boats and Hydrobikes. Buy an activity pass for a better deal (\$).

A bluebird day in Copper Mountain's Spaulding Bowl. Photo by Michael Mundt.

Summer fun at Copper Mountain includes ziplining over the resort's West Lake. Photo by Michael Mundt.

Make sure to grab fresh, warm goodness from Sugar Lips Mini Donuts (by the lake, www.sugarlipsminidonuts.com, 970.968.2520).

On the mountain, check out hiking and biking trails—Woodward Express lift hauls up mountain bikes and offers scenic charlift rides from 10 a.m. to 4 p.m.—and Colorado's only summer-snow experience, the on-mountain terrain park, where visitors can practice ski and snowboard skills. There's also the WreckTangle, a nine-element outdoor obstacle course set at the base of Copper Mountain (minimum 5 years, 36 inches, 40 pounds). www.copper colorado.com.

Georgetown

Miles from Denver: 45

Set along I-70 just 14 miles east of "the tunnel," this was once the third-largest town in Colorado, producing vast amounts of silver by the time the Colorado Central Railroad arrived in 1877. Named for George Griffith, who discovered gold in the area in 1859, the Georgetown–Silver Plume Historic District is one of the best-preserved historic mining districts in Colorado. www.georgetown colorado.org.

Georgetown Loop Railroad

Completed in 1884, the narrow-gauge steam train ride from Georgetown to nearby Silver Plume (about 2 miles west on I-70) offers an optional stop for a tour of the Lebanon Silver Mine. Roundtrip train ride is 75 minutes long; 2.5 hours with mine tour (April–Sept). Holidays include stops at Santa's Lighted Forest; Santa's North Pole Adventure includes presents and treats (50–60 minutes). 646 Loop Dr., 888.456.6777, www.georgetownlooprr.com.

Glenwood Springs

Miles from Denver: 157

Native American tribes like the Ute, Comanche, and Arapaho understood the curative nature of this area's hot springs and vapor caves long before it became a destination for health-minded travelers in the late 1880s. With the arrival of the railroads in 1887 and the 1888 opening of Glenwood Hot Springs, it quickly became a playground for the well-to-do. Today, the city located at the confluence of the Roaring Fork and Colorado River (formerly the Grand River) is home to the world's largest mineral hot-springs pool. www.visit glenwood.com.

Lodging

There are three popular state parks in the Rifle area for camping, about 27 miles west of town (technically in "The Great West" region):

Attracting photographers and movie crews from around the country, the 70-foot, triple waterfall is the centerpiece of Rifle Falls. There's also a 50-seat amphitheater, three hiking trails, a cave with a 90-foot room (bring a flashlight!), and even trout fishing. Includes 13 drive-in and 7 walk-in campsites that sit to the south along East Rifle Creek. In summer months, visitors are often turned away because the parking lot gets full quickly.

Four miles southwest of Rifle Falls is Rifle Gap State Park, home of the 350-acre Rifle Gap Reservoir, offering year-round fishing (a top ice-fishing destination), as well as boating, waterskiing, windsurfing, and swimming at a beach. There are 5 campgrounds featuring 89 sites along the reservoir's northern shore. Includes restrooms with flush and vault toilets and showers.

Six miles east is Harvey Gap, a popular day-use fishing spot for rainbow trout and northern pike (year-round), as well as smallmouth bass and perch. Only nonmotorized craft and boats with motors 20 horsepower or less. Also popular for paddle sports and swimming, in winter it's ideal for snowshoeing, Nordic skiing, ice fishing, and tubing. Three parks: 5775 Hwy 325, 970.625.1607.

Other Highlights

The smallest of Colorado's 19 hatcheries, the Glenwood Springs Fish Hatchery raises five different species of cold-water fish: native cutthroat trout, rainbow trout, brown trout, kokanee salmon, and arctic graylings. View and feed the fish (bring quarters!) at various stages of development in water troughs (raceways) before they go on to stock northwest Colorado's fishing spots. Daily 7 a.m.–3:30 p.m. 1342 CR 132, 970.945.5293.

Colorado's only active volcano, the Dotsero Crater is located about 21 miles northeast of town. To get there, take I-70 Exit 133 to Dotsero and head north on Colorado River Road to the trailhead (approximately 0.5 miles). About 3 miles roundtrip and nearly 2,000 feet of elevation gain (to around 7,300 feet), the trail leads to the half-mile-wide crater, which last erupted some 4,200 years ago.

Take a Train: The Amtrak California Zephyr trains stop eastbound and westbound in Glenwood Springs, just across the river from the vapor caves at the original 1904 train depot. Depart from Denver's Union Station; roughly a 6.5-hour journey one way (www.amtrak.com/california-zephyr-train). In 2021, the Rocky Mountaineer began offering a new luxury-train tour, the Rockies to the Red Rocks, a two-day journey between Denver and Moab with an overnight stay in Glenwood Springs.

Carbondale (and Redstone) / Basalt

www.basaltchamber.org
www.carbondale.com

Bookended by Glenwood Springs and Aspen are the small but beautiful and historic towns of Carbondale and Basalt, 13 and 23 miles southeast from Glenwood Springs, respectively. The water between these towns is called the Middle Roaring Fork, 13 miles of Gold Medal waters that are slower than other parts of the river, making it popular for float fishing trips. The Frying Pan River, aka "The Pan," also features a Gold Medal section that flows east of Basalt. Here are some area highlights:

A short drive from Carbondale on the banks of the Crystal River, the Penny Hot Springs offers a primitive soak spot along Hwy 133. Located near mile-marker 55, these springs only fit about 10–12 people. If it's too crowded, head less than 2 miles north to Avalanche Ranch (see below).

Located 16 miles southwest of Carbondale along CO Hwy 133 is the town of Redstone, home of the historic, Tudor-style Redstone Castle, built in 1902. It's also home to the Avalanche Ranch, featuring three natural hot-springs pools (92–104 degrees) designed in a tiered layout around the natural rock formations, where guests can "soak in" views of Mt. Sopris, Elephant Mountain, and the Avalanche Creek Valley. It also offers 500 feet of riverfront for fishing, as well as lodging options: four-person rooms called "studios," covered wagons (sleep 2), and an offsite house (4 miles away in Redstone). The ranch also features roughly 10 trailheads (easy to difficult hikes, no more than a 15-minute drive) and the Avalanche Pond, perfect for fishing, walking, and boating. (Canoes and 2 paddleboats for guest use.) Visit the barnyard animals including donkey and llama; play horseshoe or badminton. In winter, there's Nordic skiing, snowshoeing, ice-skating, and sledding (and free equipment for guests). On-site massage, yoga, and day passes available; 24-hour springs access except Wed. (opens after 5 p.m.). 12863 CO-133, Redstone, 970.963.2846, www .avalancheranch.com.

Located midway between Basalt and Carbondale on the Rio Grande Trail, Rock Bottom Ranch serves as the Aspen Center for Environmental Studies' midvalley hub for environmental education. This 113-acre wildlife preserve offers Farm Tours (daily in summer, weekly year-round), community dinners, and an annual Harvest Party. Produce and meat available for purchase. Open Fri., 9 a.m.–5 p.m., Sat., 9 a.m.–1 p.m., in the summer, and Fri., 9 a.m.–5 p.m., in the winter, 2001 Hooks Spur Rd., Basalt, 970. 927.6760, www.aspennature.org/location /rock-bottom-ranch.

Just 6 miles east of Marble is the Crystal Mill, an 1892 wooden powerhouse located on an outcrop above the Crystal River that's one of Colorado's most photographed sites.

Glenwood Canyon / Colorado River

Carved by the Colorado River, which glides its way through the 16-mile Glenwood Canyon into town, this area is an exceptionally beautiful outdoor-recreation destination. Visitors can bike the Glenwood Canyon Recreation Path, which runs between the Colorado River and I-70. Starting at E. 6th St. in Glenwood Springs and ending in Dotsero, the paved, relatively flat trail spans about 14.4 miles (one way). Several companies offer "bike and shuttle" combos to Bair

Ranch so you can ride one way into town, such as Canyon Bikes, 152 W. 6th St., 877.945.6605, www.canyonbikes.com.

There are also several hikes, including the Glenwood Canyon Overlook Trail, a 6.4-mile roundtrip trek ending on a ridge above the canyon. (Access trail from Dotsero Warm Springs at the east end of Glenwood Canyon. Roughly 0.5-mile in the trail splits; take the leftmost.) Four rest areas serve Glenwood Canyon—Bair Ranch, Hanging Lake (accessible only via permit; see entry on p. 85), Grizzly Creek, and No Name—each with parking areas, restrooms, picnic grounds, and hiking access.

Rafting through Glenwood Canyon is one of the most popular ways to see the area. Check out Blue Sky Adventures' Half-Day Mild Adventure ($), good for families (minimum age 3, dependent on water levels) (152 W. 6th St., 970.945.6605, www .blueskyadventure.com). Try the Whitewater Rafting LLC, two-hour "Short and Mild" tour for kids ages 2 and up, considered a good "primer" to river experiences ($) (2000 Devereux Rd., 970.945.8477, www.coloradowhitewaterrafting.com). Raft or zipline the canyon (minimum 48 inches, 65 pounds) via Glenwood Canyon Rafting (2610 Gilstrap Ct., 877.384.0445, www.raft ingglenwoodsprings.com). For a mellower float, try Turtle Tubing (located in Gypsum, about 25 miles northeast), featuring large tubes that hold 3–4 adults or multiple youth. Minimum 2 years; roughly 2.5 hours. It's best to bring food or snacks packed in a soft cooler and a shade umbrella for kiddos ($ for ages 13 and older). Colorado River trips meet in Dotsero (970.471.0547, www .turtletubing.com).

Glenwood Adventure Company offers activities such as whitewater rafting, horseback riding, off-road adventures, and even paragliding (no minimum age/weight) ($$)! It also partners with Bair Ranch, a working ranch where guests can go off the

The Giant Canyon Swing at Glenwood Caverns Adventure Park is as thrilling (read: terrifying) as it looks! Photo by Michael Mundt.

grid overnight in cabins—the Golden LeGrande Lodge sleeps 10—and tent sites. 723 Cooper Ave., 970.945.7529, www.glenwoodadventure.com.

Note: Mudslides along burn scars from the August 2020 Grizzly Creek Fire have often resulted in closure of the Glenwood Canyon area and I-70. Check conditions at www.cotrip.org before visiting.

Glenwood Caverns Adventure Park

Perched at the top of Iron Mountain, requiring a 10-minute gondola ride up, America's only mountain-top theme park is one of our family's favorites. The park includes roller coasters, an alpine coaster, a 4D theater, a laser-tag arena, food, and live entertainment such as Native American dancing. There's also the Giant Canyon Swing, the Glenwood Canyon Flyer, and a zipline. New in summer 2022: Defiance, a one-of-a-kind Gerstlauer Euro-Flight roller coaster, a 56-second adventure that "defies" convention with a record-breaking 102.3-degree free-fall drop. (Age/height restrictions vary by activity.) There are also two 40-minute cave tours: the Historic Fairy Cave Tour, originally opened in 1896, and the King's Row Tour. Cave tours and unlimited turns on rides and attractions are

The Glenwood Canyon Flyer at Glenwood Caverns Adventure Park is s perched on the edge of the canyon, 1,300 feet over the Colorado River. Photo by Michael Mundt.

(updated in 2019). In July 2019, the resort added the Sopris Splash Zone featuring Shoshone Chutes, a river ride that mimics a whitewater experience; Hanging Lake, a wade-in pool perfect for littles; and the Grand Fountain, a splash pad by day and an illuminated show fountain by night. Open daily through the summer and into the fall, weather permitting, 10 a.m.–7 p.m., and included with price of hot springs. Hot springs open year-round, 9 a.m.–10 p.m., 401 N. River St., 970.947.2955, 800.537.7946 (SWIM) for lodge reservations, www.hot springspool.com.

Glenwood Whitewater Park and Activity Area

Also called the "G-wave," this is the first man-made whitewater feature built entirely on the Colorado River. A popular spot for paddlers from May through September, it's located on the west side of town, immediately off I-70, Exit 114. Parking may be an issue during high season. (No parking on Midland Ave.) Overflow parking available ⅓-mile up Midland Avenue in the Roaring Fork Transportation Authority lot.

Hanging Lake

This National Natural Landmark located 10 miles east of Glenwood Springs along I-70 is so popular that a permit system was implemented in 2019 to limit daily visitors. A rare example of a lake formed by travertine deposition—a form of limestone deposited by mineral springs, especially hot springs—the shoreline comprises fragile travertine layers, so it's especially important to stay on the trail. Featuring a clear,

included in a Funday Pass. Hours vary by season. 51000 Two Rivers Plaza Rd., 800.530.1635, www.glenwoodcaverns.com.

Glenwood Hot Springs Resort

If you've grown up in Colorado, you know it's another rite of passage for kids to visit these famous hot springs. Established in 1888, the original red sandstone bathhouse and lodge (built for $100,000, nearly $3 million today) features the Spa of the Rockies and an athletic club, as well as a poolside restaurant, The Grill. The world's largest mineral hot-springs pool also includes the 107-room Glenwood Hot Springs Lodge

blue-green lake surrounded by waterfalls, mudslides in summer 2021 destroyed the original trail and some bridges. A redesign will likely be completed by 2024. (A temporary path may be created in the interim.) *Do not* step off the trail or enter the lake. No fishing, no dogs. High-season hikers must park at the Hanging Lake Welcome Center (110 Wulfsohn Rd.) and take the shuttle to the trailhead (or hike/bike along the Glenwood Canyon Recreation Path, about 1 mile). Cars can park at trailhead Nov.–April. Must present permit upon arrival at Hanging Lake Rest Area. Plan for about three hours for your return shuttle. Call 970.384.6309 for information. Check www .visitglenwood.com/hanginglake for updated information before visiting.

Iron Mountain Hot Springs

Just over a mile down the road from its more famous counterpart, Iron Mountain Hot Springs is situated along the Colorado River, offering 16 soaking pools (98–108 degrees) and a family pool my kids didn't want to leave. Opened in 2015, this quieter soaking alternative (operated by Glenwood Caverns Adventure Park) also offers grab-and-go food and drinks, plus adult beverages. Children 5 years and under aren't allowed in the small mineral pools; under 2 years are free. Open daily, 9 a.m.–10 p.m., 281 Centennial St., 970.945.4766, www .ironmountainhotsprings.com.

Sunlight Mountain Resort

Stats: 72 designated trails, 730 skiable acres, 3 lifts, 1 terrain park

Trail classification: 20 percent Beginner; 55 percent Intermediate; 25 percent Advanced

Base elevation: 7,880 feet

Providing free parking within walking distance of the resort's lifts, trails leading to one base-area lodge, and a full day of skiing at about half the cost of larger resorts, this is a perfect option for families. Located 12

Fast Fact: The "international monolith mystery" of 2020, where monoliths were materializing in spots around the world, hit the Roaring Fork Valley on December 8, when one appeared at Sunlight Mountain Resort.

miles south of Glenwood Springs (30 miles northwest of Aspen), it's known for its Ski, Swim, and Stay ski-vacation package, where kids 12 and under ski free (one lift ticket per one paying adult; lodging at a number of Glenwood Springs hotels). Snowmobiling is also a popular pursuit here ($$); family tours available (minimum 5 years for 1-hour tour; 10 years for 2.5-hour tour). Call for reservations: 970.945.7491. www .sunlightmtn.com.

The Yampah Spa and Vapor Caves

The only known natural vapor caves in North America, the Ute tribe that inhabited this region regarded them for centuries as a sacred place of healing and rejuvenation. Enjoy natural geothermal steam baths much like the visitors did when they first opened to the public in 1893. Spa services available. Open daily, 9 a.m.–9 p.m. Reservations recommended. 709 E. 6th St., 970.945.0667, www.yampahspa.com.

Keystone Resort

Stats: 3 mountains, 129 designated trails, 3,148 skiable acres, 20 lifts, night skiing

Trail classification: 14 percent Beginner; 29 percent Intermediate; 57 percent Advanced

Base elevation: 9,280 feet

Stretching 7 miles along the Snake River across three mountains, this resort 75 miles west of Denver is considered one of the country's most family-friendly. Starting with an easy-to-navigate layout—Dercum Mountain is a first stop from the base area with beginner and intermediate terrain, progressing in difficulty to North Peak and

The World's Largest Snow Fort at Keystone Resort offers tunnels, slides, and mazes for all ages. Photo by Michael Mundt.

Outback (as well as 5 above-tree-line bowls)—Keystone is also known for its "kids ski free" offer, where children 12 years and younger can ski and ride for free every day with two or more nights of resort lodging (no blackout dates).

It also boasts one of the nation's largest groomed skating ponds, Keystone Lake (5 acres), the state's longest ski day (Wed.–Sat., 8:30 a.m.–8 p.m.), and the most lighted trails for night skiing (15). There's also tons of fun on Dercum Mountain at Adventure Point, including the World's Largest Snow Fort, a snowy wonderland complete with tunnels, slides, and mazes for all ages (free

with lift access). Plus there's a tubing hill offering one-hour sessions every half hour beginning at noon (minimum 4 years and 42 inches; ski boots allowed). Tubing reservations recommended, 800.354.4386. Nordic skiers will find more than 9 miles of groomed trails and access to more than 35 miles of nearby trails, as well as a Nordic center offering lessons and guided hikes throughout winter (daily, 9 a.m.–4 p.m., 155 River Course Dr., 970.496.4275).

There are three base areas with lodging: River Run and Mountain House, which offer ski-out access, and Lakeside Village, perfect for visitors wanting to ice-skate or paddle the lake (summer). It's also where sleigh-ride dinners depart toward a charming homestead in the Soda Creek Valley for a hearty meal ($$). Prefer an "elevated" dinner? Head to Der Fondue Chessel at the top of North Peak (11,444 feet)—two gondola rides under a snug blanket—for an evening of Bavarian Alps food and entertainment. If you're visiting during the holiday season, check out the Keystone Lodge and Spa's Keystone Chocolate Village, an entire village with a working train and gondola made of 8,000 pounds of chocolate (22101 US-6, 970.496.4500). In summer, the Keystone Bike Park's progression-focused terrain is ideal for all riding abilities. www.keystoneresort.com.

The 1879 Silver Dollar Saloon boasts the original tile floor and custom-made bar featuring diamond-dust mirrors. Photo by the author.

Leadville

Miles from Denver: 100

Established as Leadville in 1878, the highest incorporated city in North America (10,152 feet), this mountain town nicknamed the "Two-Mile High City" resembles what it must have looked like in the late 1800s. Surrounded by Colorado's two highest 14ers, Mt. Elbert and Mt. Massive, it's the ideal headquarters for recreation in the Leadville and Twin Lakes region. See it via bike on the Mineral Belt Trail, an 11.6-mile paved trail around town (ADA accessible). www.leadvilletwinlakes.com.

Lodging

The Tennessee Pass Nordic Center and Sleep Yurts are outfitted with beds with linens, woodstoves, a kitchenette with fresh water, cookware, dishes, and dining table with chairs ($). Head over to the cookhouse for a gourmet meal in a yurt, or order catered meals for delivery. Closed for a few weeks each fall and spring. E. Tennessee Rd., 719.486.8114, www.tennesseepass.com.

Other Highlights

On the first full weekend in March, since 1949, the town has celebrated Leadville Ski Joring, where a horse and rider pull a skier through a course with gates, jumps, and rings—right down snow-packed Harrison Avenue. Fastest cowboy/girl wins!

10th Mountain Division Huts

Veterans of this elite unit were critical in developing some of Colorado's ski resorts after World War II (Arapahoe Basin, Aspen, and Vail), as well as the 10th Mountain Division Huts, scattered primarily throughout Colorado's Central Rockies (many around Vail and Leadville). Available year-round, rent the entire cabin or reserve bed space. Huts vary in design and amenities, but they offer outhouses, and the kitchens are stocked with cookware. Pack in sleeping bags, food, and beverages. Some require significant hiking or snowshoeing (or skinning) for winter access, but they're well worth the trek. www.huts.org.

Camp Hale National Historic Site

Set in a wide valley large enough for 1,000 buildings including barracks, a hospital, and weapons ranges for 15,000 soldiers, this site memorializes the US Army's 10th Mountain Division winter-training site. Built in 1942 (dismantled after World War II), its proximity to Cooper Hill and its 9,200-foot elevation made this spot off US Hwy 24 between Leadville and Red Cliff ideal for altitude training. See ruins along the 10th Mountain Division Memorial Highway (US-24, 970.945.2521). The Camp Hale Memorial Campground offers 15 campsites (vault toilets), June–Oct. Reservations required.

Leadville Colorado and Southern Railroad

Take this 2.5-hour train tour along the old Denver, South Park, and Pacific and the Colorado and Southern lines to the Continental Divide. Ride in open or closed cars some 1,000 feet up through the San Isabel National Forest to views of Mt. Elbert, Mt. Massive, and Fremont Pass, learning about Leadville's colorful past. Dogs allowed. Special tours include the Top of the Rockies Zipline and Train Ride ($$), a five-hour adventure that includes a train ride and a zipline on the same day, with an option for lunch in Leadville. 326 E. 7th St., 719.486. 3936, www.leadville-train.com.

Fast Fact: Veterans of the 10th Mountain Division, who were deployed in World War II to the Italian Alps for high-alpine fighting, founded Ski Cooper. It celebrates its history each spring with the 10th Mountain Ski Down, featuring a parade of veterans, descendants, and current military skiing down the mountain.

Leadville National Fish Hatchery

The second-oldest federally operated hatchery in the country (second to Missouri's Neosho National Fish Hatchery), here kids will enjoy feeding the fish (bring quarters!) and visiting the historic 1889 hatchery building that's used for rearing the endangered greenback cutthroat trout. Adjacent to the Evergreen Lakes Day Use Area, perfect for picnicking, the 1-mile Evergreen Lakes Nature Trail loop explains many of the natural features of the Hatchery grounds. 2846 CO-300, 719.486.0189.

Ski Cooper

Stats: 62 designated trails, 480 skiable acres, 5 lifts

Trail classification: 18 percent Beginner; 26 percent Intermediate; 56 percent Advanced

Base elevation: 10,500 feet

Smaller than its eastern neighbor, Copper Mountain, it also boasts fewer crowds and the "softest snow around," thanks to an all-natural snow base and specific grooming strategy. One of the country's oldest ski resorts (1942), this family-friendly spot offers a wide variety of terrain for all levels at a cheaper price than larger resorts. Need more adventure? The resort has added the Tennessee Creek Basin for expert levels. Or go snowcat skiing on Chicago Ridge for epic runs on wide-open powder bowls and glades. Grab food at a mountaintop yurt or make an après-ski stop at Katie O'Rourke's Irish Pub. New in 2021, the base area's Timberline Taproom features pulled-pork sandwiches, chili, soups, and Colorado beers. www.skicooper.com.

Top of the Rockies Zip Line

The only zipline in the world to fly over a train, this six-zipline adventure means jumping from an elevation of 11,500 feet (minimum 60 pounds). During winter, take the two-hour zipline tour, climbing almost

1,000 vertical feet via snow coach to the first deck. 9 a.m., 12 p.m., and 3 p.m. Add in a snowmobile tour, depending on ability. 9 a.m. departure. (Driver must be 15 years minimum with valid learner's permit; 18 years and older can carry a passenger.) In summer, combine the zipline with train tour or fishing trip ($$). 6492 CO-91, 800.247.7238, www.topoftherockieszipline.com.

Turquoise Lake

Named for the turquoise mine it once housed, this 19th-century reservoir 5 miles west of Leadville is the area's most popular boating destination. Offering motorized access on the south side or nonmotorized on the north, anglers can fish (or ice fish) for mackinaw, rainbow, and brook trout. Bikers can take an off-road adventure by parking at Sugarloaf Dam and mountain biking the 13-mile roundtrip trail that hugs the lake to the May Queen Campground, or take the paved 15-mile road that surrounds the lake (groomed in the winter, ideal for fat-biking). There are 8 lakeside campgrounds, offering nearly 300 tent/RV campsites (Turquoise Lake Rd., 719.486.0749). Or head 1 mile southeast to Sugar Loafin' RV/Campground and Cabins, offering tent/RV sites, cabins, laundry, and restrooms (2665 CR 4, 719.486.1031, www.sugarloafin.com).

Twin Lakes Interlaken Boat Tours

Considered Colorado's most beautiful resort when it was built in 1879, this spot 22 miles south of Leadville was popular for travelers in nearby mining towns such as Aspen and Leadville to ride horses, fish, and cruise the lakes via steam-powered boats. Closed in 1950, this National Historic Site is a "ghost resort" that can only be reached by foot or by one-hour, 45-minute boat tour. May–Sept., 11 a.m. and 1 p.m., weather permitting. Dogs not allowed. Water only on boat; no restrooms. Families

should bring snacks and drinks. Contact for reservations. 5585-5591 CO-82, Twin Lakes, 866.936.3654, www.twinlakesinterlakenboattours.com.

Stay awhile at the Twin Lakes Inn ($), the closest lodging to the glacial lakes and the Mt. Elbert Trailhead. (Room #3 sleeps 6!) 6435 E. Hwy 82, 719.486.9345, www.twinlakescolorado.com.

Loveland Ski Area

Stats: Two base areas, 94 designated trails, 1,800 skiable acres, 9 lifts, 1 terrain park

Trail classification: 13 percent Beginner; 41 percent Intermediate; 46 percent Advanced

Base elevation: 10,800 feet

Located 53 miles from Denver, this resort looming over I-70 West atop the Continental Divide ("the tunnel" actually goes under the ski area) has been a Colorado institution since 1936 (the state's second-oldest resort, behind Steamboat Springs' Howelsen Hill). Typically open mid-October through early May, it features two base areas: Loveland Valley, with gentle terrain for beginners, and Loveland Basin, the main area, both of which offer rental and retail shops, restaurants and bars, plus free parking. A free shuttle travels between them, 8 a.m.–4:15 p.m. Experience high adventure on The Ridge via Lift 9, which takes skiers up to 12,700 feet. www.skiloveland.com.

Fast Fact: Every Valentine's Day, the resort hosts a Marry Me and Ski Free, a group mountaintop matrimony and reception. Participating couples receive two-for-one lift tickets the day of the event.

South Park

Miles from Denver: 86 (Fairplay)

The largest and southernmost of the three high-altitude basins in the Front Range (North Park and Middle Park are in the Great West Region), this high valley between the Mosquito and Park Ranges was once home to the Ute and was a fertile buffalo-hunting ground for the Arapaho. Featuring stunning mountain passes such as Kenosha, views of surrounding 14ers and wide-open ranchlands, this central-Colorado area is one of the state's best (and quietest) areas for outdoor recreation. Designated a National Heritage Area for its landscapes, historic structures, and recreation, its largest town, Fairplay, is known in pop-culture circles as the visual basis for the television show *South Park*. It also includes the small towns of Alma, Como, Hartsel, and Jefferson.

Fairplay

Considered the Trout Fishing Capital of Colorado, this area set along the longest stretch of Gold Medal waters in the state—102 miles along the upper Arkansas River—is ideal for catching brown and rainbow trout. Used by hunters and trappers in the 1840s and later becoming a supply center for nearby mining camps during the Gold Rush, the town was established as Fair Play in 1859 (becoming one word in 1874). Set about 22 miles south of Breckenridge, it's home to one of the three "Triple Crown" burro races with its annual Burro Days.

Be sure to check out South Park City, which preserves 44 authentic buildings, including 7 buildings on the original site. Open 9 a.m.–7 p.m. Memorial Day to Labor Day. 100 4th Street, 719-836-2387, www.southparkcity.org.

Located near the center of town, Middlefork RV Park is located along the Middlefork River, offering 46 RV/tent sites, laundry, restrooms/showers, a catch-and-release trout pond (barbless hooks), and a "fun cabin" with ping pong. 255 Hwy 285, 719.836.4857, www.middleforkrvpark.com.

Located roughly 6 miles northwest of Fairplay, Alma is the country's highest incorporated town at 10,578 feet. (Leadville is the highest *city*.) Set at the base of four 14ers in Pike National Forest—Democrat, Cameron, Lincoln, and Bross—hikers can attempt to summit them all in the DeCaLiBron Loop, comprising approximately 7.5 miles and 3,700 feet of elevation. It's also home to Kite Lake, set around 12,000 feet. The above-tree campground offers 5 first-come, first-served campgrounds with picnic tables, fire rings, and vault toilets. Located 5.5 miles northwest of Alma on CR 8. One of the area's most popular summer attractions is Mosquito Pass, the highest motor-vehicle pass in North America. Off-road vehicles recommended.

Summit County

Miles from Denver: 68 (Dillon)

Featuring popular mountain destinations Dillon, Frisco, and Silverthorne (as well as Keystone, Breckenridge, and others), it's easier to mention these around their centerpiece: Lake Dillon, a freshwater reservoir set around 9,000 feet. Officially Dillon Reservoir, under control of Denver Water (for the Denver's water supply), there are roughly 27 miles of shoreline and a paved, 18-mile bike path that winds around it, which can be accessed at any point. (The reservoir is also stocked annually with 50,000 rainbow trout.)

Fast Fact: The Coney Island Boardwalk hot-dog stand in Bailey, about 40 miles northeast of Fairplay, is a 1950s-style eatery established in 1966. The hotdog is 43-feet-long; the bun 35. Open Thurs., noon–4 p.m., Fri.–Sun., noon–5 p.m., 10 Old Stagecoach Rd.

With Dillon on the east end and Frisco to the west (Silverthorne is set north of and beneath the dam), Frisco and Dillon each offer a marina; the country's highest water shuttle, the Summit Shuttle, travels between them daily (one-way or roundtrip ticket). Limited room for bikes (www.summitshuttle.com, 970.389.9336). In wintertime, the three towns' proximity to ski areas makes them popular winter headquarters.

Dillon

Built as a stagestop and trading post in the 1880s, the town moved twice to accommodate rail lines up to the 1950s, when Denver Water began searching for a place to put a new reservoir. By 1961, every resident was relocated to the town's fourth and current location to begin constructing the Dillon Dam, completed in 1963. (Many buildings were moved, but several remained, creating a "ghost town" at the bottom of Dillon Reservoir.) In exchange, the residents received a recreational amenity that continues to bring economic fortune today. www.townofdillon.com.

DILLON MARINA

Known as the highest deep-water marina in North America, it is also home to the Dillon Yacht Club, hosting several sailing events and regattas during the season. Offering SUP and kayak rentals, there are also three fishing-charter companies on-site: Big Ed's Fishing Ventures (970.389.1720, www.bigedsfishing.com), Alpine Fishing Adventures (303.885.6292, www.fishdillon.com), and Silver Flask Fishing (920.268.9918, www.silverflaskfishing.com). Rent boats, go to sailing school, or book a sunset sailing ($). Minimum 12 years old.

Adjacent to the marina is Marina Park with a playground, picnic areas, and a pavilion. (The Dillon Amphitheater is also nearby, 201 W. Lodgepole St., www.dillonamphitheater.com.) Enjoy Pug Ryan's Tiki Bar, open mid-May–early September, 11:30 a.m.–sunset (weather permitting), 970.468.2145, www.pugryans.com/tiki-bar.

The marina is open daily, Memorial Day–Sept., 9 a.m.–4:30 p.m., 150 Marina Dr., 970.468.5100, www.townofdillon.com/marina.

Three lake-area campgrounds include the Windy Point Group Campground, with two group campsites (up to 100 campers each). Lowry Campground offers 27 RV/tent sites; 3 tent-only campsites are on a first-come, first-serve basis. Includes picnic tables, campfire rings, potable water, and vault toilets. Prospector Campground features 105 sites for tents/trailers/RVs, equipped with picnic tables, campfire rings, vault toilets, and potable water.

Frisco

Established in 1873 during the Colorado mining boom, the town's pedestrian-friendly Main Street is filled with shops and restaurants. We've often stayed here in rental properties when skiing Copper Mountain because it's so close and a tad cheaper than ski-village lodging. The Summit Stage also offers free rides throughout Summit County, including to ski resorts. www.townoffrisco.com.

FRISCO ADVENTURE PARK

Located on the Frisco Peninsula, it offers year-round fun for families including a skate park, a disc-golf course, and a bike park in the summer (all free). There are also two National Forest campgrounds on the peninsula (mid-May–September): Peak One Campground, with 80 sites (tents, trailers, and RVs), picnic tables, fire rings, restrooms, and potable water, and Pine Grove Campground, offering 56 sites (tents, trailers, and RVs), vault toilets, and potable water.

In wintertime, the park features several 1,200-foot tubing lanes ranging from mellow to faster and a surface lift to whisk

you up the hill. Open 10 a.m.–6 p.m., Nov.–
mid-March; 9 a.m.–5 p.m., mid-March–
mid-April. (A free public sledding hill is
available across the street from the tubing
hill.) There's also a beginner ski/ride hill,
served by the surface lift (10 a.m.–dusk,
Dec.–mid-Mar.). Ski lessons available; kids
4 years and under ski free. The Day Lodge,
located at the base of the tubing hill and
beginner ski/ride hill, also offers food and
drink, open daily seasonally. 621 Recreation
Way, 970.668.2558. (Navigation systems
prefer "616 Recreation Way.")

Across from the tubing hill is the popular
Frisco Nordic Center, featuring nearly
17 miles of ski trails and 5 miles of snowshoe
trails, as well as rentals and lessons. Open 9
a.m.–4 p.m. The Day Lodge also offers food
and drink, open daily seasonally. (Use "616
Recreation Way" for location.)

There are also dinner or hot-cocoa sleigh
rides in winter and BBQ chuckwagon dinner tours in summer that leave from the
peninsula, offered by Two Below Zero ($),
970.453.1520, www.dinnersleighrides.com.

FRISCO BAY MARINA

Set at the eastern end of Frisco's Main
Street, this full-service marina rents everything from SUPs to canoes and boats (fishing, pontoon, sailboats), even fishing poles.
Sailing, kayak, SUP lessons, and tours available. Take a family or sunset kayak tour ($)
via Adventure Paddle Tours, located at the
marina. 844.372.3353, www.adventurepad
dletours.com. Alpine Fishing Adventures
also offers guided fishing trips, pontoon
fishing charters, and ice-fishing trips ($$).
(See information under "Dillon Marina.")
The marina's Island Grill offers food, drink,
and lake views. The marina is open daily 9
a.m.–5 p.m., mid-May–mid-Oct., 267
Marina Rd., 970.668.4334.

FRISCO HISTORIC PARK AND MUSEUM

Featuring 13 original structures dating from
1860 to 1943, this free museum campus

educates visitors about the town's Ute, min-
ing, and railroad history. Guided hikes and
tours available. Hours vary by season. 120
Main St., 970.668.3428.

THE VAIL PASS BIKE PATH

Connecting Frisco to Vail over Vail Pass
(about 10,660 feet), this popular path offers
many experiences, including riding about
14 miles from Frisco to Copper Mountain
Resort and back, or completing the full
24-mile, 1,550-foot-climb roundtrip from
Frisco's Main Street. For the price of a bike
rental, visitors can even ride a free shuttle
to the top of the pass to cruise 14 miles
downhill with companies such as Pioneer
Sports, 842 N. Summit Blvd., 970.668.3668,
www.pioneersportscolorado.com.

Silverthorne

Set in a high-mountain valley carved by the
Blue River, Silverthorne is surrounded on
two sides by National Forest and Wilder-
ness Areas. Incorporated in 1967, it features
world-class fishing holes and calm stretches
of water, attracting anglers, boaters, and
SUPers. Check out fishing-guide services
by two local companies: Cutthroat Anglers,
400 Blue River Pkwy., 970.262.2878, www
.fishcolorado.com, and The Colorado
Angler, 249 Summit Pl., 970.513.8055, www
.thecoloradoangler.com.

Campsites include Heaton Bay Camp-
ground, which fills up quickly during high
season. Located just 3 miles from Silver-
thorne on Dillon Dam Road, it offers 81
RV/tent sites, vault toilets, and potable
water. Open May–October.

Silverthorne is also a great shopping des-
tination with its Outlets at Silverthorne,
where we stop without exception en route to
Steamboat Springs for Colorado's Rocky
Mountain Chocolate Factory. www.silver
thorne.org.

Vail

Miles from Denver: 97

Once a summer respite for the Ute tribe, this world-famous ski town at the base of Vail Pass was modeled after Zermatt in the Swiss Alps and features five villages: Vail Village, connected with heated pedestrian streets winding along Gore Creek and includes Gondola One; Lionshead, the Bavarian-inspired area set at the base of the Eagle Bahn Gondola; West Vail; East Vail, just east of Vail Golf Course; and Cascade Village. A popular ski destination by the 1970s, it also offers 58 miles of paved recreational paths, 343 miles of mountain-biking trails, and 166 miles of hiking trails. Further, it's just 35 miles from the Eagle County Regional Airport (www .eaglecounty.us/airport) and offers access to free public transportation, the country's largest free system. www.vail.com.

Lodging

We've stayed in several spots in summer months, including Antlers at Vail (\$\$), a comfortable condominium hotel in Lionshead that's an easy walk to Eagle Bahn Gondola. Complimentary bike and snowshoe rentals; loaner sleds available. There's even a free shuttle to the grocery store to stock up on food for your stay (seasonally). 680 Lionshead Pl., 970.476.2471, www .reservations.antlersvail.com.

In Vail Village, the Sonnenalp Vail (\$\$– \$\$\$) offers great kids' programming (standard hotel rooms, 2-level suites, and 4-bedroom residences). A five-minute walk from the Gondola One, it's the only hotel in Vail that carries a special-uses permit with the US Forest Service, so they offer exclusive guided hiking and snowshoe trips on specific trails (hotel guests only). Our 2.5-mile family hike included a scavenger hunt for the kids. There's also a 1-mile winter snowshoe hike to a cookhouse for a four-course

meal. 20 Vail Rd., 866.284.4411, www .sonnenalp.com.

For a luxury glamping experience, visit Collective Vail, located about 30 minutes' drive northwest from Vail on 4 Eagle Ranch. The property offers two tent styles, each with linens and electricity: 6 Summit tents (\$\$), with king bed and en suite bathroom, accommodate one child age 6 and under, plus a child up to 12 years with one rollaway; and 12 Journey tents (\$), 9 with a queen bed and 3 with single beds, accommodate one child age 6 and under, and include use of shared bath/showers (private when in use). Complimentary breakfast. Enjoy farm-to-ranch cuisine at Three Peaks Lodge or delivered to your tent. Open Memorial Day–Sept. 4098 CO-131, Wolcott, 970.445.2033, www.collectiveretreats.com.

Other Highlights

The town offers some of the coolest outdoor play areas in Colorado, such as the Children's Fountain, perfect for splashing around in summer months (in front of Fuzziwig's Candy Factory in Vail Village, 223 E. Gore Creek Drive #201); Pirate Ship Park, featuring a nifty ship my kids adored (9 Hanson Ranch Rd.); and Lionshead's Sunbird, recently named one of the "World's Coolest Playgrounds" by Travel + Leisure Online for its architecture and design (555 E. Lionshead Cir.).

Vail Village boasts its own Whitewater Park, situated at the Gore Creek Promenade by the International Bridge, a popular rafting and kayaking spot in warmer months.

Set between Beaver Creek and Vail, about 8 miles southwest of the latter, Minturn offers a charming, historic downtown filled with shops and restaurants. Roughly 6 miles southeast along US Hwy 24, etched on the side of Battle Mountain, the abandoned mining town of Gilman, established in the 1880s and shut down in the mid-1980s due to toxic conditions, is worth the drive. Nine miles farther southeast rests Red Cliff, a former mining town featuring stunning views of 14er Mt. of the Holy Cross.

The Betty Ford Alpine Gardens

Named for the former First Lady and Vail resident, these free alpine gardens are the highest in the United States (8,250 feet).

Enjoy some kids' gardening or experience the "Garden's Treasure Hunt," leading visitors though the garden. Pick up treasure-hunt cards at the Schoolhouse. Open 10 a.m.–4 p.m., 183 Gore Creek Dr., 970.476.0103, www.bettyfordalpine gardens.org.

The town also honors her husband with the outdoor-entertainment venue Gerald R. Ford Amphitheater. 503 S. Frontage Rd. E., 970.476.5612, www.grfavail.com.

Lunch with Llamas

One of our most memorable experiences anywhere worldwide, our boys will never forget their roles as wranglers of llamas, ideal backcountry companions because they are typically calm and can lug up to 80 pounds of gear. Several options available,

The drive from Vail past Minturn includes an overlook at the abandoned mining town of Gilman. Photo by Michael Mundt.

The boys will never forget their jobs as llama wranglers during a Paragon Guides "Lunch with Llamas" hike in the Vail area. Photo by Michael Mundt.

including backpacking, rock climbing, hut trips, and other backcountry tours ($$$). 210 Edwards Village Blvd., b107, Edwards, 970.926.5299, www.paragonguides.com.

Piney River Ranch

Located about 12 miles north of Vail Village, this private, 40-acre retreat tucked on the shores of Piney Lake is a popular destination for families. Stay in one of nine accommodations ($–$$) that sleep 4–8, all set along the lakeshore, or in one of three 4-person glamping tents. Enjoy activities such as horseback riding ($) (minimum 8 years and 54 inches), fly-fishing, canoeing or SUPing, and hiking. The onsite Lodge Restaurant and Bar offers some of Vail's best BBQ. Summers only. 700 Red Sandstone Rd., 303.905.4439, www.pineyriver ranch.com.

Sylvan Lake State Park

Located about 31 miles west of Vail surrounded by the White River National Forest, anglers can catch rainbow, cutthroat, and brown trout; hikers will enjoy 7 miles of trails. Kayaking and canoeing but no swimming. Offers 44 campsites (tents, trailers and RVs), coin showers, and flush toilets during summer. Potable water, vault toilets year-round. Also includes 9 cabins and 3 yurts. 10200 Brush Creek Rd., Eagle, 970.328.2021.

Vail Nature Center

A 7-acre facility on a 1940s homestead, the center is one of three locations promoting environmental stewardship and sustainability. (Other locations are the Avon Tang Campus in nearby Avon and the Nature Discovery Center at the Walking Mountains Yurt at the top of Eagle Bahn Gondola, free with gondola pass). Programs include a one-hour Wildflower Walk, an Evening Beaver Pond Tour, and the Think Like a Trout program, where kids ages 8–13 learn about fly-fishing basics. Opens in spring. Prices vary by activity. 601 Vail Valley Dr., 970.479.2291, www.walking mountains.org.

Vail Ski Resort

Stats: 3 areas including the Front Side, Blue Sky Basin, and Back Bowls; 195 designated trails, 5,300+ skiable acres, 32 lifts, 2 terrain parks

Trail classification: 18 percent Beginner; 29 percent Intermediate; 53 percent Advanced

Base elevation: 8,120 feet

The third-largest single-mountain ski resort in the country (behind Big Sky and Park City), Vail is located just 100 miles west of Denver. A top destination for skiers and boarders for nearly 60 years, its back bowls, expansive terrain, and only-in-Vail views of the Gore and Sawatch mountain ranges are legendary. Nonskiing activities happen at Adventure Ridge (Epic Discovery in summer), including the mountain coaster and tubing at Eagle's Nest, open Tues.–Sat., 2 p.m.–7 p.m., during ski season ($).

Check out Emma, the world's first digital mountain assistant for real-time answers on weather, lift-line wait times, dining, and more. Available at all five of Vail Resort's Colorado properties: Beaver Creek, Breckenridge, Crested Butte, Keystone, and Vail. Text 77477.

In summertime, Epic Discovery (at Vail) becomes the headquarters for summer fun (typically opens mid-June). After a scenic gondola ride from Lionshead or Vail Village, the area offers a variety of activities, including the Forest Flyer™ alpine coaster (minimum 3 years and 38 inches; riders under 54 inches must ride with someone 16+ years old) and the Game Creek Canopy Tour, a series of 7 ziplines (minimum 10 years, 90–250 pounds). It also offers a summer tubing hill, aerial courses, bungee trampoline, and more. There's even a Mountaintop Truck Tour, an open-air adventure in a guided, off-road vehicle (minimum 4 years, 40 pounds). Prices vary. www.vail.com.

Whitewater Rafting

There are plenty of spots around Vail to raft, from the Colorado River to the Eagle and Arkansas Rivers. We took a two-hour family float down the Upper Colorado River with Sage Outdoor Adventure (in nearby Wolcott), an easy Class I and II trip that was mellow enough for my husband to ride (and get soaked) on a duckie towed behind the raft ($). The company also offers fishing, snowmobiling, fishing tours, and more. 970.476.3700, www.sageoutdoor adventures.com.

Or check out Timberline Tours' Dinosaur Discovery, combining whitewater rafting with fossil hunting ($$). 1432 Chambers Ave., Eagle, 970.476.1414, www.timberline tours.com.

Tips

It can be overwhelming for first-timer skiers or boarders heading to the slopes, especially with kids. Take some hard-earned advice:

Pay for ski/board school. I know it's expensive, and it's tough to decide which resort is best. In my experience, all offer great schools that are worth the price. It'll hurt your wallet for a few years. But by the time they revolt against lessons—my boys were about 10—they'll likely ski/ride better than you.

Use gear that fits. I promise it's better to buy or rent gear that is actually fitted to your child by a pro than borrowing from a friend temporarily. There are plenty of secondhand stores to get good deals on kids' gear, and renting is easy at any ski resort. Remember: Comfortable gear cultivates a good day on the slopes.

Keep them warm. Invest in good children's ski gloves or mittens, and always keep disposable handwarmers ready for freezing fingers and toes.

Snacks and treats go a long way. I'm a fan of keeping sugary snacks in our backpack, such as energy chews and waffles. I'm also not above bribing them with chocolate or candy.

Have fun! Parents work too hard at getting the most out of our vacation dollars. Even if the kids don't take to the slopes right away, just enjoy getting out there with your family!

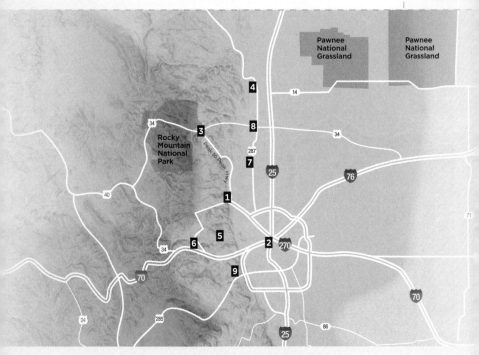

Rocky
Mountain
National
Park

Pawnee
National
Grassland

Pawnee
National
Grassland

DENVER AND CITIES
OF THE ROCKIES

Husky puppy Tasha at the top of Mt. Sanitas, a popular locals' hiking spot that offers beautiful views of Boulder and the Front Range. Photo by the author.

Boulder

Miles from Denver: 29

Marked by the geologic spectacle of the Flatirons, Boulder Valley was once the site of a Southern Arapaho village and frequented by other tribes such as the Ute. Established in 1881, it's home to the University of Colorado at Boulder (CU) Buffaloes (Buffs) and is a gateway to outdoor adventure, offering access to 300 miles of trails and 45,000 acres of open space. www.bouldercoloradousa.com.

Other Highlights

The Boulder Creek path is about 5.5 miles long and runs from Boulder Canyon on the west end to Stazio Ballfields on the east end (just past 55th Street). It offers access to the library, CU, and events around the creek, such as the Boulder Creek Festival, the unofficial start to summer.

The Fiske Planetarium, located on the beautiful CU campus (worth walking through!), is the largest planetarium

The Pearl Street Mall's West End is filled with funky shops, popular restaurants, and plenty of outdoor seating. Photo by the author.

between Chicago and Los Angeles. Open to the public, it features live talks and performances, as well as full-dome films and late-night laser shows. 2414 Regent Dr., 303.492.5002, www.colorado.edu/fiske.

The heart and soul of Boulder, Pearl Street Mall comprises four blocks closed to traffic (11th to 15th Streets). Open since 1977, it's filled with independent shops, restaurants, and street performers, including the famous Zip Code Man (David Rosdeitcher), who has memorized more than 35,000 zip codes.

The free Valmont Bike Park is a 42-acre, natural-surface cycling area featuring terrain for a variety of skills and ages. Open daily, dawn to dusk, weather permitting. 3160 Airport Rd., 303.413.7200.

Tour Operators

The Colorado Mountain School offers a range of guided backcountry adventure, including skiing, splitboarding, ice climbing, and rock climbing at Boulder's numerous renowned destinations. 633 S. Broadway Unit A, Boulder, and 341 Moraine Ave., Estes Park, 866.511.5818, www.colorado mountainschool.com.

Colorado Wilderness Rides and Guides offer a variety of adventures, including ziplining, mountain biking, whitewater rafting, fly-fishing, rock climbing and more. 720.242.9828, www.coloradowilderness ridesandguides.com.

Take a city tour on Banjo Billy's funky bus for historic and ghost tours. 1890 Telluride Ln., 720.938.8885, www.banjobilly.com.

Want to try paragliding ($$)? Check out Red Tail Paragliding, 110–210 pounds; passengers under 18 years must have a legal guardian present to sign waivers. Meetup point: 503 Locust Ave. 720.475.6405, www.redtailparagliding.com.

Boulder Reservoir

This 700-acre, multiuse recreation area set about 6 miles northeast of town is one of the best spots in the state for boating, swimming, fishing, and other lakeside recreation. The swimming area is open Memorial Day–Labor Day, 10 a.m.–6 p.m. (Lifeguards on duty. Kids under 12 must pass a swim test to swim beyond the first rope.) The marina/boat house features Rocky Mountain Paddleboard (www.rockymtn paddleboard.com/boulder), which rents

SUPs, kayaks, and canoes and offers yoga classes and paddling lessons. They'll even rent you a pontoon boat with a captain. The area includes picnic tables, fishing, and the 5.3-mile Boulder Reservoir Loop Trail. The Community Sailing of Colorado also offers sailing lessons (www.communitysailing .org). 5565 51st St., 303.441.3461, www .bouldercolorado.gov/parks-rec/boulder -reservoir.

Colorado Chautauqua

A popular US movement in adult education cultivated in the late 19th and early 20th centuries combining education with lectures, concerts, and plays, Colorado's Chautauqua institution was established in 1898. Hikers can access the iconic Flatirons—named by 19th-century pioneer women for their resemblance to metal pieces used to press clothes called flat irons—on some of Chautauqua Park's 40 miles of hiking trails. (Start at the Ranger Cottage for hiking recommendations, restrooms, and water.) The 22-acre compound also features a general store restaurant, and auditorium, which in summer hosts events such as the Colorado Music Festival. There are also 58 restored cottages for rent, ranging from studios to 3-bedroom units, all with full-size kitchens. No phones, televisions, or computers in the cottages. Wi-Fi and cell coverage available. There is limited parking in the area, so visitors are encouraged to carpool, bike, or ride the free Park to Park shuttle, available during summer weekends and holidays (runs every 15 minutes, 8 a.m.–8 p.m.). There are several stops around Boulder (www.BoulderColoradoUSA.com/Park ToPark). 900 Baseline Rd., 303.442.3282, www.chautauqua.com.

The author's dog Boris walking in Chautauqua Park, where visitors can snap the best photos of Boulder's famous Flatirons. Photo by the author.

Fast Fact: The small mountain town of Nederland is home to the Carousel of Happiness, a restored, 1910 merry-go-round with a 1913 Wurlitzer organ that's a great stop on the way back from skiing (20 Lakeview Dr., 303.258.3457, www.carouselofhappiness.org). Nederland also hosts the quirky Frozen Dead Guy Days, taking place the second weekend in March to honor Bredo Morstoel (aka Grandpa), who was cryogenically frozen after his 1989 death and is now housed on dry ice in a Nederland-based shed. The event includes coffin racing and costumed polar plunging. www.frozendeadguydays.org.

Eldorado Canyon State Park

Located just 10 miles southwest of Boulder in Eldorado Springs, this day-use park is a world-class climbing destination featuring more than 500 technical routes. Comprising two parcels—Inner Canyon and Crescent Meadows connected by the 3.25-mile Eldora Canyon Trail—it's a great spot for hiking, biking (Walker Ranch Loop), Nordic skiing, snowshoeing, and more. Closes at sunset. 9 Kneale Rd., Eldorado Springs, 303.494.3943.

Eldora Mountain

Stats: 65 designated trails, 680 skiable acres, 10 lifts, 3 terrain parks

Trail classification: 17 percent Beginner; 46 percent Intermediate; 37 percent Advanced

Base elevation: 9,200 feet

Set roughly 20 miles from Boulder in Nederland, Eldora has been considered the perfect Denver-area spot for beginners and intermediate skiers since the early 1960s. There are also three Woodward Terrain Parks, ranging from learning to freestyle zones, three restaurants, and several retail stores, as well as the Eldora Nordic Center, featuring nearly 25 miles of trails. Parking on the mountain is free but requires a res-

ervation as of the 2021 season (www.eldora.com/parking). The Regional Transportation District (RTD) offers routes to the mountain from the main Boulder station at 14th and Canyon (www.RTD-Denver.com, 303.299.6000). www.eldora.com.

Denver

While Native American tribes such as the Cheyenne and Arapaho lived for centuries on the land around what is now Denver, the 1858 Gold Rush was what brought settlers in droves, led by the famous rallying cry, "Pikes Peak or Bust!" Named after Kansas territorial governor James Denver, today's Denver-metro area is home to roughly 3 million residents and is the country's tenth-largest downtown, according to Visit Denver. There are 200 named mountains visible from Denver, creating a 140-mile

Denver's Larimer Square historic district is known for the seasonal décor that hangs above Larimer Street, such as Broncos jerseys during football season. Photo by the author.

panorama, plus it's just one hour from Loveland Ski Resort and 90 minutes from Rocky Mountain National Park. Featuring a bustling downtown in spots such as Larimer Square, Lower Downtown (LoDO), and River North (RiNo), plus three major sports stadiums within a 1-mile radius, there's a "mile-high" list of fun things to do in Denver.

Other Highlights

Hammond's Candies has been handmaking candy in Denver since 1920. Go behind the scenes on a tour of the company's factory; 30-minute tours run every half hour on the half hour, Mon.–Sat., 9:15 a.m.–2:45 p.m. Closed Wed. and Sun. 5735 Washington St., 303.333.5588, www.hammondscandies.com.

If you're visiting Denver in January, the city's National Western Stock Show, the world's largest, is held at the National Western Complex for 16 days throughout the month. 4655 Humboldt St., 303.297.1166, www.nationalwesterncomplex.com.

About 31 miles southeast of Denver lies the town of Castle Rock, recognized by the prominent rocky butte resembling a castle overlooking the town from the east side of I-25. Visitors can hike to its base on a 1.5-mile loop from Rock Park (1710 Front St., 303.814.7444). It's also home to the EDGE Ziplines and Adventures ($), featuring a 10-zipline course (70–250 pounds), a 4-story aerial trekking course (ages 4 and up), a ninja course (ages 4 and up), and more (1375 W. Plum Creek, 720.733.9477, www.theedgezip.com). www.visitcastle rock.org.

The Denver CityPass includes eight participating attractions, including the Downtown Aquarium and Denver Zoo, at up to 35-percent savings (www.citypass.com /denver). The three-day Mile High Culture Pass offers different cultural attractions such as the Denver Art Museum and exclusive discounts to other attractions,

including the Butterfly Pavilion (www.cul turepass.denver.org).

Tour Operator

Aspire Tours offers a half-day Denver Foothills Explorer that includes a stop at Red Rocks Amphitheater. Minimum age 8; younger children can be accommodated on private tours. The company also offers whitewater rafting tours and more in the Salida region. 6000 W. 38th Ave., 720.583.0654, www.aspire-tours.com.

Outdoor Denver

Featuring more than 200 parks within the city, as well as 300 acres of designated rivers and trails, Denver has much to offer outdoor enthusiasts. Here are the Top Five Best Outdoor Spots in and around Denver, created in collaboration with Visit Denver (www.denver.org):

CONFLUENCE PARK

Comprising the confluence of Cherry Creek and the South Platte River in Denver's LoDo (2250 15th St.), Confluence Park features the South Platte River's premiere whitewater chutes for kayaking, tubing, and SUPing. The Platte River Trail (Greenway Trail) is also perfect for walking or biking. Bring your own gear, or rent from nearby Confluence Kayaks (2301 7th St., Denver, 80211, 303.433.3676, www.confluencekayaks .com). Take a scenic ride along the river on the historic Denver Trolley™ (Memorial Day to Labor Day), which begins at Confluence Park (behind the REI, 1416 Platte

St.) and includes stops at the Downtown
Aquarium, Children's Museum, and
Empower Field at Mile High (www.denver
trolley.org).

DENVER BOTANIC GARDENS (AT YORK STREET)

Considered one of the top five botanic gardens in the country, here kids will especially enjoy Mordecai Children's Garden, a 3-acre haven featuring ecosystems from alpine to plains. Known for extensive programming and concerts, the gardens are especially spectacular during the holiday season with the Blossoms of Light (late November–early January). 1007 York St., 720.865.3500, www.botanicgardens.org.

DENVER ZOO

Established in 1896, the zoo is home to 3,000 animals representing around 450 species, many of which are threatened, endangered, or even extinct in the wild such as Asian elephants, Komodo dragons, and the greater one-horned rhinoceros. It also offers animal encounters and off-hour special events such as the holiday Zoo Lights, when it transforms into a colorful wonderland of more than 2-million lights. Open daily, 10 a.m.–5 p.m., 2900 E. 23rd Ave., 80205, 720.337.1400.

Bonus: Created in 1942 to develop chemical weapons during World War II, the Rocky Mountain Arsenal National Wildlife Refuge is roughly 8 miles from downtown. A 15,000-acre urban refuge that's home to 330 species of wildlife, including bald eagles, it includes roughly 10 miles of easy/moderate hiking trails and an 11-mile Wildlife Drive auto tour. Open sunrise to sunset. Visitor center open Wed.–Sun, 9 a.m.–4 p.m., 6550 Gateway Rd., Commerce City, 303.289.0930.

The Denver Botanic Gardens (at York Street) features the Mordecai Children's Garden, a 3-acre haven for kids. Photo by Michael Mundt.

RUBY HILL RAIL YARD AND RUBY HILL PARK

The country's only urban snowsports terrain park, this free attraction features 13 boxes, rails, and other features (made possible through a partnership between Winter Park Resort and Denver Parks and Recreation). Run by volunteers, it also offers a mountain-biking park and the Levitt Pavilion, an outdoor concert space featuring several free summer concerts. 1200 W. Florida Ave., 720.913.1311.

WASHINGTON PARK

A coveted neighborhood in south-central Denver filled with historic homes, the 160-acre "Wash Park," features two lakes; two flower gardens, one a replica of gardens at Mount Vernon; a 2.6-mile perimeter path for walking, running, and biking; a recreation center; picnic areas; and tennis courts. Located next to the iconic Washington Park Boathouse (opened in 1913), Wheel Fun Rentals offers a variety of rentals including surreys, water trikes, pedal boats, and SUPs (www.wheelfunrentals.com).

Denver-Area State Parks

BARR LAKE

Home to more than 350 bird species including bald eagles, spot them via an 8.8-mile, multiuse trail around the lake. The 1,900-acre prairie reservoir is also a great fishing spot for channel catfish and rainbow trout. Boats are limited to 10 horsepower, so it's a peaceful spot for kayakers and canoeists. There's also a 12-lane archery range, free with entrance. (Classes occasionally offered.) In winter, it's perfect for ice fishing, Nordic skiing, and snowshoeing. Includes a nature center, located near the south parking lot, where visitors have access to naturalists. Day-use only, 5 a.m.–10 p.m., 13401 Picadilly Rd., Brighton (26 miles northeast), 303.659.6005.

CASTLEWOOD CANYON

Set along Cherry Creek, this designated Colorado Natural Wildlife Area is ideal for bird-watching. There are also 14 miles of trails, ranging from 0.5 to 4 miles (leashed pets allowed on most trails), plus a natural amphitheater and Bridge Canyon Overlook gazebo set on the edge of the canyon. Includes 60-foot-high rock-climbing spots and views of homestead ruins. Good for Nordic skiing and snowshoeing in winter. Includes a visitor center. Day-use only, sunrise to sunset, 2989 S. Hwy 83, Franktown (37 miles southeast), 303.688.5242.

CHATFIELD

Set 24 miles southwest of the city, its centerpiece is the 1,500-acre Chatfield Reservoir, open to boating, paddle sports, swimming, waterskiing, and more. Includes four campgrounds with approximately 200 RV/tent campsites (10 group sites), some available year-round, with restrooms, showers, and laundry. The Camper Services Office offers passes, fishing, and hunting licenses. Open daily 9:30 a.m.–4:30 p.m. Includes the north and south boat ramps, a dog off-leash area, and even a model-airplane field. The Chatfield Marina features food, pontoon/fishing boat rentals, and Seagull's Restaurant (303.791.5555). The marina is open 8 a.m.–8 p.m., April–Oct. 11500 N. Roxborough Park Rd., Littleton, 303.791.7275.

Roughly 7 miles west of Chatfield, the Denver Botanic Gardens Chatfield Farms is a 700-acre, native-plant refuge and working farm located along the banks of Deer Creek. Includes a children's play area, trails, and a wildlife-observation blind. Open 9 a.m.–5 p.m., 8500 W. Deer Creek Canyon Rd., Littleton, 720.865.3500, www.botanicgardens.org.

CHERRY CREEK

Just 19 miles southeast of Denver, this destination attracts water-skiers and anglers from around Colorado. Offering 35 miles of multiuse trails, 15 paved, the campground offers 133 newly renovated RV/tent sites, plus restrooms, showers, laundry (seasonal). Abilene Loop offers the only winter camping. Includes an archery/shooting range, a swimming area, and sailing programs. The Marina at Pelican Bay offers a pub, as well as boat and jet ski rentals, Memorial Day–Labor Day (4800 S. Dayton St., 303.741.2995, www.pbcherrycreek.com). Rocky Mountain Paddleboard (follow signs for marina), located on the beach near the boat launch, offers SUP and kayak rentals, lessons, and more (4800 S. Dayton St., www.rockymtn paddleboard.com). The park often reaches capacity during high season, May–Oct. 4201 S. Park Rd., Aurora, 303.690.1166.

ROXBOROUGH

Roughly 8 miles south of Chatfield Reservoir near Littleton, this day-use area is filled with dramatic red-rock formations, earning it the nickname "Denver's Garden of the Gods." An Audubon Society Important Bird Area, it also includes a visitor center and eight trails (roughly 14 miles). In winter, it's a favorite cross-country skiing and snowshoeing destination. No pets allowed. 4751 E. Roxborough Dr., Roxborough, 303.973.3959.

Home to dramatic red-rock formations, Roxborough State Park is often called "Denver's Garden of the Gods." Photo by the author.

STAUNTON

Located within an easy drive of Denver (39 miles southwest), this park offers 30 miles of trails for hiking, biking, and horseback riding. There are also rock-climbing and fishing spots, geocache sites, and 25 walk-in, year-round campsites. Vault toilets, potable water. The park also offers track-chairs so visitors with limited mobility can explore three designated trails (reservation forms online.) Visitor center open in summer, 8 a.m.–4 p.m. Weekends only in off-season. 12102 S. Elk Creek Rd., Pine, 303.816.0912.

Estes Park

Miles from Denver: 65

The former stomping grounds of the ancient Clovis culture, as well as Ute and Arapaho tribes, the town was incorporated in 1917, two years after the national park's designation. Known as the eastern gateway to RMNP, the town's touristy Elkhorn Avenue is lined with shops, restaurants, and saltwater taffy shops. www.visitestespark.com

Lodging

Estes Park KOA Holiday is set just across the street from Lake Estes and 1.5 miles east of downtown on Hwy 34. Includes RV/tent sites plus camping cabins (sleep 4–6), showers, restrooms, and laundry. 2051 Big Thompson Ave., 800.562.1887.

The Sombrero Stables, located right next door, offers scenic horseback rides. 1895 Big Thompson Ave., 970.533.8155.

Other Highlights

The town's Riverwalk follows along Big Thompson River, which flows along the backside of Elkhorn Avenue. Spanning about 1 mile, begin at the Estes Park

Parking Structure at the visitor center (691 N. St. Vrain Ave.) and end at Performance Park (435 W. Elkhorn Ave.), where there's a natural climbing wall behind the amphitheater. Along the way, spot one of the town's 12 bronze rodent-like pikas, part of a citywide scavenger hunt.

The Estes Park Aerial Tramway opened in August 1955, offering a smooth, 3.5-minute ride up 1,100 vertical feet. Typically open Memorial Day–Labor Day, weather permitting. 420 E. Riverside Dr., 970.475.4094, www.estestram.com.

Near Sombrero Stables is the town's newest attraction, the Mustang Mountain Coaster, added in 2021. Minimum 3 years, 36 inches; 56 inches to ride alone. Open daily, 10 a.m.–7 p.m., 1180 Dry Gulch Rd., 970.672.1829, www.mustangmountain coaster.com.

Located roughly 20 minutes south of Estes Park in Allenspark along the famed Peak to Peak Scenic Byway, Camp St. Malo Visitor and Heritage Center is home to the iconic Chapel on the Rock at Camp St. Malo (1936). The main building is currently undergoing renovations, but the visitor center and church are open 10 a.m.–4 p.m. Closed Mon. Includes a gift shop, restrooms, and a 0.5-mile Stations of the Cross Trail, added in 2021. 10758 CO-7, 303.747.2786, www.campstmalo.org.

Tour Operators

Kirks Flyshop and Mountain Adventures offers fly-fishing tours, gear rentals, float trips, and backcountry llama treks. Offers a six-hour day trip, overnight pack trips, and drop service, where the llamas deliver your

Fast Fact: The area's most famous lodging, the Stanley Hotel (1909), is the inspiration for Stephen King's bestselling novel *The Shining*. 333 E. Wonderview Ave., 970.577.4000, www.stanleyhotel.com.

Fast Fact: Roughly 9 percent (30,000 acres) of RMNP was impacted by the Cameron Peak Fire (August 2020) and East Troublesome Fire (October 2020), respectively, the first- and second-largest forest fires in Colorado's history.

gear to you ($$). 230 E. Elkhorn Ave. Unit B, 970.577.0790, www.kirksflyshop.com.

Take a snowcat tour ($$) with Estes Park Outfitters to a remote mountain lodge perched at 9,200 feet. Nordic ski or snowshoe on more than 7 miles of groomed trails. Day trips are three hours, including the 90-minute layover at the lodge. Overnight and full-moon tours (5 p.m.–8 p.m.) available. 5229 Little Valley Dr., 970.215.7064, www.estesparkoutfitters.com.

Estes Park Rock Climbing offers half- and full-day guided rock climbing, including a twelve-hour adventure to summit Longs Peak ($$). 1230 Big Thompson Ave., 970.205.9226, www.estesparkrockclimbing.com.

Estes Park Visitor Center

I give the visitor center this full entry because it's a hub for the town's free shuttle system. And I can't emphasize this enough: Estes Park and RMNP are busy in the summer months through fall, when the elk-bugling mating ritual draws elk and tourists in droves, often through November. If you're not willing to start at the crack of dawn, don't even bother trying to park at Bear Lake, the kid-friendly 0.8-mile loop around the lake. Instead, use the town's free, seasonal shuttle system to avoid parking hassles, or check out the new electric trolley (since 2020). Park at one of the hubs, such as the visitor center, for one of five Town of Estes Park shuttle routes and three RMNP shuttles. (The latter operates from late May through early October.) Visitor center summer hours, starting Memorial Day week-

end, Mon.–Sat., 8 a.m.–8 p.m., Sun.,
9 a.m.–6 p.m., 500 Big Thompson Ave.,
970.577.9900 (handicapped-accessible bus,
970.586.4920), www.visitestespark.com.

Fun City / Open Air Adventure Park

I have vivid memories of riding the giant
rainbow slide as a kid whenever my parents
would drag me to Estes Park with visitors.
(Yes, I had to be dragged as a teen.)
Includes an amusement park with go-karts,
bumper boats, and a miniature golf course.
455 Prospect Village Dr., 970.586.2828,
www.funcityofestes.com.

Just across the street, the Open Air
Adventure Park features 32 aerial challenges. Axe-throwing lanes available. (Minimum 6 years, 40 pounds.) Tours daily
every 30 minutes, 9:30 a.m.–5 p.m. 490
Prospect Village Dr., 970.586.3066. Both
closed in winter.

The giant rainbow slide at Estes Park's Fun
City has been around since 1969. Photo
by Michael Mundt.

Grazing elk in the meadows of Moraine Park
are a highlight for tourists in the national park.
Photo by Michael Mundt.

Visitors seeking Colorado's expansive blue skies, verdant meadows, and craggy peaks will find them in Rocky Mountain National Park. Photo by Michael Mundt.

Kent Mountain Adventure Center (KMAC)

The all-things-extreme-backcountry guides, KMAC offers winter tours that include a full-day snowshoe ascent to the top of Flattop Mountain, avalanche and winter-camping training, and ice-climbing excursions. There are also backcountry ski schools for skiers and boarders. In warmer months, enjoy a guided hike (half- or full-day options, including hiking Longs Peak). Or take a guided via ferrata tour (4–6 hours), either the Peregrine Arete (great for kids) or the Cloud Ladder (advanced, added in summer 2021), recommended only for those with climbing experience ($$). (I've tried it, and the course is *no joke!* Younger kids, even teens, should be comfortable with heights.) Maximum 265 pounds. (Customized programming is available for kids under minimum age, roughly 11 years.) Ever wanted to sleep on the edge of a cliff? (Hard pass for me.) Try out a portaledge overnight or for "just lunch or dinner," aka a "cliffnic," a picnic at 75 feet. Includes a short hike/climb ($$). Families welcome. Minimum 8 years. KMAC is located on the Stanley Hotel property. 520 Steamer Pkwy., 970.586.5990, www.kmaconline.com.

Lake Estes

A popular recreation spot 2 miles from downtown, the area offers trout fishing, SUPing, kayaking, boating, and more. Ringed by the 3.75-mile Lake Estes Trail, there's also the Lake Estes Marina (1770 Big Thompson Ave., 970.586.2011), a one-stop resource for snacks and rentals such as pontoons, fishing gear, and bikes. Stick around for a game of horseshoes or volleyball (equipment provided). Open seasonally. To stay lakeside, check out the Estes Park Resort ($$–$$$), 1700 Colorado Peaks Dr., 970.577.6400, www.theestesparkresort.com. Across the street, Estes Lake Lodge ($) features the family-friendly Lakeside Manor, which sleeps 8. 1850 N. St. Vrain, 970.779.7455, www.esteslakelodge.com.

Rocky Mountain National Park (RMNP)

When visitors think of Colorado's expansive blue skies, verdant mountain meadows dotted with wildflowers, and alpine lakes tucked at the base of craggy peaks, RMNP is where to find it. Home to 355 miles of hiking trails, 147 lakes, and 77 mountains taller than 12,000 feet—including the state's northernmost 14er and park's highest point, Longs Peak (14,255 feet)—it's no surprise that it's Colorado's most-visited national park. Comprising one-third alpine

The boys at Sprague Lake, one of our favorite Rocky Mountain National Park destinations and a good moose-sighting spot. Photo by the author.

tundra—aka "the land above trees" that begins around 11,000 feet—the diverse ecology has earned its designation as a UNESCO international biosphere reserve and globally important bird area. It also features Trail Ridge Road, the highest continuous paved road in the United States (12,183 feet). Open roughly Memorial Day to mid-October. The 48 miles along US 34 connect the east side, Estes Park, to the west side, Grand Lake (about a two-hour drive). Colorado's second-oldest national park, RMNP earned its status in January 1915 under President Woodrow Wilson (nine years after Mesa Verde).

Take a tour to avoid permit headaches with operators such as Scot's Sporting Goods, near the Beaver Meadows entrance, offering hiking and fly-fishing tours in

RMNP ($$) (970.586.2877, www.scotssport inggoods.com). Estes Park Trolley offers a three-hour RMNP tour or a five-hour version to Trail Ridge Road (9 a.m.–2 p.m., includes cinnamon roll, coffee, and lunch) (1340 Big Thompson Ave., 970.481.8531, www.estesparktrolleys.com). Take a photographic or Hidden Valley sledding tour via Estes Park Guided Tours ($) (500 Big Thompson Ave., 970.732.7887, www.estes parkguidedtours.com).

RMNP features seven visitor/information centers, including four on the east side, one along Trail Ridge Road, and two on the west side. The two main ones, Beaver Meadows (east) and Kawuneeche (west), are open year-round, as is one campground, Moraine Park (east):

On the Estes Park side is *Beaver Meadows Visitor Center* (1967), the busiest and most famous visitor center in the park. Located right before the southeast entrance on Hwy 36, it offers restrooms and a gift shop. Open year-round, 8 a.m.–4:30 p.m. (opens 9 a.m., winter) (1000 US-36, 970.586.1206).

The Moraine Park Discovery Center, located 1.5 miles from the Beaver Meadows entrance, offers a souvenir shop and ranger-led hikes. Open in summer and fall, 9 a.m.–4:30 p.m. (3 Bear Lake Rd., 970.586.1363).

The Fall River Visitor Center, located at the northeast entrance along US Hwy 34 (5 miles west of Estes Park), features a gift shop and restrooms. Open 9 a.m.– 4 p.m; closed in winter (3450 Fall River Rd., 970.586.1206).

Sheep Lakes Information Station in Horseshoe Park is located roughly 2 miles west of Fall River Visitor Center (US Hwy 34), featuring good wildlife viewing, particularly bighorn sheep. Open 9 a.m.–4:30 p.m. Closed fall and winter.

Located along Trail Ridge Road, which crosses the Continental Divide at Milner Pass (10,120 feet), the *Alpine Visitor Center* is the highest-elevation visitor center in the National Park System (11,796 feet). It features a bookstore, restrooms, a gift shop and snack bar, the park's only restaurant, and daily ranger-led tundra walks (up to two hours). Keep in mind, it's often windy here and can be 20–30 degrees colder than town, so wear layers! Generally open late May–mid-October, 9 a.m.–4:30 p.m.; the center closes if the road does. 1000 US Hwy 36, 970.586.1206. Check road conditions and closures: 970.586.1222.

The Kawuneeche Visitor Center, located 1 mile north of Grand Lake on US Hwy 34, includes a bookstore, ranger-led activities, restrooms, six picnic tables and firepits/grills. Open year-round, 8 a.m.–4:30 p.m.; winter opens 9 a.m., closed Mon. and Tues. (16018 US-34, 970.627.3471).

Roughly 8 miles north of Kawuneeche is the *Holzwarth Historic Site*, a 1917 dude ranch that visitors can tour for a taste of early homesteading. Closed in winter.

There are five RMNP campgrounds (no lodges), many of which are booked six months in advance (970.586.1206). The first four are on the east side; the fifth is the only one serving the west side:

Moraine Park Campground (1.2 miles from the Moraine Park Discovery Center) is RMNP's only year-round campground. Surrounded by a ponderosa pine forest at 8,160 feet, it offers 244 reservable sites (101 tent-only) during the summer and 77 on a first-come, first-served basis during winter. Vault toilets, potable water year-round. Seasonal amenities include flush toilets, an amphitheater, and firewood and ice for sale. Located on Moraine Park Rd., near the Beaver Meadows Entrance on Hwy 36.

Aspenglen Campground, located near the Fall River Entrance, offers 52 RV/tent sites and includes an amphitheater, firewood and ice for sale, flush toilets, and potable water. Open late May–late September, US-34 and Old Fall River Rd.

Glacier Basin Campground, 5 miles from the Beaver Meadows Entrance Station, features 150 campsites (73 tent-only), including group campsites. Offers flush toilets, potable water, an amphitheater, and firewood and ice for sale. Open Memorial Day to Labor Day. There's an easy hike to one of the park's most popular destinations, Sprague Lake, roughly a 1.3-mile walk. The 0.8-mile trail around it is where we've spotted moose in the park.

Located 20 minutes south of Estes Park on Hwy 7, RMNP's *Longs Peak Campground* offers 26 site, tents-only (9,500 feet). Vault toilets, potable water, firewood station. First-come, first-served. Open Memorial Day–Labor Day.

Timber Creek Campground is the only west-side campground, located about 8 miles north of the Grand Lake entrance (8,900 feet), offering 98 sites (30 tent-only) with firewood for sale, an amphitheater, flush toilets, and potable water. Open summer to early fall. First-come, first-served. No shade due to a mountain pine beetle infestation.

To avoid crowds, visit RMNP in winter months for sledding and tubing in fresh powder at Hidden Valley, a closed ski area and the park's only designated sledding spot. Bring your own sled (ones with metal runners aren't allowed); no tows provided. Facilities include a warming hut, typically open on the weekends, and heated restrooms (flush/running water), located at

Catching dragonfly nymphs and high-alpine leeches at the national park's Nymph Lake. Photo by Michael Mundt.

the bottom of the hill by the parking lot (open daily). The area is also a good base camp for backcountry skiers/snowboarders, snowshoers, and Nordic skiers.

On the east side, there are free ranger-led snowshoe tours, typically in the Bear Lake region. Contact Beaver Meadows Ranger Station, 970.586.1223. On the west side, which typically receives more snow than the east, there are cross-country ski tours, a beginning snowshoe tour, and an intermediate snowshoe tour, once per week. Contact the Kawuneeche Visitor Center for days and times.

Note: As of May 2021, RMNP requires timed-entry reservations for late May through early October to mitigate crowding (www.recreation.gov). Visit www.nps.gov /romo or call 970.586.1206 for updated information.

Trout Haven Fishing Pond

Stocked with rainbow trout throughout the season (fishing rentals available), the fishing pond is just steps from the "Stump Jump" kids' obstacle course and the Meadow Mini Golf Course. Winter months include ice fishing and skating. Open 10 a.m.–6 p.m., 800 Moraine Ave., 970.577. 0202, www.trouthavenresorts.com.

YMCA of the Rockies Estes Park

Situated on 860 acres about 4 miles from the RMNP entrance, this is our favorite Estes Park lodging. Offering 9 different lodges with traditional hotel-style rooms (two queen beds) or rooms with bunk beds, there are also more than 200 heated cabins equipped with full kitchens and gas or wood fireplaces ($). Roll-away beds available for an extra fee. The property also offers families a ton of on-site activities (most at no extra cost): a family escape room; a treasure hunt throughout the property; a full-size gym for volleyball, basketball, and shuffleboard; a roller-skating rink; and an indoor swimming pool. In winter, take guided snowshoe hikes into RMNP (snowshoe rentals available) and ice-skate on a natural pond. There's also the Boone Family Mountain Center, a base camp for exploration and high-altitude activities, featuring an education nature center and a two-story climbing wall. Additionally, it's the staging and information area for hiking, fishing, mountain biking, and archery. The property also features special-programming weekends, such as a winter Mountaineering Weekend where the guests can learn about winter survival and backcountry skiing. No alcohol sales (can bring on property.) Day passes available. 2515 Tunnel Rd., 970.586.3344, www.ymcarockies.org.

Fort Collins

Miles from Denver: 65

Built in 1862 as Camp Collins to protect
travelers and settlers along the Colorado
branch of the Overland Trail, the area
thrived as an agricultural center after the
1877 arrival of the Colorado Central Railroad. Incorporated as Fort Collins in 1873,
it's home to Colorado State University
(proud Ram undergrad right here!), established in 1879, plus 50 city parks and more
than 280 miles of trails. I've always
described it as the more laid-back version
of its college-town rival, Boulder. www
.visitftcollins.com

Other Highlights

Set north of Old Town, the Poudre River
Whitewater Park offers a chance for kayak-
ers, tubers and kids of all ages to enjoy the
Poudre River. 201 East Vine Dr.

The Farm at Lee Martinez Park teaches
kids about agriculture and farm life with
animals, antique farm equipment, the
museum and farm store, and hayrides.
Pony rides available. Hours vary by season.
600 N. Sherwood St., 970.221.6665.

The Gardens on Spring Creek features 12
acres of beautiful botanic gardens and more
than 400 North American butterflies in a
tropical Butterfly House. Open daily 10
a.m.–5 p.m. (Final entry at 4 p.m.) Reservations recommended. 2145 Centre Ave.,
970.416.2486, www.fcgov.com/gardens.

Cache la Poudre River

Allegedly named for the place where
French Canadian trappers hid their gun-
powder during a raging blizzard in the
early 1800s, the Cache la Poudre (CASH la
POO-der, French for "hide the powder")
begins in RMNP along the Continental
Divide and flows down to Fort Collins.
Colorado's only nationally designated

"Wild and Scenic River," preserving rivers
with outstanding natural, cultural, and
recreational values, it's a popular rafting
(Class I–V rapids) and trout-fishing destination.

The Poudre Canyon is a busy summer
destination, and there are plenty of spots to
stay, including Bighorn Cabins, featuring
cabins that sleep 2–5 guests ($-$$) (31635
Poudre Canyon Rd., Bellvue, 970.232.6369,
www.bighorncabins.com), and Glen Echo
Resort ($), offering 17 cabins (sleep 2–6)
and 1 penthouse (sleeps 14), as well as 80
RV spots and several tent campsites. Housing units have cooking facilities, and some
include fireplaces. On-site restaurant
(closed winters). 31503 Poudre Canyon Rd.,
Bellvue, 970.881.2208, www.glenechoresort
.com. Also located in the canyon, the Poudre Rearing Unit is one of the largest trout-
egg producers in the state. Call for tours.
38915 Poudre Canyon Rd., Bellvue,
970.881.2187.

See the canyon via the Cache la Pou-
dre-North Park Scenic Byway, which connects Fort Collins to North Park. Traversing 101 miles (about three hours) through
the Poudre Canyon and over Cameron Pass
(10,276 feet), it connects to Walden's State
Forest State Park. (See "North Park" entry.)
If you'd rather skip driving, Majestic Mountains Scenic Rides offers tours along this
byway (408 Skyway Dr., 970.829.9549,
www.majesticmountainsscenicrides.com).
Take a family-friendly whitewater rafting
tour (minimum 7 years old) with Rocky
Mountain Adventures. Half- and full-day
options (1117 N. US Hwy 287, 970.493.4005,
www.shoprma.com). Or enjoy the half-day
beginner Wildwater Trip (#1) with A1
Wildwater, featuring Class II–III (a touch
of IV) rapids (minimum 7 years old) (2801
N. Shields St., 970.224.3379, www.a1wild
water.com).

Horsetooth Reservoir

This 6.5-mile-long oasis about 20 minutes west of town is a popular recreation spot for boating, fishing, swimming, waterskiing, sailing, hiking, and more. Horsetooth also offers 29 miles of hiking, biking, and horseback-riding trails on the west side of the reservoir that connect to Lory State Park trails. We especially love the hike to Horsetooth Rock, about 2.5 miles one way of moderate-to-strenuous climbing to some spectacular views. Along the east side of the reservoir is also a premier bouldering destination, Rotary Park.

There are two campgrounds with RV/tent sites: South Bay has 81 sites (some offered year-round), and Inlet Bay offers 54, with vault toilets and potable water, as well as seasonal flush toilets with showers, generally April–Oct. (www.larimercamping .com). The Inlet Bay Marina rents a variety of boats and nonmotorized equipment, from kayaks to Hydrobikes and party boats (4314 Shoreline Dr., 970.223.0140, www.in letbaymarina.com). The Horsetooth Area Information Center, located in South Bay, offers information on areas, trails, camping, boating, fishing, and more (9 a.m.–4 p.m.). 4200 W. CR 38 E., 970.498-5610.

Lory State Park

Adjacent to Horsetooth Reservoir, this 2,600-acre park features nearly 26 miles of trails for mountain biking, hiking, and horseback riding. The Corral Center Mountain Bike Park offers a variety terrain, including dirt jumps, a pump track, and skills area. Lory features 6 backcountry campsites, accessed by at least a 2-mile, one-way hike. There are many existing climbs on the granitic rocks in the Arthur's Rock vicinity and on Arthur's Rock itself. 708 Lodgepole Dr., Bellvue, 970.493.1623.

Pawnee National Grassland

Encompassing more than 193,000 acres of sky and grass, Pawnee National Grassland (PNG) is located 35 miles east of Fort Collins (25 miles northeast of Greeley). For thousands of years, the land was home to Native American tribes such as the Ute and Arapaho. But by the late 1800s, more than 1,000 homesteaders began staking claims, followed by the arrival of the Chicago, Burlington, and Quincy Railroad. Few families remained by 1960, when the PNG was established. Comprising two parcels of land—the Crow Valley Unit (west) and the Pawnee Unit (east)—it's now used for grazing, energy extraction, and recreation, especially bird-watching. 115 N. 2nd Ave., Ault, 970.834.9270.

Camping is located in the western Crow Valley Unit, nearest Ault, Grover, and Briggsdale. The area features the Crow Valley Recreation Area, a prairie oasis for some 200 bird species and a great spot for birding, hiking, and stargazing. Just head out to the grasslands with camera in hand. (Dawn and dusk are best times.) In addition to the Lee and Dorothy Rhodes Farm Implement Museum, which displays historic farm equipment, there are three campgrounds clustered together in the area:

The Crow Valley Family Campground includes 10 sites, each one for up to 8 people, with picnic tables and fire rings. Sites 2–5 are first-come, first-served. Potable water (summer), vault toilet. There's also a baseball diamond, volleyball court, and horseshoe pits.

Crow Valley Group Campground includes 3 campsites that can accommodate up to 30 people. There are picnic tables and

The challenging, 5-mile roundtrip hike to Horsetooth Rock rewards adventurers with panoramic views of Fort Collins. Photo by the author.

a small parking lot at each. Potable water (summer), vault toilets.

Located at the end of the campground road, the Steward J. Adams Education Site is a tents-only, reservation-only site that accommodates up to 100 people. Vault toilets, covered cooking shelter with electrical outlets and three picnic tables. No RVs allowed.

The campgrounds are open April–November, with reservations through late September. Flooding can temporarily close sites in spring/early summer, so check conditions before departure.

The eastern Pawnee Unit, closest to Sterling and Raymer, is home to the area's most predominant geographic feature, the Pawnee Buttes. Rising 300 feet above the prairie about 13 miles south of the Wyoming border, a 1.5-mile hiking and horseback trail leads from the parking lot to an overlook at the first butte. (The second butte is on private land, but you can walk up to it.) Restrooms at parking area. Bring binoculars to spot hawks and falcons nesting in the rocky cliffs. (Trail is open year-round, but there are some closures in the area Mar. 1–June 30 to protect nesting raptors.) You may also see arrowheads and fossils along the way. Please don't take any!

PRO TIPS

• Visit with a full tank of gas and bring plenty of water, as services throughout the area are limited.

• Most roads in the grasslands aren't paved, and they can become slick and muddy after rain.

• As a grazing area for cattle, there are many gates. Please leave them how you find them.

Red Feather Lakes

A rustic mountain village located 45 miles northwest of Fort Collins, this popular mountain destination is surrounded by the Roosevelt National Forest, ideal for enjoying kayaking, rafting, and fishing along the Cache la Poudre River. The Beaver Meadows Resort and Ranch offers several lodging options (from 1 to 35 guests), including traditional rooms, cottages, cabins, and condos, plus more than 60 RV/tent campsites. There's even a Homestead Cabin (sleeps 8) with a woodburning stove. The property includes disc golfing, hiking, horseback riding, fishing, and more. 100 Beaver Meadows Pl., 970.881.2450, www.beavermeadows.com.

The town includes North America's largest Buddhist shrine, called a stupa, the Shambhala Mountain Center (888.788.7221, www.shambhalamountain.org), as well as Deadman Lookout Tower, a 55-foot-tall tower set at 10,700 feet, a National Historic Lookout Register built in the 1930s. Climb the 72 steps toward stunning views. Open most summer days 10 a.m.–4 p.m., starting early July. It's run by a volunteer staff, so call ahead to ensure it's open: 970.295.6700.

Golden

Miles from Denver: 15

The town's friendly Old West charm is evident in the sign arching over its main drag, Washington Avenue, welcoming visitors: "Howdy, Folks! Welcome to Golden." Founded in 1859, Clear Creek runs down its center, a scenic setting for outdoor lovers. Home to the world's largest single-site brewery, Coors, and renowned Colorado School of Mines, it's also the gateway to the "Rockies Playground" along I-70 West. www.visitgolden.com.

Lodging

Set at 7,700 feet and spanning 58 acres within Genesee Mountain Park (home to the bison herd; see next page), Chief Hosa Campground opened in 1918 as "America's first motor-camping area." Offering approximately 60 RV/tent sites, it includes restrooms, potable water, and showers. Open May–late Sept. Across the street is the Chief Hosa Lodge, a National Historic Site offering amazing views. Reservations must be made through Denver Parks and Recreation. 27661 Genesee Dr., 303.526.1324, chiefhosa@denvergov.org.

Other Highlights

Appearing in late 2020, a small family of geometric triceratops now roam the grasslands on private land north of town around the intersection of 56th Avenue and CO Hwy 93. The small herd is the work of Golden sculptor Pat Madison. The land happens to be for sale, however. Spot them while you can!

Formed about 60 million years ago from lava flow, the city's iconic North Table Mountain and its sister mesa, South Table Mountain, offer 15+ miles of trails and endless views.

Roughly 20 miles northwest of town are the twin casino towns of Black Hawk and Central City. Popular destinations for gamblers, they have a free tramway that shuttles tourists to and from each (less than 2 miles).

The City of Denver owns the bison herd located roughly 10 miles west of Golden at Genesee Park off I-70. View roughly 30 descendants of the country's last wild bison herd—brought to Colorado in 1914 from Yellowstone National Park—by following signs to the "Buffalo Overlook" (Exit 254). Visitors can camp at the area campground. (See "Lodging" below.)

Drivers heading west from Golden along I-70 may notice a spaceship-like structure to the south, perched high on a mountain around Genesee (about 10 miles southwest). Known as the "Sleeper House" for its appearance in Woody Allen's 1973 sci-fi comedy "Sleeper," it's now a private residence my kids have always called the "UFO house."

The free Mines Museum of Earth Science at the Colorado School of Mines features 15,000 square feet of rocks, minerals, and fossils, including an authentic triceratops trackway. Open Mon.–Sat., 9 a.m.–4 p.m., Sun., 1 p.m.–4 p.m. 1310 Maple St., 303.273.3815, www.mines.edu/museumof earthscience.

Golden offers an extensive and interconnected trail system of 24 miles that includes the popular Triceratops Trail, a 1.5-mile gravel hiking route that includes invertebrate tracks and traces of dinosaurs, birds, mammals, insects, and plants. (Maintained by Dinosaur Ridge, detailed under "Morrison" entry.)

The free Golden History Museum and Park features an 1800s homestead, barn, and chicken coop, as well as the 1876 Guy Hill schoolhouse that served the needs of Golden Gate Canyon families until 1951. Open Thurs.–Sat., 10 a.m.–2 p.m. Park is always open. 923 10th St., 303.278.3557.

A joint venture of the Colorado

Fast Facts: August 2021 marked the opening of the 1.75-mile Gateway segment extension, a multiuse, paved trail that clings to the mountainside into Clear Creek Canyon, offering fantastic mountain views and hiking access to a restored wooden flume. The segment is part of the Peaks to Plains Trail, a 65-mile paved pathway that will one day stretch from the South Platte River in Denver to the Clear Creek headwaters at Eisenhower Tunnel. 20050 US Hwy 6.

America's favorite candy, Jolly Rancher, was founded in Golden in 1949 by Bill and Dorothy Harmsen. The free Golden History Museum features artifacts and history on the candy and gives samples to visitors. Open Thurs.–Sat., 10 a.m.–2 p.m., 923 10th St., 303.278.3557, www.goldenhistory.org.

Mountain Club and the American Alpine
Club, the Bradford Washburn American
Mountaineering Museum features exhibits
on mountaineering history. Visitors can
cross a crevasse and pick a route up Everest.
Open weekdays 10 a.m.–4 p.m. (6 p.m.
Wednesday), Sat., noon–5 p.m, closed Sun.,
710 10th St., 303.996.2747, www.mountain
eeringmuseum.org.

Fly high above Golden in one of the
area's most popular pursuits: paragliding
($$). Visit Golden recommends local outfit-
ters Colorado Paragliding, which has flown
with kids as young as 6 years but goes on a
case-by-case basis (720.583.4731, www.colo
radoparagliding.com); and Paraglide Tan-
dem, minimum 18 years old (303.800.7572,
www.paraglidetandem.com).

Buffalo Bill Museum and Grave / Lookout Mountain Preserve and Nature Center

Perched above Golden on the top of Look-
out Mountain is the final resting place of
William Frederick Cody, aka "Buffalo Bill."
Open 9 a.m.–5 p.m. during high season
(987 1/2 Lookout Mountain Rd.,
303.526.0744, www.buffalobill.org). A
1-mile mountain trail connects the museum
to the Lookout Mountain Preserve and
Nature Center, connecting visitors with the
natural world through interactive exhibits,
a hands-on playroom, and more. Open
Tues.–Fri., noon–4 p.m. (closed Mon.),
weekends, 11 a.m.–4 p.m. (closes 5 p.m.
summer weekends) (910 Colorow Rd.,
720.497.7600). Next door (900 Colorow
Rd.) is the historic Boettcher Mansion
mountaintop estate, built in 1917 as a sum-
mer home and hunting lodge for wealthy
businessman Charles Boettcher. Tour the
interior with period furniture and décor
(720.497.7630).

Clear Creek Whitewater Kayaking Park

A 0.25-mile course created for recreational
canoeing and kayaking—paddlers should
be proficient on fast-moving, cold water,
particularly during high-flow season—it's
also the site of several competitions, includ-
ing the Junior Olympic Championships.
Rocky Mountain Paddleboard offers a 2.5-
hour evening introduction to whitewater
paddleboarding ($$), which includes gear
rental. Mid-May–early Oct. Closed-toe
shoes required. Minimum age 12. (www
.rockymtnpaddleboard.com). The whitewater park is south of the Golden Community
Center, just across the street, which offers
convenient parking. 1470 10th St., 303.384.
8100.

Colorado Railroad Museum

Featuring some 100 locomotives and more
at the base of North Table Mountain, the
museum allows kids to walk through the
cars, ring a locomotive bell, and ride an
actual train. During the holiday season, the
museum re-creates the acclaimed children's
book and movie on The Polar Express™
Train Ride ($), complete with the story's
sights and sounds, an actual train ride, a
golden souvenir ticket, and hot chocolate.
Pajamas encouraged. 17155 W. 44th Ave.,
303.279.4591, www.coloradorailroad
museum.org.

Golden Gate Canyon State Park

Tucked 16 miles northwest of town is this
popular destination for Denver-area families. Featuring the 100-mile view of the
Continental Divide from the Panorama
Point Scenic Overlook, there are also more
than 35 miles of trails (mountain bikes and
horses are allowed on multiuse ones),
including the Beaver Trail, a moderate, 2.8-
mile loop that traverses aspen groves
toward views of the Indian Peaks

Wilderness Area. It also offers rock-climbing routes, six stocked fishing ponds, and a variety of lodging options. There are 2 campsites: Reverend's Ridge, with 97 RV/tent sites (year-round), features flush toilets, shower, and laundry facilities (seasonal); reservations required. Aspen Meadows offers 35 tent sites with vault toilets and potable water; open mid-May–mid-October. In the backcountry (1- to 3-mile hikes), there are also 20 tent sites and 4 shelters (sleep up to 6). Reservations required. Group campsites, yurts, and 6-person cabins available, even a 4-bedroom, 2-bathroom guesthouse with full kitchen, linen service, and gas fireplaces (horses welcome). Two electrical RV sites are also available. 92 Crawford Gulch Rd., 303.582.3707.

Idaho Springs

Miles from Denver: 33

Marked by the Charlie Taylor water wheel on the south side of I-70 at the base of Bridal Veil Falls, Idaho Springs is the site of the first significant finding of the Colorado Gold Rush. Home to around 2,000 residents today, the Victorian town is a popular destination for its hot springs, historic mines, and access to Mt. Evans. It also boasts the first Beau Jo's Pizza (opened in 1973, 1517 Miner St., 303.567.4376, www.beaujos.com), creators of Colorado-style pizzas, with thick crusts that *must* be dipped in honey. Clear Creek, one of Colorado's most popular commercially rafted rivers (Class II–V rapids), runs right through town. www.thisisidahosprings.com

Lodging

The Squaw Mountain Fire Lookout Cabin, perched at 11,000 feet and roughly a 35-minute drive southeast of town, is available for

There may have been bribery involved in convincing the boys to summit their first 14er, Mt. Evans, near Idaho Springs. Photo by Michael Mundt.

rent year-round. The 14-by-14-foot living space includes an electric stove, a refrigerator, heat, beds, table and chairs, dishes, and incinerating toilet. Sleeps 4. (Visitors must clean and maintain toilet.) No potable water. In summer, temperatures range from 30 to 70 degrees; winter visitors will need to ski or snowshoe up to 3 miles and bring winter-camping gear. Not recommended for young children. For summer access, take CO Hwy 103 via Forest Road 192.1 to a small parking area at the end of the road. High-clearance vehicle recommended. Park in the designated "Lookout Parking" without blocking gate. Hike 1 mile up a steep dirt road to the lookout. 303-567-4382.

Other Highlights

New in December 2020, the town transformed part of its football field from Gold-Digger Field into the Frozen Fire Ice Rink at Digger Field. Made of synthetic ice or "Glice," it can be skated on year-round. Rentals available. Hours vary, but Friday Music Nights are 4:30 p.m.–8 p.m. Gold-Digger Stadium, 932 Miner St., www.clearcreekrecreation.com.

Head 750 feet into the mountain on a one-hour tour of the Phoenix Gold Mine, a functioning mine operated by Al and Dave Mosch, part of Colorado's oldest continuous gold-mining family. Then pan for gold in a creek with the help of actual miners. Times vary by season. Kids ages 3 and under are free. 800 Trail Creek Rd., 303.567.0422, www.phoenixmine.com.

Tour Operators

AVA Rafting and Zipline offers the full-day Clear Creek Gold Rush + Zipline package ($$), featuring 6 ziplines and 4 additional elements, including the 50-foot freefall. After a break for lunch (bring one or grab a bite in town), enjoy a whitewater adventure that includes Class III rapids (minimum 6 years, 40 pounds). 431 Chicago Creek Rd., Ste. 1, 970.423.7031, www.coloradorafting.net.

Argo Mill and Tunnel

Head 120 feet into the mountain and walk in miners' shoes in their historic workplace (1893-1943), the town's number-one attraction. Finders of any gems or minerals—peridot, amethyst, even gold—are keepers! Two-hour tours. Open daily, 10 a.m.–6 p.m., 2350 Riverside Dr., 303.567.2421, www.argomilltour.com.

Echo Mountain Resort

Stats: 16 designated trails, 85 skiable acres, 3 lifts, 1 terrain park, night skiing

Trail classification: 5 percent Beginner; 75 percent Intermediate; 20 percent Advanced

Base elevation: 10,050 feet

Established in 1960 as Squaw Pass Ski Area, Echo Mountain opened in October 2016. One of Denver's closest ski resorts (36 miles), it comprises mostly intermediate runs. There's also a tubing hill with six lanes and a conveyor lift. Night tubing available Wed.–Sat. until 7 p.m. One-hour time slots; minimum 36 inches. Day tubing hours vary. The resort also features two eateries, a mountain lodge, and equipment rentals. Night skiing available Tues.–Sat. until 9 p.m. Special passes for ski bikes and uphill skiers available. www.echomntn.com.

Indian Springs Resort

Considered sacred by the Ute and Arapaho Indians long before gold was discovered, it opened to the public for health baths in 1863, hosting numerous famous names such as Walt Whitman and Bo Diddly. The property includes a mineral water swimming pool (90–100 degrees), open daily 9 a.m.–10 p.m.; gender-specific geothermal caves, ages 16+ only, 7:30 a.m–10:30 p.m.; spa treatments available. Accommodations include rooms and cabins ($–$$). 302 Soda Creek Rd., 303.989.6666, www.indianhotsprings.com.

Lawson Adventure Park and Resort

Located in Dumont between Idaho Springs and Georgetown, this year-round resort features an aerial challenge course, a private zipline, and a via ferrata (minimum 12 years old). Play disc golf or ride inside a Zorb (a 9-foot sphere) down a mountain course. The Upper Park (ages 5–12) includes a gyro-sphere and climbing wall. Choose adventures such as snowshoeing to St. Mary's

Glacier, a scenic, 1.5-mile, easy-to-moderate hike about 30 minutes from town, or whitewater rafting Clear Creek in summer. Accommodations include 8 furnished tiny homes/cabins with a bedroom, bathroom, sleeper sofa, and kitchen. There are also 5 camping yurts with heat and access to a heated bathhouse with showers, restrooms, and electrical plugs. The Base Camp Grill and Bar offers food year-round; a food truck was added in 2021. 3440 Alvarado Rd., 720.779.2595, www.lawsonadventurepark.com.

Mt. Evans

One of only two Colorado 14ers where visitors can drive to the summit (Pikes Peak is the other), Mt. Evans (14,264 feet) is the closest 14er to Denver. After a moderate-to-strenuous hike approximately 2.9 miles from Summit Lake to the top, we hitched a ride down from the parking lot to our car at Summit Lake. Our kids' first 14er hike when they were ages 6 and 8, it took about three hours (and lots of bribery) to summit. Note: In summer 2021, the Mt. Evans Recreation Area began requiring timed-entry reservations to mitigate crowding (www.recreation.gov).

The closest camping is at Echo Lake Park, home of the scenic Echo Lake that sits at 10,600 feet at the base of Mt. Evans. Popular for hiking and fishing, it has 17 sites, 10 for RVs and 7 for tents, all equipped with fire ring and picnic table. Vault toilets, potable water. Firewood for sale (mid-June–September). Fishing available year-round. To get there, take CO Hwy 103 for 13 miles

---

Fast Fact: The Mount Evans Scenic Byway—28 miles along State Hwy 103 from Idaho springs to the summit, climbing more than 7,000 feet—is the highest paved road in North America. Nicknamed the "road into the sky," it's typically open Memorial Day through Labor Day.

---

from Idaho Springs. 303.567.3000.

Located adjacent to the campground is the historic Echo Lake Lodge (1926), which offers a restaurant and gift shop (no lodging). 13264 State Hwy 103, 303.567.2138, www.echolakelodgeco.com.

Longmont

Miles from Denver: 38

Established in 1870 as the "Chicago-Colorado Colony" by a group of prominent Chicago men who selected the area for its farmland, it was called "Longmont" in 1871 after Longs Peak. Set within 40 miles of Denver, Boulder, Fort Collins, DIA and Estes Park, Longmont was considered a quiet agricultural town when I was growing up here. Now it's a vibrant Certified Creative District boasting a historic Main Street, unique restaurants, and more than 15 craft breweries, which you can visit via my favorite transportation mode: a Brewhop Trolley (www.brewhoptrolley.com). www.visitlongmont.org.

Other Highlights

Home to Colorado's largest sky-diving facility, here you're bound to see parachuters dropping from the sky toward terra firma if you're on the west side of town. Minimum 18 years old. Mile-Hi Skydiving Center, Vance Brand Airport, 229 Airport Rd., Hangar 34G, 303.702.9911, www.milehiskydiving.com.

Tour Operators

You can't miss the hot-air balloons dotting the early morning sky in summer and fall (best times May–Nov.), led by Fair Winds Hot Air Balloon Flights, launching about 20 minutes south of town in Lafayette. 2140 North 107th St., 303.939.9323, www.hotair balloonridescolorado.com.

Agricultural Heritage Center at the Lohr-McIntosh Farm

Get a glimpse of agriculture history (1900–1925) in this 1909 furnished farmhouse. Animals on site April–October include chickens, pigs, draft horses, and sheep. Hours vary. 8348 Ute Hwy, 303.776.8688.

Adjacent to the center to the south is the popular recreation area McIntosh Lake Nature Area, aka "Lake Mac," perfect for nonmotorized paddle sports such as SUP-ing. There's also a 3.3-mile loop around the lake. Open one hour before sunrise until one hour after sunset. 1905 Harvard St., #3.5.

Dickens Farm Nature Area

New in 2019, this float course along the St. Vrain Creek is perfect for tubes, kayaks, SUPs, and more. There's even a BMX/Mountain Bike Area. Located between Main and Martin Streets along the St. Vrain Creek, we park behind Dick's Sporting Goods (210 Ken Pratt Blvd.), or the put-in on Boston St., set about 0.2 miles west of Shoes and Brews (63 S. Pratt Pkwy., Unit B). Float to the 119 Trailhead (parking lot directly across the street from the Elevated Longmont dispensary, 9800 N. 119th St.).

Rent tubes or tube/shuttle combo via Adventure West, located in the parking lot behind Pinocchio's Incredible Italian Restaurant (210 Ken Pratt Blvd., #260). Open Fri.–Mon., 10 a.m.–5 p.m., 720.722.1645, www.adventurewestco.com.

Lyons

Situated 12 miles northwest of Longmont (16 miles north of Boulder), Lyons is set in the foothills en route to Estes Park. The historic downtown area features restaurants, shops, a soda fountain, the original Oskar Blues Brewery (creator of the famous Dale's Pale Ale), and Planet Bluegrass, a 20-acre outdoor concert venue (500 W. Main St., 303.823.0848, www.bluegrass.com/planet).

We never tire of spotting bald eagles at St. Vrain State Park, near our Longmont home. Photo by Brody Mundt.

It's also home to a whitewater park along the North St. Vrain River, as well as the popular LaVern M. Johnson Park, with 16 RV sites (year-round) and 17 tent sites (mid-April–mid-October). Offers showers, restrooms, and potable water (ice rink in winter, open daily, 10 a.m.–9 p.m., weather permitting; must bring skates). There's also a playground and plenty of catch-and-release fishing along the river. 600 Park Dr., 303.823.6150, www.reserveamerica.com.

Stay at the world's largest tiny-house destination, WeeCasa Tiny House Resort ($), offering 23 miniature abodes (sleep 2–6). 501 W. Main St., 720.460.0239, www.weecasa.com.

Popular hiking spots include Hall Ranch Open Space, including the moderate, 2-mile Button Rock Trail and the 1-mile Antelope Trail (31635 CO-7); Heil Valley Ranch's moderate, 2.3-mile Overland Loop or easy 0.9-mile Schoolhouse Loop (63 Red Gulch Rd.); and Rabbit Mountain Open Space, featuring the easy, 2.2-mile Indian Mesa Trail and moderate, 1.5-mile Little Thompson Overlook Trail (15140 N. 55th St., 303.678.6200). Our favorite Lyons spot is Button Rock Preserve's 2-mile hike to Ralph Price Reservoir. A popular fly-fishing spot for brown trout along the North St. Vrain Creek, it also has a creekside fishing pier located just past the entrance gate. Restrooms available (CO Hwy 80).

Sandstone Ranch Visitors and Learning Center

Learn about early pioneer life at this historic property (1860), offering guided bird walks, history tours, and free programming. Open Mon., 9 a.m.–noon, May–Aug. Call for off-season hours. The area is part of the Sandstone Ranch Community Park and Nature Area, which includes playgrounds, athletic fields, and a skate park. It's also along the St. Vrain Greenway trail system, featuring a paved, 8-mile trail spanning from Golden Ponds Nature Area (Third Avenue, west of Hover St.) to Sandstone Ranch. 3001 CO-119, Longmont, 303.651.8404.

St. Vrain State Park

An urban oasis just a 10-minute drive from my home, we spent many hours here during the pandemic shutdown, snapping photos of birds—ospreys, bald eagles, blue herons, and pelicans, to name a few—and walking around the park's 11 ponds. Featuring 15 species of fish such as bluegill, perch, and pike, it's a popular fishing spot (ice fishing in winter); anglers and photographers crowd the area's 4 fishing piers in summer months. (Blue Heron Reservoir has a boat ramp for wakeless boating, 10 hp or less.) There are 87 RV/tent sites, about half available year-round, and the camper-services building offers year-round showers, restrooms, and potable water. 3525 Hwy 119, Firestone, 303.678.9402.

Union Reservoir Nature Area

I live about 1 mile from this 736-acre body of water (7 miles west of I-25), one of only a few natural lakes in Colorado. (In 1903, the Union Ditch Company began drilling a tunnel to release water into the St. Vrain Creek, making Union a true reservoir.) A popular windsurfing spot, it also offers good fishing for walleye, trout, and crappie, as well as wakeless boating and a swim beach. A dog off-leash area is located on the reservoir's south side, and there are several picnic areas. The Union Sailing Club is one of Colorado's largest and most active sailing clubs, (www.UnionSailingClub.org); Rocky Mountain Paddleboard offers SUPs and kayaks rentals, SUP yoga (Fri., 5:30 p.m., Sun., 8:30 a.m.), and full-moon and sunset paddles (www.rockymtnpaddle board.com/longmont, 720.943.1132). Reservoir hours vary by season, May–Labor Day, 6 a.m.–9 p.m., 461 CR 26, 303.772.1265.

The fishing ponds at Longmont's St. Vrain State Park attract a variety of birds, including the shy great blue heron. Photo by Colin Mundt.

Wild Animal Sanctuary

Surrounded by the farmlands of Keenes-burg (about 37 miles southeast of Long-mont), this sanctuary rescues large preda-tors that have been "ill-treated, for which their owners can no longer care, or which might otherwise be euthanized." Offering habitats and care facilities for about 600 animals among three locations (one in Southeast Colorado, another in Texas), the facility's 1.5-mile elevated walkway over-looks habitats for lions, bears, wolves, and more than 90 tigers and other animals res-cued from Joe Exotic's Oklahoma facility, made famous by the 2020 Netflix docuseries *Tiger King*. One of its most popular fund-raising events is the Into the Wild Running Festival, featuring family-friendly 5K and 10K races. 2999 CR 53, Keensburg, 303.536. 0118, www.wildanimalsanctuary.org.

Loveland

Miles from Denver: 52

Established in 1877 along the new Colorado Central Railroad near its crossing of the Big Thompson River, it's most famous as Sweet-heart City, dating back the 1940s when the city launched a Valentine Re-Mailing Pro-gram. Still practiced today, the city receives more than 100,000 Valentines that are handstamped by volunteers with a Valen-tine's Day verse, then remailed to their intended recipients. The town also boasts more than 25 city parks, as well as two sculpture parks, the Benson Sculpture Gar-den (1125 W. 29th St., 970.962.2327) and the Chapungu Sculpture Park featuring 82 Zimbabwean masterpieces (located just east of the Promenade Shops at Centerra off US Hwy 34 (www.chapunguatcenterra.com). www.visitloveland.com.

Other Highlights

Set 20 miles east is the town of Greeley, home to the University of Northern

Colorado and the state's renowned Western festival Greeley Frontier Days. Started in 1922, the 12-day event around the Fourth of July attracts 250,000 visitors and offers rodeo events, music performances, and car-nivals. Island Grove Regional Park, 501 N. 14th Ave., www.greeleystampede.org.

In 2019, the town debuted the Loveland Love Locks Sculpture, the largest of its kind in the United States. Located at the visitor center, stop inside to buy a lock, engrave it, and place on the sculpture if you choose. Open Mon.–Sat., 8:30 a.m.–3:30 p.m., 5400 Stone Creek Cir., 970.667.3882. A second sculpture, the Hearth Arch, was added in 2020 near Lake Loveland. West Lake Park Rd., 970.962.2727.

Located in the foothills of Loveland, Bless Your Heart Ranch offers horse-train-ing services and goat adventures ($), such as a private hike with a goat. Half-day and full-day options (best for ages 8 and up). 4718 Lonetree Dr., 720.684.8920, www .blessyourheartranch.com.

Boyd Lake State Park

This 1,700-acre lake features power zones for water-skiers and wakeboarders and no-wake zones for paddlers and anglers, who can fish for bluegill and smallmouth bass. Guided fishing trips available via Brad Petersen Outdoors (www.bradpetersen .me), NOCO Fishing Outfitters (www.noco fishing.com), and Fishful Thinker (www .fishfulthinker.com). The swimming beach offers a pavilion with rinsing showers and restrooms, a playground, picnic tables, and a snack bar, as well as SUP rentals from Mountain Rentals (www.mountainrentals inc.com). The Boyd Lake Marina, open in summer, offers boat and waverunner rent-als, a full-service gas dock, snacks, and fish-ing and camping supplies (4430 N. CR 11-C, 970.663.2662, www.boydlakemarina .com). There are 148 RV/tent sites (some year-round) that include restrooms with showers, playground equipment, and horseshoe pits. The park's paved trail along the water's edge is part of the 22-mile loop around Loveland. The Boyd Lake State Park Visitor Center is open 9 a.m.–4 p.m. 3720 N. CR 11-C, 970.669.1739.

Carter Lake Reservoir

Set at 5,760 feet in the foothills about 15 miles southwest of Loveland, "Carter" is a popular spot for sailing, waterskiing, swimming, and rock climbing—even scuba diving. Fishing is especially popular here, including for walleye, bluegill, and yellow perch. There are also two hiking trails: Fawn Hollow Trail, a 1-mile easy trek on the lake's east side, and Sundance Trail, a 3.5-mile trail along the western side. There are five campgrounds, some sites available year-round: Big Thompson, South Shore, North Pines, Eagle Campground, and Carter Knolls Campground (www.larimer camping.com). The Carter Lake Marina, located on the north shore, offers boat rentals and a store with snacks and lake-day essentials (4011 S. CR 31, 970.667.1062, www.carterlakemarina.com). The Natural Resources Administrative Office, offering information on all the county open spaces and parks, is open 9 a.m.–4 p.m., 1800 S. CR E., 970.619.4570.

Sylvan Dale Guest Ranch

This family-owned and -operated dude ranch (since 1946) offers vacations in summer and fall and horseback riding year-round. Enjoy the Game Courts with tennis, pickleball, shuffleboard, foursquare, and basketball; a Game Room for billiards, ping-pong, or foosball; volleyball courts and horseshoe pits; a heated pool; and several hiking trails. Take a scenic trail ride or hayride. Offers cabins that sleep 2–10 ($). 2939 N. CR 31D, 970.667.3915, www.sylvan dale.com.

Morrison

Miles from Denver: 18

Home to part of the Dakota Hogback extending from Wyoming to New Mexico that includes Dinosaur Ridge, this was a favorite campsite for Native American tribes before settlers arrived. Founded in 1859, Morrison's tourism industry took off in the early part of the 20th century, when John Brisben Walker operated a hotel and developed attractions at Red Rocks. Home to several restaurants and antique stores, it was recognized in 1976 as a Colorado Historical District. www.town.morrison.co.us.

Lodging

About 10 miles northeast of town in Lakewood is the Best Western Denver Southwest, aka "The Dino Hotel," which features museum-quality fossil casts such as Brachiosaurus femurs and on-site Paleo Joe's Bar and Grill. There's also a Jurassic dig pit with real fossils and a swimming pool designed in the shape of the Western Interior Cretaceous Seaway, a shallow inland sea that covered much of North America

The lobby of "The Dino Hotel" in Lakewood resembles an old-school explorer's club, complete with museum-quality fossil casts. Photo by Michael Mundt.

The legendary Red Rocks Park and Amphitheatre in Morrison is the world's only naturally occurring, acoustically perfect amphitheater. Photo by the author.

My kids enjoyed chipping away at a real fossil specimen at the Morrison Natural History Museum. Photo by Michael Mundt.

(including Colorado) about 85 million years ago. Enjoy breakfast-hour chats at the interactive fossil table. My boys *loved* staying here. 3440 S. Vance St., 303.989.5500, www.bestwesterndenver.com.

Other Highlights

Opened in 1963, The Fort is a full-scale adobe replica of Bent's Old Fort near La Junta. (See "La Junta" entry.) Offering a menu inspired by the trappers, traders, and Native Americans who traveled along the Santa Fe Trail, the eatery is known for its game meat such as elk and buffalo. 19192 CO-8, 303.697.4771, www.thefort.com.

Dinosaur Ridge

The site where Golden professor Arthur Lakes discovered the first stegosaurus fossils in 1877, it features more than 250 real dinosaur tracks. Visitors can head to the hillside for a 3-mile, self-guided tour. (Download an audio tour that highlights ten stops.) Or take a 45-minute guided bus tour to view fossils and geological highlights, which leaves from the Main Visitor Center (on the east side). The property also offers exhibits, an outdoor kids' dig area, life-size dinosaur models, a picnic area, and allosaurus bones under a pavilion. 16831 W. Alameda Pkwy., Morrison.

On the west side, the Discovery Center serves as a visitor center for Dinosaur Ridge (right next to Red Rocks). See fossil replicas and a 24-foot-long trackway from southern Colorado made by a duck-billed dinosaur. Hours vary. 17681 W. Alameda Pkwy., Golden, 303.697.3466, www.dino ridge.org.

Morrison Natural History Museum

View baby stegosaurus tracks and touch fossils throughout the museum's hands-on exhibits via a self-guided or one-hour guided tour. My boys especially loved their chance to chip away rock on a real fossil specimen, just like real paleontologists. Open 10 a.m.–4 p.m., 501 CO-8, 303.697.1873, www.mnhm.org.

Red Rocks Park and Amphitheatre

It's hard to overstate the reverence Coloradans hold for this venue, the world's only naturally occurring, acoustically perfect amphitheater. Hosting world-renowned headliners such as the Beatles in 1964 and U2 in 1983, when the band famously recorded its "Sunday Bloody Sunday" video, it officially opened in 1941. Concerts are the main draw, but there are other events such as yoga classes, as well as free hiking and biking during the day. (The 1.4-mile Trading Post Loop Hiking Trail takes visitors through rock formations, valleys, and a natural meadow.) There's also a free visitor center and the Colorado Music Hall of Fame (located at the Trading Post just to the east, down the hill about 100 yards from the main stage). Summer nights offer Film on the Rocks, where my boys first watched *The Goonies*, a perfect opportunity for a picnic dinner under the stars. (The park is also located right next door to the western side of Dinosaur Ridge.) 18300 W. Alameda Pkwy., 720.865.2494, www.redrocksonline .com.

PIKES PEAK WONDERS

Buena Vista

With the Arkansas River coursing through this historic mountain town, flanked by the Sawatch Mountain Range to the west (with fourteen 14ers!) and the San Isabel National Forest to the east, it's no wonder the town is named "beautiful view" in Spanish. Originally settled in 1864, it was named Buena Vista (BV) in 1879 by citizens with the idea to "Americanize" the name to sound like the English word "beautiful." This spot nicknamed "Bewnie" is a wildly popular outdoor destination for its access to the Arkansas River and Collegiate Peaks Wilderness, boasting eight 14ers and the highest average elevation of any wilderness in the Lower 48.

Lodging

Snowy Peaks RV Park and Rentals offers 8 tent sites, 90+ RV sites, 2 lodge rooms (4 guests), and even 5 RVs for rent. 30430 US-24, 719.395.8481, www.snowypeaksrvpark.com.

The Buena Vista KOA Journey features RV and tent sites, plus cabins and a glamping tent. April–Oct., 27700 CR 303, 719.395.8318.

For a more remote experience, stay in nearby Nathrop (about 15 minutes away) at the Antero Hot Springs Cabins ($$). Nestled along Chalk Creek in the San Isabel National Forest, there are 3 cabins, each with a private hot-springs pool. Spa treatments available. No dogs. 16120 CR 162, info@anterohotsprings.com, www.anterohotsprings.com.

Other Highlights

Head to the Jumpin' Good Goat Dairy to check out goat cheeses and some mama goats with their kids. Visit the country store and take a one-hour guided tour of the farm (Wed., Fri., and Sat., 10 a.m. and 11:30 a.m. tours). Store is open Wed.–Sat., 10 a.m.–4 p.m., 31700 US-24, 719.395.4646, www.jumpingoodgoats.com.

Dating back to the late 1800s, the Historic Turner Farm and Apple Orchard serves as a living-history museum. Tour through buildings such as the 1910 farmhouse, and celebrate Apple Fest the second Saturday in September (10 a.m.–4 p.m.). Includes apple-pie contests and entertainment. Open Memorial Day–September, Fri. and Sat., 11 a.m.–4 p.m., 829 W. Main St.

Ever heard of rockhounding? This recreational practice of collecting rocks, gems, fossils, and more from natural environments (where legal) is popular in the gem-rich area around BV and Salida. More than 100 different minerals and gems from aquamarines to topaz are found here, specifically around Mt. Antero (a 14er just west of BV), which was featured on a 2019 *Treasure Hunter* Travel Channel episode.

Did you know that because of its temperate, arid climate, BV is often called the "banana belt" of Colorado? Technically defined as a larger geographic region that enjoys warmer weather, the Arkansas River Basin from BV through Salida to Pueblo encompasses the belt.

AVA Rafting and Zipline

This operator offers extensive activities: a private zipline, a via ferrata, and lodging (5 rustic cabins that sleep 4–5 and 8 campsites, restroom access, grills, picnic tables; pet-friendly with extra fee). Rafting tours range from beginner to Class V adventures.

Fast Fact: Chaffee County, home to BV and Salida, boasts the greatest number of 14ers in the country at twelve, celebrated each fall in BV with a "14er Fest," which features activities including bike rides, seven-hour hikes, and a 14K race. www.14erfest.org.

Beautiful mountain views like this driving south from Buena Vista are what earned the town its name. Photo by Michael Mundt.

(Minimum age varies by trip.) The private Granite Via Ferrata includes a zipline to the starting point and rappelling above the Arkansas River (minimum 6 years, 40 pounds). Multiday trips available include fly-fishing, horseback riding, and rock climbing ($–$$). Tours available in other locations such as Breckenridge and Aspen. 40671 US Hwy 24, 970.423.7031, www .coloradorafting.net.

Browns Canyon National Monument
Designated by President Barack Obama in 2015, this secluded canyon carved by the Arkansas River between the Mosquito Range and Collegiate Peaks is Colorado's newest national monument. Its Gold Medal waters feature brown and rainbow trout, and most visitors see the area via whitewater raft.

Kids will love the Browns Canyon Colorado Adventure Park and Ziplines, owned and operated by Noah's Ark Whitewater Rafting Co., an aerial playground along the river featuring a big drop swing. Try the Park and Paddle tour that includes a rafting trip and the aerial course ($$). Aerial course offered at night, 7:15 p.m. (23910 US Hwy 285, 719.395.2158, www.brownscanyon adventurepark.com). Or take a "Family

Float" with River Runners Browns Canyon ($). Minimum 3 years, 35 pounds. 24070 CR 301, 719.395.2466, www.whitewater.net /rafting-buena-vista-colorado.

Buena Vista Whitewater Park

This Arkansas River playground set east of the historic district—the state's largest whitewater park—features man-made water structures such as Staircase Wave and Uptown Wave for kayaks, rafts, SUPs, and more. The area also offers a disc-golf course, pump track, and climbing walls. The 0.6-mile Arkansas River Trail provides great views of the river action. 715 E. Main St., 719.395.1939. Learn how to catch a wave via SUP with the Rocky Mountain Outdoor Center ($$). Basic SUP lessons available, as well as guided whitewater, hiking, climbing tours, and more (23850 US Hwy 285 S., 719.395.3335, www.rmoc.com).

Head across the Arkansas River pedestrian bridge, which connects the River Park to extensive hiking and biking trails on the east side of the river, such as the Whipple Trail System and Midland Railroad Bicycle Trail, a singletrack trail following a former railroad track, roughly 19 miles roundtrip.

Cottonwood Hot Springs Inn and Spa

Once a spiritual gathering place for the Ute tribe, these springs set about 6 miles west of BV are known for their medicinal and therapeutic value. Offers four pools (and a cold plunge) ranging 94–100 degrees; two private hot tubs for rent. Dry sauna available. Accommodations include a lodge, cabins (with private soaking pools), tent sites, and more (even a 5-bedroom house!). No phones, TV, WiFi, refrigerators. Spa services available. Soaking hours: 8 a.m.–midnight. Kids ages 16 and under must be accompanied by adult after dark. 18999 CR 306, 800.241.4119, www.cottonwood-hot -springs.com.

Mount Princeton Hot Springs Resort

Located in Nathrop 9 miles south of BV, generations of Ute Indians came to this spot for winter camping grounds, where fresh drinking water and hot bathing water were plentiful. Today, it's a perfect destination for families, featuring a full-service boutique hotel, the Hillside and Cliffside hotel rooms, and more than 20 log cabins.

Soak in the odor-free geothermal waters, which include the upper pools (75 degrees), a 400-foot waterslide, and an infinity pool (100 degrees), open daily 10 a.m.–5 p.m., Memorial Day–Labor Day. Year-round facilities, open daily 9 a.m.–9 p.m., include the historic bathhouse (1867), with a soaking pool (105 degrees) and an exercise pool (90 degrees), and several springs along Chalk Creek (70–120 degrees); the Spa and Club, featuring a relaxation pool (99

Buena Vista's river trail is the perfect spot to watch riders catch waves on the Arkansas River. Photo by the author.

degrees) and cascading pools (100–107 degrees) (both ages 16+), plus a fitness room and classes; and the Princeton Market, which sells camping accessories, snacks, souvenirs, gasoline, and more, open daily 9 a.m.–8 p.m. (according to website). Day passes and private soaks available. (Fair warning: The automated phone system is so difficult to use, I'd suggest just visiting the website for information/reservations.)

Located roughly 1 mile from the springs, Mt. Princeton Hot Springs Riding Stable features trail rides, two-hour sunset rides, Saturday-night hayrides, and more. Minimum 5 years old. Under 5 years can take a pony ride (14582 CR 162, Nathrop, 719.395.3630, www.coloradotrailrides .com).15870 CR 162, 719.395.2447, Nathrop, www.mtprinceton.com.

St. Elmo

Located 16 miles west of Nathrop (about 20 miles southwest of BV), St. Elmo is one of the best-preserved ghost towns in the West.

Perched nearly 10,000 feet in the heart of the Sawatch Range, it was founded in 1880 as a booming gold and silver mining town with the creation of the Chalk Creek Mining District. Today more than 40 buildings remain, including a saloon and courthouse/ jail, old boardwalks, and a museum inside the restored, one-room schoolhouse. If you have time, explore the Mary Murphey Mine, as well as Hancock, a ghost town located about 5 miles south of St. Elmo. (The main drag is dotted with OHVs headed to Hancock or Tincup Pass.)

Several services are offered in the town, including the St. Elmo General Store, featuring souvenirs and snacks (seasonally), and renting out a 3-person cabin (719.395. 2117, www.st-elmo.com). Visitors can also stay at a B&B, the Ghost Town Guest House ($), located across from the general store. Two-day minimum; no dogs (www.ghost townguesthouse.com). Or rent one of 2 cabins at Chalk Creek ($). Three-day minimum in summer. Pets with fee. (Contact

More than 40 buildings remain in the ghost town of St. Elmo, which thrums with activity and visitors in the summer months. Photo by the author.

The Royal Gorge Cabins each include an indoor-outdoor fireplace and a personal cornhole game. Photo by Michael Mundt.

Doug Baumgardner, dougscabins@yahoo.com, or call 719.398.3261, www.cabinsatchalkcreek.com.)

Campsites in the area include the Iron City Campground. No reservations; 15 sites, vault toilets during peak season, June 1–Sept. 30. The Chalk Lake Campground offers 18 sites, vault toilets and water, some reservable (18668 Chalk Creek Dr.). Finally, Mt. Princeton offers 17 campsites, some with reservations. Water and vault toilets (719.539.3591) (USDA Forest Service).

Cañon City

Miles from Denver: 114

Founded in 1860 on the heels of Colorado's Gold Rush, the lead and silver discovered in nearby Leadville (120 miles northwest) prompted a rush to establish rail access to the area, establishing the region as a hub for transcontinental rail travel by the 1890s. Although passenger train service ceased in 1967, today it's a tourism mainstay. But the biggest attractions here are the Royal Gorge

and the Arkansas River, with its Class III–V whitewater rapids and Gold Medal waters. www.canoncitycolorado.com

Lodging

We stayed at one of the area's newest facilities, Royal Gorge Cabins, located 5 miles north of the Royal Gorge Bridge and Park (about 9 miles from the city). Owned by Echo Canyon River Expeditions—which sits across the street from the cabins, next to the company's restaurant, 8 Mile Bar and Grill—the property features 9 luxury cabins (6 2-bedroom and 3 1-bedroom) complete with indoor-outdoor fireplace and patio seating, as well as a personal cornhole game and hammock (plus a kitchenette, WiFi and TVs). There are also eight glamping tents—four each of double and single queen beds—and one, two-person log cabin, Pine Creek. 45054 W. US Hwy 50, 800.748.2953, www.royalgorgecabins.com.

Just down Highway 50 are the colorful Royal Gorge Riverside Yurts ($), featuring 10, each with 2 queen beds, a patio, and an open-air kitchen (bring dishware, towels, food), plus 3 Airstream trailers that sleep 4 (restrooms and showers nearby). Owned by Royal Gorge Rafting and Zip Line Tours (www.royalgorgerafting.net), visitors can also plan adventures during their stay. 41746 W. US Hwy 50, 719.250.6404, www.royalgorgeyurts.com.

Or check out the Royal Gorge/Cañon City KOA Holiday, offering RV/tent sites, 11 cabins, a pool, dog park, and more. 559 CR 3A, 719.275.6116.

Other Highlights

Hike or bike the Canyon Rim Trail, part of the 17-mile Royal Gorge Trail System (www.royalgorgeregion.com/royal-gorge-park-trails-system/). Take a stroll along the Arkansas Riverwalk Trail, a gravel path following the river for more than 7 miles. Bikes, horses and dogs permitted. Or visit the Riverwalk's newest addition: the Cañon City Whitewater Kayak and Recreation Park. (Centennial Park is a good starting point, 221 Griffin Ave.)

Opened in 2020, Jason and Ashley Shepperly's Shepperly Farm Petting Zoo is one of the city's newest tourism destinations. Home to more than 127 animals for visitors to snuggle—like piglets and burros—all proceeds benefit the animals. Can be used for private events. Call for hours. 3240 Grandview Ave., 719.232.1772, www.shepperlyfarm.com.

NEW IN 2021

The Yard is a mountain-bike skills park featuring two lines and man-made features like jumps and rollers. Not for beginners. Open dawn to dusk. Access via the Arkansas Riverwalk Trail east of Centennial Park (221 Griffin Ave.). And the 1-mile Point Alta Vista trail traverses four restored train trestles, offering one of the best views of the gorge. To get there, take US Hwy 50 west, turning south at CR3A on eight-mile hill toward the Royal Gorge Park. Travel 1.25 miles and turn right into the parking area. Look for the Point Alta Vista Trail map and pedestrian gate. Dogs must be leashed.

Arkansas River

Whether peering at it from 1,000 feet above from the Royal Gorge Bridge, fly-fishing along its banks or riding its churning waters, the Arkansas River is a must-see destination in this area. Boasting Colorado's longest stretch of Gold Medal Trout

Take a Drive: Head for Skyline Drive, a 2.6-mile, one-way drive beginning 3 miles west of the city off US Hwy 50, offering one of the best views of the town, river valley and mountains—even a set of 10 tracks thought to be from a group of ankylosauri (www.royalgorgeregion.com/skyline-drive/).

Fast Fact: With more than 20 antique shops along Main Street, the small town of Florence (9 miles southeast of Cañon City) is known as the "antique capital of Colorado." But it's also home to the only United States Penitentiary Administrative Maximum Facility (ADX) or "Supermax," nicknamed the Alcatraz of the Rockies, housing notorious criminals like Mexican drug lord Joaquín "El Chapo" Guzmán and Oklahoma City bomber Terry Nichols.

waters (102 miles), many visitors come for its whitewater. (Roughly 20 different rafting companies are headquartered here.) We opted for the Echo Canyon River Expeditions' half day Bighorn Sheep Canyon trip ($), a mix of Class II–IV rapids. (The Family Float itinerary is an option for kids ages 4 and up.) 45000 W. US Hwy 50, Cañon City, 800.755.3246, www.raftecho.com.

Mueller State Park

Set in the shadow of Pikes Peak, this park is home to 44 miles of trails for mountain biking, hiking, or horseback riding (snowshoeing and Nordic skiing in winter). Roughly 15 miles north of Cripple Creek, the park includes a visitor center, a backcountry trout pond, 4 geocaches, picnic sites, and 3 furnished log cabins (2-, 3- and 4-bedroom). There are also 134 tent/RV campsites, including 22 walk-in tent sites, a reservable group campground, and 2 equestrian sites, in addition to restrooms, showers, laundry, and water. 21045 Hwy 67 S., Divide, 719.687.2366.

A view of the mighty Arkansas River and the Royal Gorge from America's highest suspension bridge. Photo by Michael Mundt.

Royal Gorge Bridge and Park

A 10-mile-long chasm carved into granite by the Arkansas River, the area was home for centuries to the Ute tribe before being discovered in 1806 by Lieutenant Zebulon Pike during his Louisiana Purchase exploration. One hundred years later, the land was ceded to the city, and the country's highest suspension bridge (nearly 1,000 feet high) was built in 1929. Known as America's Bridge, visitors can walk 1,260 feet across it toward the Plaza Theater, showing a movie on the gorge's history; Tommy Knocker Children's Playland; and Aerial Gondolas, carrying passengers 2,200 feet across the gorge.

For the adrenaline junkies, there's America's highest zipline, the Cloudscraper Zip Line (ages 10 and up; other restrictions apply); the Royal Rush Skycoaster, where passengers are sent in a free-fall swing deemed the "World's Scariest Skycoaster" (42–82 inches tall); and the via ferrata, offering guided climbing routes for all levels (minimum 10 years old). Reservations recommended. Most activities are an additional cost to the entrance fee. 4218 County Rd., 3A, 719.275.7507, www.royalgorge bridge.com.

Royal Gorge Dinosaur Experience

Featuring fossils and casts of dinosaurs, as well as a paleo lab to view unearthed fossils, here most of the excitement is outdoors: life-size animatronic dinosaurs such as Tyrannosaurus Rex move and make noise as visitors pass. There's also a Dinosaur Wild Walk, a kids' dig pit, or the T-Rex Terror Ropes Course (minimum 48 inches). Includes a little kids' course. 44895 W. US Hwy 50, 800.209.0062, www.dinoxp.com.

Royal Gorge Route Railroad

Running on tracks alongside the Arkansas River since 1879 ($), it's considered the most famous portion of the Denver and Rio Grande Western Railroad. We missed this two-hour scenic ride due to COVID-19, but hopefully someday we'll get to eat a gourmet meal and experience the Murder Mystery or Santa-themed train rides. 330 Royal Gorge Blvd., 719.276.4000, www.royalgorge route.com.

Colorado Springs

Miles from Denver: 71

Long before Zebulon Pike's "discovery" of Pikes Peak, the Ute, Cheyenne, and Arapaho tribes were drawn to the area's springs in what is today's Garden of the Gods Park. (The "springs" are actually in Manitou Springs.) Today, Colorado's second-largest city is home to the Air Force Academy and five bases, and it is headquarters of the US Olympic and Paralympic Committees (and training centers), earning its nickname "Olympic City USA." www.visitcos.com.

Lodging

There are tons of options in the city, but families especially love visiting Great Wolf Lodge. With its indoor water park, climbing wall, ropes course, and more, it's a popular "staycation" destination. 9494 Federal Drive, 844.553.9653, www.greatwolf.com /colorado-springs.

For a luxurious stay, visit the Broadmoor. (See entry on p. 142.)

Other Highlights

The world's largest private insect collection (more than 7,000 species) is housed at the May Natural History Museum of the Tropics (aka May Natural History Museum). Opened in 1952, it's marked by a giant, roadside statue of a West Indian Hercules Beetle nicknamed "Herkimer." Open daily 9 a.m.–6 p.m., May–Oct., 710 Rock Creek

The Ranch at Emerald Valley is an all-inclusive retreat set at 8,200 feet. Photo by Michael Mundt.

Canyon Rd., 719.576.0450, www.colorado springsbugmuseum.com.

The Golden Eagle Campground is located on the property, offering more than 200 campgrounds for tents to RVs, 12 miles of hiking trails, and lakes for fishing. www .campingincoloradosprings.com.

The US Olympic and Paralympic Training Center is open for tours year-round, beginning daily at 9 a.m. (Sun., 11 a.m.). Call for seasonal hours ($). 1 Olympic Plaza, 719. 866.4618, www.teamusa.org/csotc.

Pair your visit with the new US Olympic and Paralympic Museum (about 2.5 miles from Training Center), which opened July 2020, considered one of the world's most accessible and interactive museums. Open 10 a.m.–5 p.m., Sat., 9 a.m.–6 p.m. ($$) 200 S. Sierra Madre St., 719.497.1234, www.uso pm.org.

The town of Larkspur, 32 miles north of Colorado Springs, comes alive mid-June through early August with the Renaissance Festival, becoming a 16th-century village featuring minstrels and maidens, jousters

and musicians. It's also home to the newly renovated Jellystone Park™ at Larkspur, with cabins, RV and tent sites, a water park, a miniature golf course, dining, and more. 650 Sky View Ln., 720.325.2393, www.sun rvresorts.com.

Air Force Academy

Open to the public daily from 9 a.m.–5 p.m., head through the North Gate at the Barry Goldwater Visitors Center for information on self-guided tours and the property's 23+ miles of unpaved trails. The Eagles Peak Trail, about 3 miles roundtrip (challenging), offers incredible views of the academy and city. The Stanley Canyon trail, approximately 2 miles (one way), offers views of the city and Stanley Canyon Reservoir (difficult). There's also the Falcon Trail, a 13-mile loop that's easy to hike short stretches and catch a glimpse of the horse stables. Note: Closed during the pandemic; be sure to contact the visitors center for updated tourist information before visiting. 2346 Academy Drive, 719.333.2025, www.usafa.edu.

Learn about "the sport of kings" at Broadmoor Falconry Adventure, which is open to the public. Photo by Michael Mundt.

The Broadmoor

Mining magnate Spencer Penrose and his wife, Julie, are credited with bringing this renowned pink-stucco property known as "Grand Dame of the Rockies" to her current glory in 1918. Set around 6,200 feet at the base of Cheyenne Mountain, it offers two championship golf courses, eighteen restaurants, a 5-star spa, three swimming pools, a movie theater, a bowling alley, and more. There's also a free shuttle to the adjacent Cheyenne Mountain Zoo. (See "Cheyenne Mountain Zoo" entry on the opposite page.) 1 Lake Ave., 719.623.5112 or 855.634.7711, www.broadmoor.com.

THE WILDERNESS EXPERIENCES

For more rustic luxury lodging, check out one of the Broadmoor's mountain properties, including Cloud Camp, located 3,000 feet above the main resort atop Cheyenne Mountain at the site of Spencer Penrose's Cheyenne Lodge. After a quick drive up the mountain via shuttle, mule ride, or hike—an elevation gain of 2,000 feet beginning at the famous Will Roger's Shrine of the

Sun—guests can stay at the camp while enjoying access to the main property's amenities. Anglers can experience the hotel's Fly Fishing Camp, pairing guided fishing with deluxe lodging and dining, located 75 minutes west of the Broadmoor along the Tarryall River. Dude-ranch lovers will enjoy the Ranch at Emerald Valley, an all-inclusive retreat set at 8,200 feet. Surrounded by Pike National Forest, visitors can hike, fish, horseback ride, and more. Take a quick archery lesson, practice fly-fishing in one of two small lakes (canoes and kayaks are available), and soak in one of the two hot tubs. For an extra fee, there's also the City Slicker Experience, a real-life cattle drive at the nearby Elk Ranch. Cookout nights are Wed. and Sat., featuring a down-home dinner of barbecued meats and sides, desserts and s'mores.

These Broadmoor activities are open to the public:

FALCONRY ADVENTURE

Known as "the sport of kings" and designated by UNESCO as an Intangible Cultural Heritage of Humanity, this program is the only one of its kind in Colorado. Get up close with the property's majestic birds such as Harris's hawks and peregrine falcons. Learn about the sport's 4,000-year history, then take a "hawk walk" to learn what it's like to get "hawk slapped." (It doesn't hurt.) Beginner and intermediate experiences available (about 90 minutes each; must complete beginner course first). One of *the* coolest things my family has ever experienced! Minimum 5 years old. 719.471.6168.

SEVEN FALLS

Tumbling 181 feet down the head of this box canyon in seven leaps, the falls can be seen from the top of the 224-step staircase or the Eagle's Nest viewing platform, which offers elevator access. Or hike one of two short trails: a 1-mile trek to Inspiration Point for a spectacular view of the city or a 30-minute walk to Midnight Falls, formed by springs and snowmelt from Pikes Peak. There's also the Seven Falls souvenir shop; the Rockhounds at the Eagles Nest, featuring minerals and fossils from around the world; and the 1858 food truck. Parking at 1045 Lower Gold Camp Rd.; purchase tickets at gate. Open Thurs.–Mon., 10 a.m.–6 p.m.

SOARING ADVENTURES

Set in secluded South Cheyenne Canyon above Seven Falls, nicknamed the "Grandest Mile of Scenery in Colorado," it comprises 10 ziplines among two courses, the Woods and the Fins. Choose one or a combination of both. We completed the Fins course, a three-hour adventure traversing Seven Falls Canyon that included walks across custom-built suspension bridges. It also requires a controlled 180-foot rappel to the canyon floor at the end—the only part that scared me! Weight requirements: 90–250 pounds. 719.471.6167.

Cheyenne Mountain State Park

A former ranch set beneath Cheyenne Mountain, there are 23 miles of easy-to-moderate hiking and biking trails, and

Visitors can hand-feed lettuce to the giraffes at Cheyenne Mountain Zoo. Photo by Michael Mundt.

another 6.7 miles rated difficult to extreme. Stop at the Trail's End Visitor Center for information on guided nature hikes, geocaching, Junior Ranger programming (ages 7–12), and mystery hikes. The campground includes 51 RV campsites and 10 tent sites, a camper-services store (mid-April–mid-October), showers, and laundry. 410 JL Ranch Heights, 719.576.2016.

Cheyenne Mountain Zoo

Located adjacent to the Broadmoor, at 6,714 feet, it's the country's highest zoo. Established in 1926 by Spencer Penrose as the Cheyenne Mountain Zoological Society to house his exotic animals, it includes the Mountaineer Sky Ride, a chair-lift-style ride that offers spectacular views of the zoo and city. Enjoy the brand-new "Water's Edge: Africa!" exhibit for the zoo's Nile hippos and African penguins. And be sure to feed the zoo's famous giraffe herd, said to be the largest in any zoo. (Hat wearers be warned: one hungry fella snatched my friend's straw one right off her head!) Open 9 a.m.–5 p.m. 4250 Cheyenne Mountain Zoo Rd., 719.633.9925, www.cmzoo.org.

Flying W Ranch

Get a taste of the Old West with one of the area's most beloved destinations, operating as a tourist spot since 1953. Destroyed in 2012 by the Waldo Canyon Fire, it reopened in 2020, once again offering its famous chuckwagon suppers, complete with home-cooked BBQ, baked beans, and biscuits. Listen to sing-alongs hosted by the Flying W Wranglers and watch Native American dancers perform (about 3 miles north of Garden of the Gods). Chuckwagon Rd., 719.598.4000, www.flyingw.com.

Garden of the Gods Park

The most-visited attraction in the Pikes Peak region, the area's red-rock formations are a must-see for visitors. Set at the base of Pikes Peak, the National Natural Landmark offers some 21 miles of trails for hiking, biking, and horseback riding. Naturalists provide 45-minute walks daily, 10 a.m. and 2 p.m., or visitors can simply drive through it. Stop at the Trading Post for coffee, restrooms, and a map (324 Beckers Ln., 719.685.9045). The Visitor and Nature Center is located across the street. Open Mon.–Thurs., 9 a.m.–3 p.m., Fri.–Sun., 9 a.m.–5 p.m., 1805 N. 30th St., 719.634.6666, www.gardenofgods.com.

For climbing tours (90 minutes to 6 hours), contact Front Range Climbing ($$) (1676 S. 21st St., 719.632.5822, www.frontrangeclimbing.com). Segway, Jeep, and 1909 Trolley tours available via Adventures Out West ($–$$) (719.578.0935, www.advoutwest.com). E-bike tours offered through Amp'd Adventures ($). Ages 11 and up (719.590.6500, www.ampdadventures.com). Horseback tours available via Academy Riding Stables ($). Ages 8 and up (888.700.0410, www.academyridingstables.com). Rock Ledge Ranch Historic Site, adjacent to the park, offers living-history programs Wed.–Sat., 10 a.m.–5 p.m., Sun., 1 p.m.–5 p.m. (3105 Gateway Rd., 719.578.6777, www.rockledgeranch.com).

For nearby lodging, the Garden of the Gods Resort and Club is a 4-star property located just three minutes away. 3320 Mesa Rd., 800.329.4607, www.gardenofthegods resort.com.

Or stay 2 miles away in one of 17 rooms at the Glen Eyrie Castle and Conference Center, considered a "Christ-centered property" (alcohol- and marijuana-free). A 67-room, English Tudor–style structure built in 1871 by Colorado Springs founder General William Jackson Palmer, it's also open to the public. Daily tours, 1 p.m. Castle teas take place in the Music Room, Wed.–Fri., 11 a.m. and 2:30 p.m.; weekends, 11 a.m., 1 p.m., 3 p.m. Reservations required for both. 3820 N. 30th St., 719.265.7050, www.gleneyrie.org.

Paint Mines Interpretive Park

This landscape of colorful hoodoos and spires is located about 30 minutes east of the city. Named for the brightly colored bands of oxidized iron compounds exposed in the rocks, likely used by Native American tribes for ceramic paints, the Paint Mines Trail is an easy 3.4-mile walk for all skill levels. Interpretive signs and restrooms. Dawn to dusk. *Do not* climb or walk on the rocks! 29950 Paint Mine Rd., Calhan, 719.520.6375.

Pikes Peak

While I don't outline all of the state's 14ers, Pikes Peak is an exception. With more than a half-million annual visitors, the 14,115-foot peak (the official tourism elevation) is not only the most visited summit in North America; it's also one of only two Colorado 14ers that you can summit via car: a 19-mile drive along the Pikes Peak Highway. (Mt. Evans, near Idaho Springs, is the other.) And it's the only one that visitors can summit by train. (See "Manitou and Pikes Peak Cog Railway" entry.) If you prefer a strenuous hike, Barr Trail is roughly 13.5 miles one way, with some 7,500-foot in elevation gain. (It may take the fittest person 10 hours roundtrip, so it's best to start before daylight.) The Barr Trail Lot in Manitou Springs requires reservations; cost is $20. (See "Manitou Incline" entry for parking/shuttle options.) Stop for refreshments and restrooms at Barr Camp, 6.5 miles from the trailhead. Or stay for the night (bunkhouse and tent-camping options). Meals available. Overnight reservations required (www.barrcamp.com). Bike Pikes Peak via Adventures Out West with their Pikes Peak by Bike tour, 19.5 miles (6 hours) of "pure mountain-bike heaven." Breakfast and lunch included. Minimum 12 years ($$) (719.578.0935, www.advoutwest.com).

Cripple Creek

Miles from Denver: 114

Once the summer hunting grounds for the Ute tribe, this mountainous playground at the base of Pikes Peak was the site for the biggest (and last) mining boom in the late 19th century. Eventually known as the "World's Greatest Gold Camp," the downtown was decimated in an 1896 fire, replaced by red-brick buildings that remain standing on Bennett Ave. Filled with restaurants, shops, and hotels, it attracts modern-day "prospectors" to its nine casinos. This is a gambling town, which means kids under 21 cannot enter a majority of the buildings. But its history and proximity to the national monument make it worth the visit. www.visitcripplecreek.com.

Lodging

We stayed about 6 miles northeast of town at the KOA Cripple Creek, the highest KOA (10,000 feet), complete with a kid-sized train play area. Our cabin was ideal for chilly, high-country evenings. 2576 CR 81, 719.689.5647.

There are also a handful of lodging options in Victor (4 miles) and several in

---

Fast Fact: Cripple Creek maintains its own herd of donkeys, said to be descendants of the Gold Rush era. (Once miners left the area, their beasts of burden were often let loose.) The local Two Mile High Club hosts the annual Donkey Derby Days the last full weekend in June to fund the animals' veterinary services and food. The club also raises funds with leaf-peeping tours the last two weekends of September. Can't spot the beloved animals roaming the streets? Ask a local, especially the town bus drivers, who'll likely know their whereabouts. www. cripplecreekdonkeys.com.

Woodland Park (26 miles). It's also an easy day trip from Colorado Springs (34 miles).

Other Highlights

The Cripple Creek Heritage and Information Center showcases the area's gold-camp history; local geology, flora, and fauna; and recreation opportunities. Open daily, 9 a.m.–5 p.m., 9283 S. Hwy 67, 877.858.4653.

The scenic town of Lake George, a former stagestop located 22 miles northwest of Cripple Creek, is home to two state parks: Spinney Mountain, home to Spinney Mountain Reservoir, a 2,500-acre lake formed by the South Platte River that boasts Gold Medal waters, popular for fishing, boating, sailboarding (with wind gusts of 30–40 mph), and bird-watching (closed in winter), and Eleven Mile, which features more than 300 campsites with laundry, a marina, and more. Eleven Mile manages services for both parks, so both are listed at the same address and phone, despite being 9 miles apart: 4229 CR 92, 719.748.3401.

There's also the Puma Hills Mountain Retreat, offering a lodge with kitchen (sleeps 11), a cabin with kitchen (sleeps 4), 24 glamping tepees (sleep 2–4), 2 Conestoga wagons, 3 geodesic domes, and even a bubble tent with a queen bed. Bedding, heated mattress pads, and electricity in all structures. Bathhouse with restrooms and showers available. Primitive sites with provided tents also available. Chef on staff; meal plans offered. 20859 CR77, 727.455.8791, www.pumahills.com.

Colorado Wolf and Wildlife Center

Located in nearby Divide (19 miles northwest of Cripple Creek), this nonprofit sanctuary for wolves and wild canines offers one-hour tours that end with a group "wolf howl." Kids' tour ideal for ages 6–11; full-moon tours and up-close encounters also available. Daily tours at noon, 2 p.m., and 4 p.m., mid-May–early Sept.; low season, noon and 2 p.m. ($–$$$) 4729 Twin Rocks Rd., 719.687.9742, www.wolfeducation.org.

Cripple Creek and Victor Narrow Gauge Railroad

The colorful, open-air train departs from an 1894 vintage depot, transporting guests past abandoned and working mines toward views of the mountains and Cripple Creek. Trains depart every 70 minutes, 45-minute rides, 10 a.m.–5 p.m., mid-June–early September. Depot includes a snack/gift shop. 520 E. Carr Ave., 719.689.2640, www.cripplecreekrailroad.com.

Florissant Fossil Beds National Monument

Did you know Colorado was once home to giant redwood trees? See petrified proof roughly 3 miles south of the tiny town of Florissant (16 miles northwest of Cripple Creek). One of the richest fossil deposits in the world, most of which you can't see, the area's crown jewels are the petrified tree

The crown jewels of Florissant Fossil Beds National Monument near Cripple Creek are the petrified redwood stumps scattered throughout. Photo by the author.

stumps scattered throughout the meadows and pine forest around the visitor center. There are remnants of trees as high as 230 feet tall, including "Big Stump" and three interconnected stumps called the "Redwood Trio." See them via a shaded 0.5-mile loop near the visitor center, or head toward the meadow's 1-mile Petrified Forest Loop. 15807 CR 1, 719.748.3253, www.nps.gov/flfo.

Gold Mine Tours

Descend 1,000 feet underground with a Mollie Kathleen Gold Mine tour, named for the first woman to find gold here. Ride an underground tram-air locomotive and experience the cacophony of mining equipment. Less than 0.25-mile of walking on level ground required. Open daily, 9 a.m.–5 p.m., 9388 Hwy 67, 719.689.2466, www.goldminetours.com.

Visitors can see a working gold mine at the Cripple Creek and Victor Gold Mining Company, watching heavy equipment as they work in the large surface mine (the largest mining operation in the continental United States). Proceeds benefit the Victor Lowell Thomas Museum, located in nearby Victor. Mon. and Wed.–Sat., 10 a.m. and 1 p.m. Open Memorial Day Weekend–Labor Day. Minimum 5 years; closed-toe shoes required. 3rd and Victor Ave., 719.689.4211, www.victormuseum.com/MineTours.htm.

Shelf Road

Climbing aficionados will want to visit the Shelf Road, a dramatic, vertical "shelf" of limestone cliffs (up to 100 feet tall), roughly 7 miles southwest of Cripple Creek. Part of the 130-mile Gold Belt Tour Scenic Byway that includes Cripple Creek, Victor, Florissant, Florence, and Cañon City, certain stretches of it require four-wheel drive. (Phantom Canyon, also on the byway, is a good destination for beginner climbers.) Take a guided, half-day (4-hour) tour with Front Range Climbing ($$), 1676 S. 21st St.,

Colorado Springs, 866.404.3721, www.front
rangeclimbing.com.

Manitou Springs

Miles from Denver: 76

Considered sacred by the Native American
tribes who settled at the base of Pikes
Peak—including Cheyenne and Arapaho—
they believed the eruption of bubbles in the
town's numerous mineral springs were the
breath of the Great Spirit, Manitou. Eventually those mineral springs and clean mountain air established the area as a health
resort by the 1890s, attracting medical pro-
fessionals and tubercular patients. Revital-
ized in the 1980s as a National Historic District, the downtown draws visitors to its
galleries, shops, and restaurants. www.man
itousprings.org.

Other Highlights

The Rainbow Falls Historic Site is a popular
spot because of its accessibility to the
waterfall. With an easy, 0.1-mile walk amid
red rocks surrounding Fountain Creek, the
area was once home to the Tabeguache or
Sun Mountain people, the spiritual leaders
of Ute tribe. Visitors can also see the historic 1934 Highway 24 Bridge into Manitou
Springs, listed on the National Register of
Historic Bridges. Open 10 a.m.–4 p.m.,
April–Oct., US-24, Cascade, 80809,
719.520.7529.

. Local lore says the town is filled with
witches practicing the pagan Wicca reli-
gion, which seems more urban legend than
fact. Recently when I told a neighbor I was
visiting Manitou Springs, she teased that I
would join a coven, or a group of witches
who meet regularly. I'll never tell.

The town's annual Emma Crawford Coffin Races and Festival pays homage to
Crawford, who died from tuberculosis in

Fast Fact: Taste each of the eight springs that
gave the town its name via a self-guided
walking tour. Grab a map at the Manitou
Springs Heritage Center, 517 Manitou Ave.,
and begin sampling the naturally carbonated
water, each with a distinctive taste. BYOG
(glass)!

1891. Her last wish was to be buried near
the top of Red Mountain, but harsh winter
and spring rains launched her coffin down
the mountain in 1929. The town has hon-
ored her each October with the festivities
since 1995. www.emmacrawfordfestival.
com.

Cave of the Winds Mountain Park

Open since 1881, the main draw at one of
Colorado's oldest tourist attractions is the
cave tours, including the Discovery Tour, a
45-minute journey through 15 "rooms," and
the Lantern Tour, a 90-minute "adventure
of the past," complete with lanterns and
ghost stories (minimum age 6 years).
Newer attractions include an all-ages aerial
adventure, the Wind Walker Challenge
Course, set on the rim of a 600-foot drop
into Williams Canyon; the Bat-a-Pult ($), a
1,200-foot, roundtrip zipline through the
canyon (42-inch minimum-height require-
ment; 48 inches to ride alone); and a 3.5-
hour via ferrata course ($$), geared toward
inexperienced climbers (minimum 12 years
old; guests 12–17 must be accompanied by
an adult). Younger guests will enjoy pan-
ning for gold or riding the Stalactykes
Adventure Slide. But the biggest adrenaline
junkies will want to ride on the on the Ter-
ror-dactyl, falling more than 150 feet into
the canyon. The views are amazing! Open
daily, 10 a.m.–5 p.m., 100 Cave of the
Winds Rd., 719.685.5444, www.caveofthe
winds.com.

Manitou and Pikes Peak Cog Railway

Climbing to the top of Pikes Peak since 1891, the railway shut down in 2017 for updates—costing $100 million for new trains, tracks, a depot, and more—and reopened in May 2021. Owned by the Broadmoor, the world's highest and longest cog train transports visitors 9 miles through Pike National Forest and canyons to above tree line, ending at the peak's summit: 14,115 feet. The trip lasts about 3 hours—70 minutes each way plus a 40-minute stay at the top. Be sure to visit the new Pikes Peak Summit Visitor Center and taste the world-famous doughnuts, a recipe that's allegedly been used since 1916 and can only be made at high altitude. Railway parking costs $10. 515 Ruxton Ave., 719.685.1045, www.cograilway.com.

Manitou Cliff Dwellings

Writer and lecturer Virginia McClurg dismantled and relocated the 40-room structure from McElmo Canyon near Cortez in southwestern Colorado to its current site in Cliff Canyon. Open since 1907, they were reassembled using concrete mortar instead of the mud/clay used by the Ancestral Puebloans, allowing visitors to walk inside the 1,000-year-old dwellings. Hours vary seasonally. Located adjacent to Cave of the Winds. 10 Cliff Dwellings Rd., 719.685.5242, www.cliffdwellingsmuseum.com.

Manitou Incline

If you want to feel like a local, climb this 1-mile, 2,768-step incline that first opened in 1907 as a cable-car track, which begins around 6,500 feet and gains about 2,000 feet in elevation (located across from the

Walk inside Ancestral Puebloan homes at Manitou Cliff Dwellings, transported from Southwest Colorado in the early 1900s. Photo by the author.

cog railway). Downhill use of the incline is strongly discouraged, so the descent includes a 4-mile hike down the Barr Trail. (There are two bailout points: railroad ties #395 and #1300.) Keep in mind this is a very popular destination, so parking is difficult. The nearest spot is Iron Springs Chateau Parking, $10/car (four hours), cash only. Must get a parking pass from the attendant. 444 Ruxton Ave. Or park at 10 Old Man's Trail at the Hiawatha Gardens building ($1/hour) and take the city's free shuttle, which runs daily throughout the city, 6 a.m.–8 p.m., roughly every 15 minutes. Reservations (free) have been required since the pandemic, available seven days in advance, 6 a.m.–6 p.m. Other parking options and reservations details here: www .coloradosprings.gov/parks/page/manitou -incline.

Pueblo

Miles from Denver: 114

Established in 1842 as a trading post known as Fort Pueblo, this city nestled along the Arkansas River is the last major hub along the I-25 corridor before heading southbound out of Colorado. Incorporated as Pueblo in 1861, the city grew with the arrival of railroads; three years later, more than 2,000 people gathered in what is now Pueblo for a horse exhibition, which developed into the first Colorado State Fair in 1872—four years before Colorado became a state! An important manufacturing center in the Arkansas Valley, it was nicknamed "Steel City" for being one of the major steel-producing cities in the country.

Colorado's seventh-largest city also features a vibrant art scene as a Creative Corridor, but it's most famous for its green chiles, celebrated annually the last weekend in September at the Chile and Frijoles Festival. www.pueblochamber.org.

Other Highlights

The El Pueblo History Museum illustrates the area's many cultural and ethnic groups through unique exhibits, such as a re-created 1840s adobe trading post and plaza, as well as the archaeological excavation site of the city's original 1842 El Pueblo trading post. Mon.–Sat., 10 a.m.–4 p.m., 301 N. Union, 719.583.0453, www.historycolorado .org/el-pueblo-history-museum.

Located in downtown, the Pueblo Whitewater Park is a half-mile stretch of the Arkansas River featuring eight drops, perfect for kayaking or SUPing. Located at Chappa Place and Pearl Street; main access on 4th Street, takeout on Union Avenue. Parking is available in a lot on the south side of the Main Street Bridge or along Corona Street. Rent SUPs and tubes at The Edge Ski, Paddle, and Pack, open Mon.– Fri., 10 a.m.–6 p.m. (5 p.m. Saturdays). 107 N. Union Ave., 719.583.2021, www.edgeski andpaddle.com.

South of Pueblo are the small towns of Colorado City (27 miles) and Rye (33 miles), both popular headquarters for recreation around the San Isabel National Forest. Stay at one of many camping spots, such as the Pueblo South / Colorado City KOA (RV and tent sites, cabins) (I-25 South, Exit 74, 719.676.3376). Rye features Camp Jackson-YMCA of Pueblo, which offers "Family Camp" weekends in summer months (9126 CO-165, 719.543.5151, www.puebloymca.org /programs/camp-jackson). It also boasts one of Colorado's coolest attractions, Bishop Castle, called "The Largest One-Man Construction Project in the Country." Building on land he bought in 1959 at age 15, Jim

160-foot-high Bishop Castle (near Pueblo), a one-man construction project built by Jim Bishop since 1969, is one of Colorado's most unique attractions. Photo by the author.

Bishop has used over 1,000 tons of rock to create his stone masterpiece: a 160-foot-high castle featuring several towers, stained-glass windows, and a fire-breathing dragon. Donations recommended. 12705 CO-165, www.bishopcastle.org.

The city boasts an outdoor neon-sign "museum," Pueblo Neon Alley, with more than 20 neon signs glowing 24/7 in a Union Avenue Historic District alleyway. Dubbed the "greatest assembly of neon art west of Times Square and east of the Las Vegas Strip." 125 W. B Street, 719.544.0020, www.puebloneonalley.com.

Historic Arkansas Riverwalk

This 1-mile stretch along the Arkansas River modeled after the famous San Antonio version is filled with shops, restaurants, and more than 50 pieces of artwork. Enjoy a stroll along the paved path, or take a 30-minute boat ride through the channel to learn about the riverwalk's history (pedal boats, gondola rides, and "booze cruises" also available). 101 S. Union Ave. and S. Victoria Ave., 719.595.0242, www.pueblo riverwalk.org.

Lake Pueblo State Park

Located in the plains and sunbaked bluffs of the Pueblo West area, Lake Pueblo (aka Pueblo Reservoir) sits along the Arkansas River, featuring 60 miles of shoreline that draw visitors for water sports, boating, and fishing; the river below the dam is perfect for kayakers, rafters, and tubers. Offering nearly 400 campsites (and 150 picnic sites) among three campgrounds—Northern Plains and Juniper Breaks on the north shore and Arkansas Point on the south—there are also two marinas, Northshore and Southshore, as well as the Rock Canyon Swim Beach (northeast end of lake). Two mobile companies are authorized to rent out watercraft and deliver to guests at the south boat ramp, near the Southshore Marina: Pueblo Jet Ski Rental (719.248.6826, www.pueblojetskirental .com) and Laketime Rentals, for SUPs and kayaks (719.494.6884, www.laketime -rentals.com). (Both businesses require reservations.)

The area is also a good mountain-biking destination, with a network of 45 miles of trails marked like ski trails (green, blue, and black), named the South Shore Trail Network (located on the south shore, adjacent

Fast Fact: Pueblo's most prized contribution to the food world is the "slopper," an open-faced cheeseburger smothered in green chile. Locals are quick to offer their favorite "slopper stops," including Gray's Coors Tavern (515 W. 4th St., 719.544.0455) and Sunset Inn (2808 Thatcher Ave., 719.564.9841).

The plains and sunbaked bluffs of Lake Pueblo State Park feature a popular network of mountain-biking trails. Photo by the author.

to Arkansas Point Campground). Keep in mind that the trails' loose shale may be challenging for less experienced riders. 640 Pueblo Reservoir Rd., 719.561.9320.

Nature and Wildlife Discovery Center River Campus

Nature and Wildlife Discovery Center's sister property to the Pueblo Mountain Park Campus (see "Pueblo Mountain Park / Horseshoe Lodge" entry), the River Campus is a nature preserve along the Arkansas River offering community and educational programs, special events, and more. Campus is open daily 6:30 a.m.–7 p.m. (9 p.m. in summer). 5200 Nature Center Rd., 719.549.2414, www.hikeandlearn.org.

About a five-minute walk away is the Raptor Center, where 200 birds of prey are rehabilitated and released to the wild annually. By appointment only. 719.529.2327.

Pueblo Mountain Park / Horseshoe Lodge

Located about 27 miles southwest of Pueblo in Beulah, this 611-acre park (owned by the City of Pueblo) is perfect for families seeking mountain solitude without the overhead of camping. Managed by the Nature and Wildlife Discovery Center, with a mission to connect kids and communities with nature, the property's West Wing features 11 rooms of various sizes and amenities: 4 rooms with en-suite bathrooms; 7 rooms with 4 community bathrooms to share. (All are compost toilets and coin-operated showers.) Four "family rooms" accommodate up to 4 guests. (Simple continental breakfast included.) There are also 6 miles of trails including the easy 0.95-mile Devil's Canyon Trail, some that connect with longer ones in the adjacent San Isabel National Forest. Two-hour private guided hike or snowshoe tours available ($). 9112 Pueblo Mountain Park Rd., Beulah, 719.485.4444, www.hikeandlearn.org.

There are two sister properties along the Arkansas River: the River Campus and Raptor Center. (See "Nature and Wildlife Discovery Center River Campus" entry.)

Pueblo River Trail System

Featuring more than 30 miles of trails for walking, running, or biking, the system meanders along the Arkansas River from the North Entrance of Lake Pueblo State Park to the Colorado State University Pueblo Campus (2200 Bonforte Blvd.).

Need a bike? I rented one for a day at Great Divide Ski Bike and Hike, Mon.–Fri., 9:30 a.m.–5:30 p.m.; Sat., 9 a.m.–5 p.m., 400 N. Santa Fe Ave., 719.546.2453, www.greatdividebike.com.

Pueblo Zoo

Set in Pueblo's City Park, it's about one-third the size of the Denver Zoo (25 acres versus 80), but it's also about half the price of entry. Plus the flat, paved grounds make it easier for younger kids (and strollers) to negotiate. Visit outdoor exhibits for unique animals such as red pandas (the only zoo in the state to see them) and Watusi cattle (those oversized horns!). Indoor habitats include the San Esteban Island chuckwalla and Rodrigues Island fruit bats. Outside food is allowed, so it's perfect for a picnic. 3455 Nuckolls Ave., 719.561.1452, www.pueblozoo.org.

Salida

Miles from Denver: 142

Known as the "Heart of the Rockies," Salida (pronounced Sal-EYE-da) is home to Colorado's largest National Historic District (136 preserved buildings). It's also a Certified Creative District featuring a variety of artists, from pottery to metal and fiber arts. A neighbor 25 miles south of Buena Vista (biking enthusiasts often bike to BV from here or vice versa), it's also a gateway to the Arkansas River and surrounding mountain wilderness. The paved Salida Trail, a 4.6-loop for biking and walking, is a good way to see the town.

Lodging

Four Seasons RV Park boasts 1,000 feet of Arkansas River access. 4305 US Hwy 50, 719.539.3084, www.fourseasonsrvpark.biz. About 7 miles from Monarch Mountain is Monarch Spur RV Park and Campground: 30 RV sites, 15 tent sites, 2 cabins (capacity 4–6). 18989 W. US Hwy 50, 719.530.0341, www.msrvpark.com. Set 2 miles from the Arkansas Headwaters Recreation Area, the Amigo Motor Lodge is a newly renovated boutique hotel from the 1960s. Stay in a traditional hotel room or an Airstream with names like "Francis" and "Velma." 7350 US Hwy 50, 719.539.6733, www.stayamigo.com.

Other Highlights

The Mt. Shavano Fish Hatchery (or Trout Rearing Unit) is a great way to learn about and witness the life cycle of trout. Visit the Arkansas Headwaters Recreation Area, 307 W. Sackett, for advice and maps.

Located along 1,200 feet of the Arkansas River in downtown Salida, the Whitewater Park includes four features or "play holes" for kayaking, rafting, and tubing. Watch the action from the paved trail, roughly 1.5 miles one way. Parking available on Sackett

Ave. (Take F St., left on Sackett Ave.) The next block offers parking spaces to the left of the boat ramp; spots also available on ramp.

Rent tubes, SUPs, and more at Totally Tubular River Rentals, first-come, first-served. Open Memorial Day–Labor Day, 9 a.m.–7 p.m. daily, 240 N. F St., www.totally tubularsalida.com.

Arkansas Headwaters Recreation Area (State Park)

Comprising portions of Browns Canyon National Monument, as well as more than 100 miles of Gold Medal fishing waters, the area has 8 campgrounds (tent pads, picnic tables, vault toilets) and several picnic sites. Bring your own watercraft, or contact one of several outfitters in the area. Hiking, biking, and horseback riding, as well as extensive OHV trails. Guided hikes available with an amateur geologist. Reservations required (e-mail ahra@state.co.us). 307 Sackett Ave., 719.539.7289.

Ever tried gold panning? This is a great spot! Get supplies in nearby Nathrop at the Rock Doc at Prospectors Village, 17897 US Hwy 285, 719.539.2019, www.therockdoc.net.

Captain Zipline Aerial Adventure Park

Three different adventures await visitors ($–$$), starting with the state's largest, the Canyon Aerial Course, with 120 different elements of varying difficulty such as swings and a flying snowboard. Two hours of "free play" (minimum 8 years, 70 pounds, with restrictions). The lost Canyon Zipline Tour offers tours over the stunning gorge (minimum 6 years, 55 pounds). Try the via ferrata, featuring four routes from "easy" to "extreme" (minimum 55 pounds, 60 inches). 1500 CR 45, 719.207.4947, www .captainzipline.com.

Monarch Mountain

Stats: 66 designated trails, 800 skiable acres, 7 lifts, 2 terrain parks

Trail classification: 24 percent Beginner; 27 percent Intermediate; 49 percent Advanced

Base elevation: 10,790 feet

This ski area in the Sawatch Mountain Range is famous for deep snow, great tree skiing, and backcountry snowcat territory. Perfect for families seeking solace away from the crowds, it's set on the Continental Divide at Monarch Pass, about 20 miles west of Salida. Free parking, and runs flow back to a single base area. Monarch Cat Skiing operates on an adjacent 1,000+ acres, offering chutes, bowls, and trees. Take a break from the slopes on the tubing hill (minimum 36 inches); children ages 6 and under must be accompanied by an adult (riding separately). Go dog sledding with Monarch Dog Sled Rides ($$), featuring a half-hour ride on a sled surrounded by 13,000-foot peaks (75-minute sessions). Daily 9 a.m., 11 a.m., 1 p.m., 3 p.m. (times adjusted during Daylight Saving), 719.207.1150, www.monarchdogsledrides .com.

In spring, celebrate the end of the season with the resort's signature Kayaks on Snow race, the only contest featuring kayakers racing competitors down a snowy course. In warmer months, ride to the top of Monarch Pass (11,312 feet) via the Monarch Crest Scenic Tramway, May through fall (www .monarchcrest.net). www.skimonarch.com.

Salida Hot Springs Aquatic Center

Offering two pools channeled from springs located 8 miles away from the facility, the center has fresh water piped in continually, so there's no need for chlorine in the six-lane lap pool or small leisure pool. ($) Private soaking pools and fitness classes available, including learning to roll and recover a kayak. Weekdays, 6 a.m.–7:30 p.m.;

weekends, 10 a.m.–5:30 p.m., 410 W. Hwy 50, 719.539.6738, www.salidarec.com.

Tenderfoot Mountain

The town's natural landmark set across from the Arkansas River at the end of historic F Street, Tenderfoot Mountain—also referred to as "S Mountain" for the large, white "S" located toward the top—is filled with accessible hikes and rides. Closest to town are the Arkansas Hills Trails and Salida Mountain Trails, a network of 23 dirt trails in a stacked-loop design, where the lower trails are the easiest and increase in difficulty as you climb higher (mountain biking or hiking). Head to the summit (around 7,500 feet) via the Tenderfoot Mountain Overlook Trail, about 6.6 miles roundtrip. Or simply drive Spiral Drive to the top instead.

Wet Mountain Valley

Miles from Denver: 146 (Silver Cliff)

Comprising two towns, Westcliffe and Silver Cliff (Custer County), this valley is home to more than 200 miles of hiking and biking trails and about fifty alpine lakes. It also offers access to a cluster of five 14ers known as the Crestone Group, including the Crestone Needle and Humboldt Peak. Shielded by the stunning Wet Mountains and Sangre de Cristo Range, the towns are protected from light pollution, the ideal setting to make them the ninth Dark-Sky Community in the world (first in Colorado). The Custer County Welcome Center is located on the corner of Main Street and CO-69 in Westcliffe, 107 N. 3rd St. The Media Room provides information and inspiration about the area's mountains and stars. 719.480.7230, www.visitwetmountainvalley.com.

Lodging

Wet Mountain RV Park, located just off Main St., features 22 RV sites and 3 cabins, each with full beds, a refrigerator, and a microwave. The studio offers a queen bed, table and chairs, a sink with water, and kitchenware. 816 Main St., 719.371.7165, www.wetmtnrv.com.

Other Highlights

Enjoy public star parties at the Smokey Jack Observatory in Westcliffe, featuring a retractable roof with a high-powered telescope. (Private star parties can also be reserved.) Located on the southwest corner of Bluff Park, west end on Main St., 719.398.1284, www.darkskiescolorado.org/events.

Experience an Amish hayride (30- and 60-minute rides), horseback rides, and pony and cart rides via Sunset Ranch. Reservations required for hayrides. 3038 Hwy 96, Silver Cliff. Call Freeman Miller, 719.239.0154, or e-mail valleywide@sle.email.

Hike past three 13ers—Comanche Peak, Venable Peak, and Spring Mountain—on the Comanche-Venable Trail Loop, a moderate, 12.3-mile trek that includes a thrilling walk along a ledge called Phantom Terrace. For a shorter journey, turn back after reaching Venable Falls, about 2.5 miles up the trail. The loop begins at the Alvarado Campground, offering RV/tent sites and spots for equestrian campers. CR 140, Westcliffe, 719.269.8500.

MYSTIC SAN LUIS VALLEY

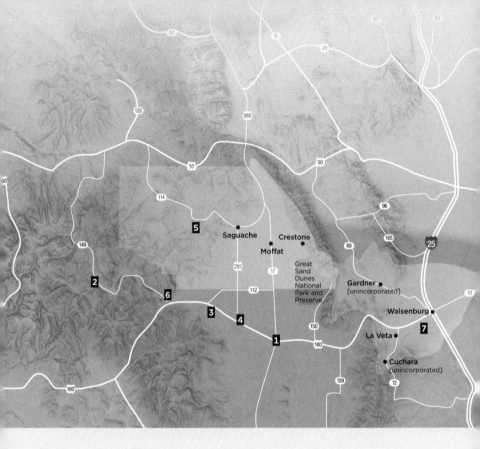

MYSTIC SAN LUIS VALLEY

Alamosa

Miles from Denver: 235

Native American tribes such as the Clovis (of New Mexico) hunted big game here, followed by Spanish explorers. But what drew settlers was the gold and silver discovery in 1870 near Summitville (a ghost town about 58 miles west of Alamosa), followed by the 1878 arrival of the Rio Grande Railroad. Established that year as Alamosa, Spanish for "cottonwood grove," it was soon the supply and cultural center of the valley. Home to Adams State University (ASU) since 1921 and a gateway to Great Sand Dunes National Park and Preserve, Alamosa is the region's largest city. www.alamosa.org.

Lodging

The Sand Dunes Swimming Pool and Campground, situated about 32 miles west of the national park visitor center in Hooper, offers RV/tent sites and cabins, plus a hot-springs pool (98–102 degrees) and a 24-person therapy pool (108–9 degrees). 1991 CR 63, 719.378.2807, www .sanddunespool.com.

Other Highlights

Once under the command of Kit Carson, the Fort Garland Museum and Cultural Center, located about 25 miles east in Fort Garland, was built in 1858 primarily to protect settlers against attacks by Native American tribes. Visitors can walk the parade grounds, tour the adobe buildings, and more. Open Mar.–Oct., 9 a.m.–5 p.m., Nov.–Dec., 10 a.m.–4 p.m. Closed Jan. and Feb. 29477 CO-159, Fort Garland, 719.379.3512.

Set about 41 miles southeast of Alamosa, San Luis is Colorado's oldest town. Populated primarily by Hispanic families who settled here in 1851, this spiritual mecca is home to the Shrine of the Stations of the Cross, a 0.5-mile trail to view 15 bronze sculptures of Christ's passion and resurrection (located on San Pedro Mesa at the junction of Hwys 159 and 142). Visitors can even stay in a former convent, now the El Convento Inn, a B&B with 4 guest rooms (2 beds in each), owned and operated by the Sangre de Cristo Parish. 512 Church Pl., 719.992.0122, www.sdcparish.org/el-con vento-inn.

Colorado Gators Reptile Park

This working fish farm and reptile refuge just 17 miles north of town opened in 1977 as a tilapia farm (for stocking ponds and aquaponic systems and for human consumption). The owners bought 100 baby alligators in 1987 to take care of their stinky "dead fish" problem, and it's since transformed into an exotic-animal refuge and education center that families love visiting.

Touch tortoises, meet Morris the Hollywood alligator from *Happy Gilmore*, and feed "gator chow" to the alligators. Earn a "Jr. Handler" certificate during the reptile-handling class (minimum age 4). Learn about and handle a variety of reptiles, including snakes and lizards ($). Visitors over 18 can sign up for a gator-wrestling class ($), learning how to catch an alligator (2–8 feet long), and earn a "Certificate of Insanity." (No, there's no muzzle. Yes, you can get injured.) But handling them is not just for sport; the alligators need to be checked for wounds and receive medication if necessary, so it helps manage the animals' health. Hours vary by season (roughly 9 a.m.–5 p.m.). 9162 Ln. 9 N., Mosca, 719.378.2612, www.coloradogators.com.

Cumbres and Toltec Scenic Railroad

Located roughly 28 miles southwest of Alamosa in Antonito, the Cumbres and Toltec Scenic Railroad ($$) was established in 1880, considered the longest and highest narrow-gauge train still running. Take a

64-mile day trip through wilderness in the mountains of Colorado and New Mexico in the Victorian elegance of a deluxe parlor car or the budget-friendly coach. Lunch stop included. The train operates primarily in the summer and fall, but there is also a Christmas train, conditions permitting. 888.286.2737, www.cumbrestoltec.com.

Great Sand Dunes National Park and Preserve (GSDNP)

There is something otherworldly about driving up to the unique landscape of the state's newest national park (2004), a vast stretch of sand tucked at the base of the stunning Sangre de Cristo Mountains, the tallest dunes in North America. Covering approximately 39 square miles and rising up to the highest, Star Dune, which towers 755 feet (five dunes top 700 feet), they emerged after ancient lakes dried up, scientists now believe. No matter how you explain their enormity, it's impossible to comprehend until you hike into them.

Begin your visit at the visitor center, offering exhibits, back-porch viewing with telescope, restrooms, and snacks. Open 8:30 a.m.–5 p.m., Memorial Day Weekend–Labor Day Weekend, 9 a.m.–4:30 p.m., nonsummer months. 11999 CO-150, Mosca, 719.378.6395, www.nps.gov/grsa.

The park encompasses a variety of geography, from tundra to forest and wetlands, in addition to the sand dunes. There's even Medano Creek at their base—*médano* is Spanish for "sand dune"—a seasonal stream that's often high enough for tubing.

Families with younger kids may not get any farther than the creek, but you'll still get amazing views of the dunes.

There are two main hikes in the sand: High Dune on the first ridge, about 2.5 miles roundtrip, about two hours, and Star Dune, roughly 6 miles roundtrip, about eight hours of hiking. For the latter, start from the Dunes Parking lot, trekking roughly 2 miles south along the Medano Creek Bed until the pyramid-shaped dune comes into view; follow a ridge to summit. Some hikers even use snowshoes to prevent sinking. Having hiked maybe 30 minutes to a sledding spot, I can attest that it feels impossible to get traction in regular footwear.

Here are some boarding/sledding dos and don'ts:

If you're a parent of toddlers or younger, *do* allow them to splash in Medano Creek instead of plodding up what feels like mountains of quicksand. If you insist, *don't* walk farther than the small hills at the base, where families tend to congregate. You'll get plenty of sightseeing there with fewer objections from the kiddos, plus the dunes are less steep. Keep in mind, sand is much less

Walking toward Medano Creek, which sits seasonally at the base of the Great Sand Dunes. Photo by the author.

forgiving than snow, and sledding or boarding them can be quite dangerous. If your children are game, *do* allow them to attempt boarding or sledding the dunes with products designed specifically for the task (which also require special wax). *Don't* bring traditional snow sleds such as plastic saucers, which won't work. We rented a two-person sled and boards in town at Kristi Mountain Sports, 3223 Main St., 719.589.9759, www.kristimountainsports.com.

Do wear socks/shoes, at the very least. At its peak, the sand can reach 150 degrees, and I cannot emphasize enough how uncomfortable it feels in your shoes. (It's better to hike in early morning or evening.) I would also suggest wearing a cloth face covering to protect against inevitable wind gusts and sledding/boarding spills. (Did I mention how much dirt will end up on your body?) *Don't* forget sunscreen!

Certified in 2019 as an International Dark Sky Park, camping here is especially popular. Here are some options:

The Great Sand Dunes Oasis, located just outside the park, includes 90 RV/tent sites, showers, a restaurant, laundry, a store, cabins, and even traditional lodge rooms ($). Gear rentals offered, including sleds, boards, and mountain bikes. 7800 Hwy 150 N., Mosca, 719.378.2222, www.greatdunes.com.

Zapata Falls Campground is a primitive, BLM-managed campground located 11 miles south of the park's visitor center (9,000 feet in elevation). Includes 24 sites (one group), vault toilets, no potable water. First-come, first-served. Open year-round. The North Fork South Zapata Trail (#868), set just above the campground in the day-use area, leads to a mildly steep, 0.5-mile hike to the campground's namesake, Zapata Falls, a 25-foot waterfall sheltered in a rocky crevasse. 719.852.7074.

Sledding or boarding the dunes requires products designed specifically for the task. Prepare to get very dirty. Photo by Michael Mundt.

Located 19 miles west of the visitor center in Mosca, the *Rustic Rook Resort* offers glamping in furnished canvas tents, as well as Wi-Fi, a dog park, hot breakfast, on-site dining, night-sky viewing programs, and more. 13254 Lane 5 N., 719.270.1356, www.rusticrookresort.com.

UFO Watchtower

Set 23 miles north of Alamosa, this unique site opened in 2000 as a joke, when owner Judy Messoline gave up cattle ranching. Having heard neighbors' stories of unusual sightings in the San Luis Valley, she capitalized on her prime location, opening a campground and building the 10-foot watch tower. Be sure to walk through the "healing garden," where visitors have left "pieces of their energies" (aka "trinkets"). The year-round campsite offers primitive sites on the valley floor, set adjacent to the tower and store. No reservations required. CO-17, Center, 719.378.2296 or 805.886.6959, www.ufowatchtower.com.

The UFO Watchtower near Alamosa is one of the quirkiest impromptu stops in Colorado. Photo by Michael Mundt.

Creede

Miles from Denver: 259

Incorporated in 1892, this was the last silver boom town in Colorado in the 19th century. Mining remained the town's main economy until 1985, when the last producing mine closed. Today it draws tourists with its mining history, 1890s storefronts, beautiful scenery, and plenty of year-round recreation. www.creede.com.

Lodging

The Antlers Rio Grande Lodge and Riverside Restaurant, set on 70 acres, offers RV sites, cabins, and rooms ($) in the 1800s-era lodge. Includes a game room, a hot tub on the river, laundry facilities, fly-fishing on the Rio Grande, a private stocked fishing pond, and farm animals. Opens mid-May, 26222 Hwy 149, 719.658.2423, www.antlerslodge.com.

Other Highlights

Creede boasts the largest fork in the United States, measuring 40 feet long and more than 600 pounds, located at the Cascada Bar and Grill and Cabins (offers 6 cabins that sleep up to 6). Open late May–early Sept. 981 La Garita St. (Hwy 149), 719.658.1033, www.cascadagrill.com.

It's also home to the world's only underground firehouse, Creede's actual fire station. Tours available by request. 1201 N. Main St., 719.658.2211.

The town's Silver Ice Park offers two

skating ponds, a warming hut, a skate shack complete with equipment free for public use, and lights for nighttime skating (Dec.–Feb., weather permitting). 904 S. Main St.

Started in 2017 to honor the town's 125th birthday, the Creede Donkey Dash takes place the second Saturday in June, featuring a 10-mile burro race that begins and ends on Main St.

The Underground Mining Museum features a museum and community center that are both completely underground. One of Creede's most popular attractions, it comprises a series of rooms and tunnels blasted into the cliff face of Willow Creek Canyon, offering visitors a taste of the miner's experience. Open Tues.–Sat., 10 a.m.–3 p.m. Guided tours are only available during the summer. Reservations required at least one day ahead. 503 Forest Service Rd., #9, 719.658.0811, www.undergroundmining museum.com.

A focused Creede Donkey Dash participant with his furry running partner. Courtesy Western Pack Burro Ass-ociation, Michael Mewes.

Wheeler Geologic Area

Located about 8 miles east of Creede, this eroded outcropping of volcanic-ash layers is the result of eruptions from the La Garita Caldera some 25 million years ago. Nicknamed "City of Gnomes" for its unique rock structures, it was designated as Colorado's first national monument in 1908.

The area is tough to access, though, requiring a full day to reach via an 8-mile hike or mountain-bike ride along East Bellows Creek Trail (#790), or a 14-mile 4x4

Fast Fact: Creede is one of seven communities in this area named in Colorado Tourism's best spots for stargazing. Sharing characteristics of high elevation and low humidity, the other communities include Lake City, Crestone, Great Sand Dunes, Cuchara, La Veta, and Colorado's first certified International Dark Sky Communities, Westcliffe and Silver Cliff. (Ridgway received the designation in 2020.)

---

track requiring a jeep/ATV (after which visitors must still walk about 1 mile to the site). The main access is via Pool Table Road, roughly a 10-mile, windy dirt road that will take about 30 minutes to drive, depending on road conditions. The road ends at Hanson's Mill, an area featuring restroom facilities and primitive campsites, where you'll park. Dispersed camping is allowed around but not in the geologic area. The best season is June through September. Call or check the Forest Service website for conditions and availability ahead of time because there is no cell service outside of town (719.852.5941). To get to Pool Table Road from Creede, drive east on E. 7th St. toward La Garita St. for 269 feet. Turn right at the first cross street onto CO-149 South and follow for 7.3 miles. Turn left onto Pool Table Road, FR600.

Del Norte

Miles from Denver: 218

Set along the Continental Divide, this former Old Spanish Trail stagestop and mining town established in 1892 is named for the Rio Grande del Norte or "large river of the north." Pronounced "Del NORT" (instead of the Spanish pronunciation, "NOR-tay"), it's located near several attractions, including Wolf Creek Ski Area (35 miles) in Pagosa Springs and the Great Sand Dunes (47 miles). www.delnorte colorado.com.

Lodging

The Mellow Moon Lodge is an "eco-chic" boutique property that opened in 2019. Centered on outdoor enthusiasts, it includes an on-site bike shop and is located just minutes from the Del Norte trail system. Dog- and family-friendly, the property offers 15 rooms, including a family suite featuring beds for six, a kitchenette, even kids' toys and books. Guests can also fly-fish on the 2 miles of private Gold Medal waters located at the Rio Grande Club and Resort and can golf on the property's 18-hole course (in South Fork, 0285 Rio Grande Club Trail, www.riograndeclubandresort.com). 1160 Grand Ave., 719.207.0747, www.mellowmoonlodge.com.

Other Highlights

The Rio Grande County Museum Cultural Center features exhibits on Native American rock art, horno baking, fur trappers, Hispanic settlers, and more. Open Tues.–Fri., 10 a.m.–4 p.m., Sat., 10 a.m.–3 p.m., 580 Oak St., 719.657.2847.

Del Norte offers the accessible 200-acre Lookout Mountain Park Trails System, named for the 8,475-foot promontory on the south edge of town. Offering almost 8 miles of natural-surface, single-track

Colorado's Official Sport: Pack-Burro Racing

A nod to 19th-century miners who used donkeys or "burros" (Spanish) to carry tools and supplies as they prospected for gold, silver, and other valuable ores, the sport of pack-burro racing was designated Colorado's official "Summer Heritage Sport" in 2012. It allegedly developed in the 19th century, when two miners found gold in the same location and raced each other back to town to stake their claim, leading their burdened animals by rope as they ran.

Modern pack-burro races offer strict rules: You cannot ride the burro and must lead it via a rope up to 15 feet long. The animals carry a pack saddle holding 33 pounds of traditional mining gear that must include a pick, gold pan, and shovel. Other gear can be hauled—clothing, water, food—not to exceed 33 pounds. Cruelty to the burro is prohibited.

The race season takes place late May through September in eight Colorado towns that also host burro-themed events and festivals: Georgetown, Idaho Springs, Creede, Victor, and Frederick, as well as three "Triple Crown" races in Fairplay, Leadville, and Buena Vista. Distances vary, from as short as 5 miles up to Fairplay's 29-mile race, which includes a summit of Mosquito Pass (13,185 feet). www.packburroracing.com.

trails for hikers, runners, bicyclists, and equestrians, the challenging 1-mile trail to the summit gains 600 feet in elevation, ending in breathtaking views of the valley.

Explore a section of the Old Spanish National Historic Trail—a trade route used from 1829 to 1848 between Santa Fe and Los Angeles that traversed parts of Colorado, Utah, Arizona, and Nevada—just 6.5 miles east of town on Hwy 160 (roughly equidistant from Monte Vista). The parking area at the trailhead includes a monument and interpretive marker dedicated to the trail. From the memorial, travel about 0.8 miles to the south on the dirt road and take the first open road to the east; travel 0.4 miles through a small ravine toward the wagon tracks and interpretive panel.

Penitente Canyon

This BLM Special Recreation Management Area was named after the 19th-century Penitente Brotherhood, which used the canyon as a place of worship and created its unique, artistic feature: a pictograph of the Virgin of Guadalupe painted high on a cliff. Offering some 300 rock-climbing routes (some south-facing ones can be climbed year-round), the area also has roughly 20 miles of foot, horse, and bike trails, including a 1.5-mile hiking-only loop along Penitente Canyon Trailhead to views of the pictograph and 1800s wagon-wheel ruts.

Penitente Canyon Campground offers 15 RV/tent sites, 2 group sites, and vault toilets. Potable water available at the well house about 0.7 miles east of Penitente near CR 38A, May–Oct. (Bring water because the well isn't always functional.) Includes a picnic shelter, an interpretive kiosk, and toilets in the canyon's day-use area. There are also three primitive sites around Witches Canyon Trailhead. Pack in, pack out. 719.852.7074. To get there from Del Norte, travel northeast on Hwy 112 to CR 38A. Turn north and stay on road for about 8 miles until spotting signs for the canyon.

Near Penitente is La Garita Arch, a natural, high rock arch surrounded by unique volcanic rock structures (also called La Ventana or the Natural Arch). From Penitente travel south on County Road 38A 3.5 miles, turning west at County Road A32 (aka FS Road 660). The sign there says Old Woman's Creek/Natural Arch; travel A32 about 4 miles. Turn north on FS Road 659; the terminus of 659 is the trailhead to the arch, a very steep, approximately 0.1-mile climb. The road can be rough—summer is the best season—so a high-clearance vehicle is recommended. It's possible to park near the base of the arch to view it.

Monte Vista

Miles from Denver: 217

Set near the center of the San Luis Valley between several 14ers in the Sangre de Cristo Range to the east and 13ers in the San Juan Mountains to the west, it's clear why this town's name means "mountain view." Set at the junction of Hwy 160 and Hwy 285, the town was incorporated in 1886. Offering a downtown that's a National Historic District, filled with plenty of shopping and dining, the town invites visitors to "Experience the Full Monte." www.monte vistachamber.org.

Other Highlights

In July, the town hosts the state's oldest pro rodeo, the Ski-Hi Stampede, a Wild West experience that has taken place since 1919. 2389-2499 Sherman Ave. (Ski Hi Stadium), 719.852.2055, www.skihistampede.com.

Set along the Colorado Birding Trail, the Home Lake State Wildlife Area is also a great fishing hole. To get there from town, head 1.5 miles east on Sherman Ave.

Monte Vista National Wildlife Refuge (NWR)

Established in 1952, the NWR provides a safe place wildlife and migratory birds dependent on wetland habitat. (The refuge is one of three managed under the umbrella of the San Luis Valley NWR Complex, along with Alamosa and Baca NWRs.) Home to more than 200 several species of birds, including the American avocet, cinnamon teal, and white-faced ibis, it's most famous for the more than 23,000 sandhill cranes that stop in the valley to feed and rest during their spring and fall migrations. Best viewing is from early March through November, when water is available to flood the wetlands. Walk, bike, or drive along the 3.5-mile Wildlife Drive, walk the Meadowlark Nature Trail, or view wildlife from several pullouts along Hwy 15 and County Road 8S. Open one hour before sunrise to one hour after sunset. The Monte Vista Crane Festival takes place in early March (since 1983), offering tours, photography workshops, and more (www.mvcranefest.org). NWR address is 6120 Hwy 15. But staff are located at the Alamosa NWR Headquarters Office, 7824 El Rancho Ln., Alamosa, 719.589.4021, www.fws.gov/refuge/monte_vista.

Saguache County

Miles from Denver: 207

Encompassing rich mining history and traces of the Old Spanish Trail, these high-desert lands are home to robust agricultural and ranching communities. Offering access to rushing rivers and the Sangre de Cristo and San Juan Mountains, nearly half of the land is designated as wilderness or backcountry. www.saguachetourism.com.

Other Highlights

The town of Crestone is a prominent spiritual center that features a Zen center and a Hindu temple, a few Tibetan Buddhist centers and more. It was designated as an International Dark Sky Community in May 2021. www.townofcrestone.colorado.gov

In the ranching community of Moffat, stay overnight at Joyful Journey Hot Springs Spa in a hotel room ($), yurt, or tepee (or RV/tent site). Offers three natural hot-springs pools (98–108 degrees), fitness classes, and spa services (28640 CR 58 EE, 719.256.4328, www.joyfuljourneyhotsprings.com). Or head to the town's Valley View Hot Springs, a nature sanctuary featuring six ponds, a hot tub, and a swimming pool (93–107 degrees), plus RV/tent campsites (some reservable), rooms, and trails. Kids are welcome, but the all-ages pools are clothing-optional. Owned and operated by the nonprofit Orient Land Trust, here visitation is managed via quota. Reservations recommended (64393 CR GG, 719.256.4315, www.olt.org/vvhs).

Once a trading post on the Old Spanish Trail that flourished as a supply center for the surrounding mining camp, the town of Saguache (pronounced "su-WATCH") is considered the northern gateway to the San Luis Valley. Visit the Saguache County Museum, comprising seven rooms with history about Ute Native American chief Ouray and wife Chipeta, railroad mogul Otto Mears, Spanish settlers, and more (405 8th St [US Hwy 285], 719.655.2557). Stay 1 mile south of the town at the Saguache Camp and Lodge, which offers 6 rooms (sleep 2–6) (21495 US Hwy 285, 719.850.2473, www.saguachelodging.com).

South Fork

Miles from Denver: 234

Set at the confluence of the South Fork and Rio Grande Rivers at the eastern edge of the San Juan Mountains, this was the summer home of the Ute tribe for centuries until settlers established farms and ranches in the 1800s. Incorporated in 1992 as South Fork, one of Colorado's youngest towns, its location near Gold Medal waters on the Rio Grande River, the San Juan and Rio Grande national forests, Wolf Creek Ski Area, and Colorado's largest wilderness area, the Weminuche Wilderness, make South Fork a prime recreation destination. www.southfork.org.

Lodging

The Lazy Bear Cabins offers 9 2-bedroom cabins (sleep up to 6) and 1 1-bedroom (sleeps up to 4), all with full kitchens and a bathroom. 29257 US-160, 719.873.l443, www.lazybearcabins.com.

The Blue Spruce Lodge offers a comfortable stay in basic rooms, luxurious suites, or rustic cabins. 29431 US Hwy 160, 719.480.1858, www.sprucelodges.com.

Or stay in the Rio Grande National Forest at the Alder Guard Station (1910), located 2 miles north of town along Alder Creek. Includes bathroom and full kitchen, electricity, hot water, furnishings, utensils, and woodstove (the only heat). Five single beds and a futon. Must bring linens or sleeping bags. Maximum five nights. Pack

Fast Fact: Located near the Continental Divide (approximately 17 miles west, at the top of Wolf Creek Pass), South Fork was Colorado's first designated Continental Divide Trail Gateway Community (in 2015), which welcomes travelers along the 3,100-mile route between Canada and Mexico.

in, pack out. From South Fork, head northwest 1 mile on State Hwy 149 until crossing the Rio Grande. Turn right on CR 15, then travel east slightly more than 1 mile until the Forest Road 610 sign. Turn left and go north 2 miles to the guard station. Park behind it at the trailhead. 719.657.3321 or 719.852.5941 (Mon.–Fri. only).

Tour Operator

Mountain Sports is a one-stop-shop retailer for gear rentals and adventures such as fly-fishing with South Fork Anglers and Rio Grande Angler (Creede) and rafting with Mountain Man Rafting (owned by 8200 Mountain Sports). Open Sun.–Thurs., 7:30 a.m.–5:30 p.m., Fri. and Sat. until 6 p.m., 30923 W. Hwy 160, 719.873.1977, www.8200mountainsports.com.

Beaver Creek Reservoir

Featuring 114 acres of water in the Rio Grande National Forest, Beaver Creek Reservoir is one of 80 lakes and reservoirs in the area. It features a boat ramp (motors allowed but no wakes) and plenty of opportunities to fish for rainbow and brown trout. From town, travel 1 mile west on US Hwy 160. Turn left and go south on Forest Road 20 (Beaver Creek Road). Travel Forest Road 20 for 6 miles to the upper end of Beaver Creek Reservoir; the ramp and parking are on the west side of the road. Continue another 13 miles to Poage Lake, where a 0.25-mile hike gets you to the scenic lake.

Spanish Peaks Country

Miles from Denver: 205

Geologically distinct from the Sangre de Cristo Mountains to the west, these are a pair of prominent points known to the Comanche tribe as *Wahatoya*, or "the twins" (or "the brothers" or "the sisters"). Comprising Walsenburg and La Veta (plus unincorporated Cuchara and Gardner), the area is rich in Native American and Hispanic culture, as well as significant mining history. www.spanishpeakscountry.com.

There's an annual star party each June, the Rocky Mountain Star Stare, on 35 acres called "Starry Meadows" near Gardner. (La Veta and Cuchara also host events.) Set between the Sangre de Cristo and Wet mountain ranges (7,612 feet), the illuminating event attracts more than 350 amateur and professional astronomers, family, and friends. Food vendors, tent/RV camping available ($). www.rmss.org.

Highway of Legends Historic and Scenic Byway

An easy segue from I-25, I drove the 82 miles north from Trinidad to Walsenburg (about two hours), meandering along Hwy 12 past mining towns, geologic highlights, and the San Isabel National Forest. Favorite highlights include Cokedale's coke ovens, once used for smelting coal; Monument Lake and its Monument Lake Resort, with a 20-room lodge, 13 cabins, and RV/tent campsites and other amenities (4789 CO-12, Weston, CO 81091, 719.868.2226, www.monumentlakeresort.com); and

Stonewall's literal "stone wall" called the Dakota Sandstone Formation. Free audio tour here: www.spanishpeakscountry.com /highway-of-legends-audio-tour.

Lathrop State Park

Established in 1962 as Colorado's first state park, this spot set among the pinyons and junipers on the prairie (3 miles west of Walsenburg) offers panoramic views of Spanish Peaks. There are two bodies of water: Martin Lake, offering a swimming beach and fishing for trout, walleyes, and bluegills, and Horseshoe Lake, crystal clear and wakeless, also filled with fish such as largemouth bass and rainbow trout. The only state park in Colorado featuring a nine-hole golf course, it also offers an archery practice range, a miniature-golf course, and 13 geocache sites. Provides primitive and electrical campsites, toilets, showers, laundry facilities, and potable water. The Hogback Nature Loop Trail (1.3 miles) is popular for all skill levels. 70 CR 502, 719.738.2376.

Mission: Wolf

Set in the Sangre de Cristo Mountains, this peaceful sanctuary for captive wolves and wolf-dog crosses is worth the long drive. Housing roughly 40 animals, the property is also an example of sustainable living, with solar-powered electricity and hot water, organic greenhouses, buildings made from recycled materials, and vehicles powered by vegetable oil. 13388 CR 634, Westcliffe, 719.859.2157, www.missionwolf.org.

Mountain View Sanctuary

The first two rescue animals at this animal sanctuary in Walsenburg were goats Jake and Elwood, and there are now more than 40 "residents" including goats, donkeys, and reptiles. Open 8 a.m.–10 p.m., 719.470. 0449, www.mountainviewsanctuary.org.

The Highway of Legends Historic and Scenic Byway along Hwy 12 from Trinidad to Walsenburg (or reverse) features several stops, including the former mining camp of Cokedale and its coke ovens that were used for smelting coal. Photo by the author.

Located roughly 12 miles northwest of Trinidad, the Ludlow Massacre site features a memorial honoring the men, women, and children who died in the conflict over miners' working conditions. Photo by the author.

Parker-Fitzgerald Cuchara Mountain Park

Opened in the early 1980s as a ski resort, Panadero Resort closed in 2000, leaving 50 acres at the base open for recreational opportunities in the San Isabel National Forest. Activities include an 18-hole disc golf course, human-powered skiing and snowshoeing—even a full-moon celebration, the "Howl and Growl" event—and sledding and hiking on old ski trails. The former ski rental office has also been transformed into a day lodge that's open to visitors on select weekends and holidays (can be booked for special events). 946 Panadero Ave., www.thecucharamountainpark.org.

PIONEERING PLAINS

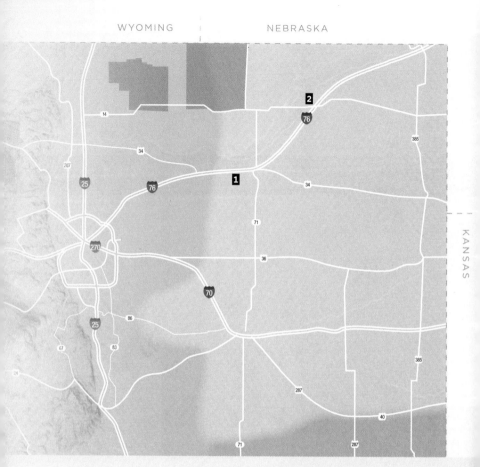

KANSAS

PIONEERING PLAINS

1 Fort Morgan

2 Sterling

Fort Morgan

Miles from Denver: 82

Established in the 1860s as a US military defensive post against attacks by Native Americans who were defending against encroachment on their lands, it was named in 1866 after the commanding officer, Christopher Morgan. An agricultural hub set on the high plains northeast of Denver, it's especially proud of its most famous Fort Morgan High School graduate (1921): big-band musician Glenn Miller, whom the town celebrates each June at SwingFest, featuring swing-dance lessons and performances. www.morgancountytourism.com.

Other Highlights

Offering beautiful views of the South Platte River, the 11-arch Rainbow Bridge (completed in 1923) is one of the last few bridges of its kind, earning its place on the National Register of Historic Places. See it from Riverside Park (1600 Main St.), which also features trails, a disc-golf course, and picnic shelters.

The town's Bobstock Music Festival is a free, three-day event in July that features regional bands and headliners such as Loverboy and Young MC. City Park, 414 Main St., www.bobstockmusicfestival.com.

Jackson Lake State Park

This "oasis on the plains" just 22 miles northwest of Fort Morgan attracts migrating birds such as long-billed curlews and whooping cranes. It's also a great spot for boaters, jet- and water-skiers, and anglers fishing for walleye, perch, and rainbow trout (and ice fishing). There's an OHV track (1.5 mile, on south side of park), two

Visitors to this region can expert dazzling night skies like this (in Peetz), far away from city light pollution. Photo by Elizabeth Fehringer of Elizabeth Jane Photography.

geocaching sites, and a swimming beach. The lake's west side offers a boat ramp and marina, and its designation as an International Dark Sky Park means prime night-sky viewing. Includes roughly 250 RV/tent campsites (many year-round), showers, toilets, laundry, and potable water. Reservation only. The visitor center is open daily, 8 a.m.–4 p.m. A 1.75-mile trail begins there and runs north to Northview Campground. 26363 CR 3, Orchard, 970.645.2551.

Sterling

Miles from Denver: 128

Home of Native American tribes including the Arapaho, Cheyenne, and Pawnee, it also features the South Platte Section of the Overland Trail. A branch called the "super-highway" of the high plains, here thousands of prospectors crossed en route to gold and silver mines in California (and later, Colorado). Established in 1881 with the arrival of the Union Pacific railroad, the town incorporated as Sterling in 1884 still uses Union Pacific and Burlington Northern railroads to service primary industries, largely agriculture. www.exploresterling.com.

Lodging

Located off of I-76, Buffalo Hills RV Park offers more than 50 RV/tent sites, as well as restrooms, showers, and laundry. 22018 US Hwy 6, 970.522.2233, www.buffalohills rvparks.com.

Other Highlights

Located in a replica of an old fort house, the Overland Trail Museum features a 14-building village including a 1910 barn housing a two-headed calf. Kids will also love panning for "gold." Open Mon.–Sat., 9 a.m.–5 p.m., summer; Tues.–Sat., 10 a.m.–4

p.m., winter. 110 Overland Trail, 970.522.3895. Across the road is the Overland Trail Recreation Area, featuring a fishing pond and multiuse trails.

Area Highlights

In the town of Limon, situated roughly 91 miles southeast of Denver, the Limon Heritage Museum and Railroad Park exhibits include a prairie living room and kitchen, Plains Indians tepee, and more. 701 1st St., 719.740.0782, www.limonmuseum.com.

The city is also home to the Limon Wetlands, providing a "refueling station" for migrating birds such as the yellow-headed blackbird and green-winged teal. Reach them via the Doug Kissel Fishing Ponds—located just south of Main St.—on a 0.5-mile trail to an interpretive kiosk and gazebo overlooking the wetlands.

The small town of Wray boasts the Wray Museum, featuring an extensive Paleo-Indian (minimum 5000 BC) exhibit that's one of the only permanent Smithsonian exhibits outside of Washington, DC. Open Tues.–Sat., noon–4 p.m., 205 E. 3rd St., 970.332.5063.

If you're planning to visit the area, Our Journey are the Central Plains experts on area museums, National and State Register sites, golf courses, swimming pools, and more. www.ourjourney.info.

Jumbo State Wildlife Area

Located on the Jumbo State Wildlife Area 37 miles northeast of Sterling (in Julesburg), Jumbo Reservoir is a popular warm-water fishing spot for crappie, bluegill, and more. (Fishing is possible year-round.) In warmer months, roughly mid-April through September, the reservoir is open to boaters 30 minutes before sunrise to 30 minutes after sunset. (Off-season, any use of nonmotorized boats must be hand-launched, such as kayak or canoe.)

The author's uncle Tom Fehringer during a sunset fishing outing at North Sterling State Park.
Photo by Elizabeth Fehringer of Elizabeth Jane Photography.

Camping regulations may change. Contact the Brush field office for more information, 970.842.6300. CR 95.

North Sterling State Park

The 3,000-acre North Sterling Reservoir offers sailing, jet skiing, waterskiing, and views of expansive bluffs and prairie. In addition to warmwater fishing, from walleye to bluegill, it also features the Cottonwood Cove Swim Beach and the 3.5-mile South Shoreline Trail for hikers, bikers, and horseback riders. There's a boat ramp and marina offering water-sports rentals, plus an archery range. The park also features 141 RV/tent campsites in 3 campgrounds, each with a picnic table, shade shelter, and fire ring; they include restrooms, coin-operated showers, and laundry facilities (April–Oct.). 24005 CR 330, 970.522.3657; marina, 970.466.2279.

Prewitt State Wildlife Area

Located in Merino just 13 miles from Sterling, Prewitt Reservoir is a warmwater fishing destination for saugeye, crappie, and more. Nonwake boating is permitted; sailing and windsurfing are allowed in July and August. There are no established campgrounds, but dispersed camping is permitted around the property year-round. No amenities except trash cans. Hwy 6, Merino. 970.842.6300.

CANYONS AND PLAINS

CANYONS AND PLAINS

Comanche National Grassland

Miles from Denver: 254

Comprising more than 440,000 rural acres of prairie grasslands and intricate canyons, this area is one of the state's best-kept secrets. Split into two sections—the Timpas Unit in La Junta (about 187,000 acres) and the Carrizo Unit in Springfield (more than 257,000 acres, near the Oklahoma border)—Comanche National Grassland (CNG) offers plenty of trails for hiking, biking, and horseback riding (no guided tours for the latter). Offering a bounty of archaeological highlights, its biggest bragging right is the dinosaur tracks in Picket Wire Canyonlands, the largest site in North America. It's also a popular birding destination, serving as home to more than 250 species including the lesser prairie chicken (*very* rare), red-tailed hawk, and golden eagle. And let's not forget the tarantulas! (See "Tarantulas" entry.)

Timpas Unit

The following two sites are part of the Timpas Unit, 1420 E. 3rd St., La Junta, 719.384.2181.

PICKET WIRE CANYONLANDS

It's rumored that 16th-century Spanish soldiers died without receiving last rites in this region while seeking lost treasure, essentially banning them to Purgatory, earning the river the Spanish name "El Rio de Las Animas Perdidas en Purgatorio" (River of Lost Souls in Purgatory). French fur trappers referred to the area as "Purgatoire" (pronounced pur-gah-TWAR), which settlers eventually corrupted to "Picket Wire." Today the river and its canyon are called by both names: Purgatoire and Picket Wire. Open via Withers Canyon Trailhead, the area is perfect for hiking, mountain biking, and horseback riding. Hike anywhere from

1 mile to 17 miles past ruins of the Dolores Mission and Cemetery, Native American rock art, the 19th-century Rourke cattle ranch, and the pièce de résistance: the Purgatoire River track site, with more than 2,000 tracks from apatosarus and allosaurus imprinted in the river valley 150 million years ago. Motorized access is not permitted except for full-day, guided auto tours, 8 a.m.–4 p.m. on Saturdays in May, June, Sept., and Oct. Visitors must provide their own four-wheel-drive, high-clearance vehicle. Tours begin at the La Junta Forest Service office, 719.384.2181. Reservations at www.recreation.gov or call 877.444.6777.

Hikes from Withers Canyon Trailhead (roundtrip): Withers Loop Trail, 1 mile; Purgatoire River, 2 miles; Hispanic Cemetery, 7.8 miles; Track Site, 11.2 miles, with difficult hike on rugged terrain (2 vault toilets); Rourke Ranch, 17 miles. This area is also a popular area for spotting tarantulas during mating season. (See "Tarantulas" entry.)

Primitive campsites, all with vault toilets, are available at Withers Canyon Trailhead (4 sites), Picket Wire Corrals (3 miles from trailhead), Timpas Picnic Area (1 group site), and Vogel Canyon (parking area only).

VOGEL CANYON

Featuring sandstone canyons carved by a tributary of the Purgatoire River, Native Americans lived here for thousands of years, evidenced by their rock-shelter remnants and rock art (dating back 300–800 years). The Barlow and Sanderson Stage line also traversed the area in the 1870s, leaving ruins of Santa Fe Trail stage stations, homesteads, and corrals. There are also two permanent springs at the bottom of the canyon, supporting wildlife such as jackrabbits, coyotes, and pronghorn. Includes four hiking trails (roundtrip): Overlook Trail to an overlook, wheelchair-accessible, 1 mile; Canyon Trail to see ruins, overlook, spring, rock art, 1.75 miles;

Mesa Trail to see ruins, 2.25 miles: and Prairie Trail, to see stage tracks, 3 miles.

Carrizo Unit

The following two sites are part of the Carrizo Unit, 27204 Hwy 287, Springfield, 719.523.6591.

CARRIZO CANYON

Ideal in spring and fall for bird-watching species such as the black-chinned hummingbird and greater roadrunner, pecked-style animals (petroglyphs) adorn the canyon walls, and there's a 0.5-mile loop trail (and a 300-foot wheelchair-accessible trail). There are three picnic shelters and a vault toilet, and it's a good fishing hole for channel catfish. Primitive camping is allowed in the grassy spots around the picnic area.

PICTURE CANYON

Just north of the Oklahoma border, there are both petroglyphs and pictographs, as well as evidence of ancient rock shelters. Hiking along Arch Rock Trail is a 4-mile loop, offering three picnic sites and one vault toilet. Primitive camping is allowed around picnic areas. Its most unique feature is Crack Cave, containing prehistoric drawings that are illuminated by sunlight for about 10 minutes at sunrise during the spring and autumn equinoxes. It's sealed except for those seasons and can only be visited on a guided tour with Canyon Journeys. Overnight backpacking trips available. 719.643.5414, www.canyon-journeys.com.

La Junta

Miles from Denver: 176

Located along the Arkansas River at the northern edge of Comanche National Grassland's Timpas Unit, the former grounds for the Arapaho and Cheyenne became one of the most important stopping

spots for travelers, trappers, and explorers along the Santa Fe Trail. As the railroad began replacing the trail farther west, La Junta became a construction camp for the Santa Fe Railroad. By 1879, it became the headquarters for the Santa Fe Railroad's Colorado Division, becoming in 1881 La Junta, Spanish for "the junction" or "meeting place." Today this farming and ranching town is a great stop for experiencing Old West history and the beauty of the grasslands. www.visitlajunta.net.

Other Highlights

The Koshare Museum, located on the Otero Junior College campus, houses Native American art and artifacts considered to be among the finest in the world. Built in 1949 with the efforts of a Boy Scout group, the museum also has an attached kiva with a roof spanning 60 feet across created with logs weighing over 40 tons, the largest self-supported log roof in the world. Open daily, noon–5 p.m., 115 W. 18th St., 719.384.4411, www.koshares.com.

About 20 miles northeast of La Junta lies Las Animas and the Boggsville Historic Site, the first nonfortified settlement in southeast Colorado. Located near the confluence of the Arkansas and Purgatoire Rivers about 2 miles south of town, the site includes reconstructed homes with period furnishings. The town also celebrates its heritage each year the last Friday of April with Santa Fe Trail Days. Open Tues.–Sat., 11 a.m.–3 p.m., 28120 Hwy 101, 719.456.1358, www.bentcountyheritage.org/boggsville.

Bent's Old Fort National Historic Site

Set roughly 8 miles northeast of La Junta along the Santa Fe Trail, this "Castle of the Plains" where the buffalo-fur trade was pioneered is one of the best historic destinations I've visited in Colorado. Once an important commercial, social, military, and cultural destination for Native Americans, Mexicans, and Americans along the United States–Mexico border (demarcated by the Arkansas River), it remained a pivotal trade point for 16 years until it was destroyed in 1849. (Bent built his "new" fort near Lamar in 1853. Located on private property without an official address, it's marked well with signs, about 1.5 miles south of US Hwy 50. www.thegreathighprairie.com/bents-new-fort.) Reconstructed in 1976 in time for the country's bicentennial, the adobe structure resembles the original, along with living historians setting the scene. A 0.25-mile trail runs from the parking lot to the fort; Bent's Old Fort National Historic Site Trail follows along the river through cottonwood trees, about 1.5 miles. Open daily 9 a.m–4 p.m., 35110 Hwy 194, 719.383.5010, www.nps.gov/beol/index.htm.

Lamar

Miles from Denver: 207

Situated along in the lower Arkansas Valley area called Big Timbers, this area was a source of water for nomadic tribes that followed bison herds across the plains, and home for centuries to the Plains Apache and Comanche. The town's location along the banks of the river also drew settlers traveling the Santa Fe Trail (parallel to US Hwy 50), the trade route linking New Mexico and Missouri, crossing Colorado in the southeast. In 1907, the arrival of the Atchison, Topeka, and Santa Fe Railway drew homesteaders. Today, it's a great family destination with spots like the Willow Creek Park, offering a skate park and frisbee golf course, as well as the Lamar Loop, a 6.2-mile trail around the city for running, biking, or walking. www.thegreathighprairie.com.

Living historians help re-create the fort's sights, sounds, and smells at Bent's Old Fort National Historic Site near La Junta. Photo by the author.

The Amache Museum in Granada, just three minutes from the former camp, features several belongings donated by survivors. Photo by the author.

One of Colorado's largest birding festivals takes place in Lamar each February during the High Plains Snow Goose Festival, when the birds descend on southeastern Colorado during their migration to winter roosts. Includes programs, seminars, and tours to birding spots such as Two Buttes Reservoir, 36 miles south of Lamar, and Picture Canyon and Carrizo Canyon, both in Comanche National Grassland. (See "Comanche National Grassland" entry.)

Lodging

I stayed at the Sundance–High Plains RV Park and Cabins, set at the southern tip of Lamar off Hwy 287. There are several lodging options: 22 RV sites; 2 tent sites; 7 rooms or "cabins" decorated in various themes such as "Fisherman" with standard amenities; and a primitive cabin with queen, twin, and full (pullout) beds. Property includes laundry, showers, and restrooms. What truly sets the property apart, though, are owners Derek Mudd and Richard Taylor, who are happy to share their expertise with guests. 29151 US Hwy 287, 719.336.1031, www.sundance-highplains.com.

Fast Fact: The town boasts "the oldest building in the world," a service station built by W. G. Brown in the 1930s out of petrified wood (circa 175 million years ago), which he pilfered from Emick Ranch (about 20 miles south of Lamar). No longer used as a gas station, the building at 501 N. Main St. remains a quirky roadside attraction.

Camp Amache

Also called the Granada Relocation Center, this National Historic Landmark is located about 2 miles west of Granada, a small farming community 17 miles east of Lamar. Set along the historic Santa Fe Trail near the Colorado-Kansas border, it's one of 10 sites where the US government imprisoned more than 120,000 Japanese Americans during World War II following the December 1941 bombing of Pearl Harbor.

Although it was demolished after the war, several building foundations remain, as well as reproductions of a barracks, rec hall, and watchtower. (Free audio driving tour at www.amache.org.) Open daily, 8 a.m.–7:30 p.m. The Amache Preservation Society—established in 1993 by John Hopper, history teacher and dean of students at Granada High School—maintains the site and provides free, private guided tours. Contact the school directly: 719.734.5492. The Amache Museum in Granada is also worth a stop (109 E. Goff Ave.). CR 23 5/10, www.nps.gov/places/granada-relocation-center.htm.

John Martin Reservoir State Park

Located in the small town of Hasty (21 miles west of Lamar), this is southeastern Colorado's largest body of water. A major site along the Colorado Birding

A reproduction of a watchtower at Camp Amache, a former WWII Japanese-American internment camp located near Lamar. Photo by the author.

Trail—a network of 54 trails throughout the state where there is plenty of watchable wildlife—nearly 400 species of birds have been documented here. Anglers can also catch fish from the shore, and there are plenty of boating, waterskiing, and windsport opportunities. In winter, there's also camping, ice fishing, and ice-skating. There are two boat ramps and two campsites, Lake Hasty and The Point Campground, with more than 200 sites. The popular Red Shin Trail is a 4.5-mile loop featuring Native American carvings, historic canals, and more. 30703 CR 24, Hasty, 719.829.1801.

Sand Creek Massacre National Historic Site

Located roughly 37 miles northeast of Lamar (near Eads), this sacred site was once a camp along Sand Creek where more than 200 Cheyenne and Arapaho people were killed by US soldiers. On the morning of November 29, 1864, despite ongoing peace talks between the tribes and the US government, nearly 700 volunteer soldiers led by Colonel John Chivington slaughtered the tribespeople, primarily women, children, and the elderly. When I visited, I was worried my phone navigation was misleading me along dirt roads, since there was very little signage. (It's better marked from the east entrance off CO Hwy 96.) But I arrived at the ranger station and visitor center, a 0.5-mile walk to Memorial Hill, offering a view of a distinct thicket of cottonwood trees surrounded by farmland behind which the massacre took place. (Visitors aren't allowed to the site; cars can drive to the memorial.) A 1.5-mile hiking trail starts near the memorial site (4 miles roundtrip from the ranger station).

To be clear, it's a somber place to visit—akin to how I felt at the 9/11 Memorial in New York—so be prepared to answer kids' tough questions about our country's

Fast Fact: The Sand Creek Massacre site hosts an annual Spiritual Healing Run-Walk, a 173-mile relay run from the site to Denver, representing the route used by soldiers returning to Denver after the massacre.

treatment of Native Americans. Open Thurs.–Mon., 9 a.m.–4 p.m., Mar. 1–Oct. 31; Mon.–Fri., Nov. 1–Feb. 28., 1301 Maine St., Eads, 719.438.5916, www.nps.gov/sand.

Trinidad

Miles from Denver: 195

Considered the cultural, social, and economic capital of southeastern Colorado, Trinidad is centrally located between Santa Fe, New Mexico, and Denver (roughly 190 miles to each). Colorado's southernmost stop on the Santa Fe Trail before heading over Raton Pass into New Mexico, the town's culture blends the history of Native American tribes, settlers, and coal miners. With access to outdoor areas and a charming Victorian downtown featuring red-brick paved streets, Trinidad is a fantastic headquarters for exploring Southern Colorado. It's also home to Colorado's newest state park (2020), Fishers Peak State Park, featuring the iconic flat-topped mountain overlooking the town. (Open sunrise to sunset with limited access during development.) www.visittrinidadcolorado.com.

Other Highlights

The Louden-Henritze Archeology Museum features a dinosaur-track exhibit and artifacts from the nearby Trinchera Cave, where prehistoric humans lived for thousands of years. Free, open Mon.–Thurs., 10 a.m.–3 p.m., Trinidad State Junior College, 600 Prospect St., 719.846.5508, www.trinidadstate.edu.

Charming downtown Trinidad combines Victorian history with modern artistic touches, including murals like this one. Photo by the author.

Fast Fact: The town was known for five decades as the Sex Change Capital of the World thanks to Dr. Stanley Biber, who pioneered sex-reassignment surgery there from 1969 through 2003, when he handed over the business to OB/GYN surgeon Dr. Marci Bowers. She relocated to California in 2010.

The Trinidad Trolley offers free, 45-minute tours daily. Running Memorial Day–Labor Day, they depart from the Colorado Welcome Center hourly: Mon.–Thurs., 10 a.m.–4 p.m., Fri. and Sat., 10 a.m.–6 p.m., Sun., noon–5 p.m., 309 Nevada Ave., 719.846.9512.

About 12 miles northwest of Trinidad lies the site of the Ludlow Massacre, the result of a labor uprising when Colorado Fuel and Iron (CFI) coal miners began protesting dangerous working conditions. Throughout the strike, coal miners and their families lived in makeshift tent colonies like the one here. On April 20, 1914, the Colorado National Guard and CFI guards attacked it, killing 25 people, including 11 children. The site features a monument, photos, and storyboards. CR 44.

Trinidad Lake State Park

Perched around 6,300 feet in the foothills of the Sangre de Cristo Mountains, this scenic lake offers a semidesert climate for year-round recreation. In addition to water sports such as jet skiing and waterskiing, sailing and boating, the lake offers anglers

opportunities to catch fish including rainbow and brown trout, walleye, and crappie. There's even a six-lane archery range on-site. (The Highway of Legends Historic and Scenic Byway, State Hwy 12, passes the north side of the park.) There are two campgrounds:

Carpios Ridge Campground offers 63 RV/tent sites, plus laundry, showers, and flush toilets. Four trails are accessible from here (roundtrip): Carpios Cove, 1 mile; Park View Trail, 1.2 miles, wheelchair-accessible, featuring an amphitheater, a functional horno (adobe oven), and a Native American archaeology site; Levsa Canyon Trail, 1-mile loop; and Reilly Canyon Trail, 0.5 miles on Levsa Trail, 9 miles total, to the historic town of Cokedale.

The South Shore Campground features 10 sites with water and one vault toilet. There are two accessible trailheads (roundtrip): South Shore, 5 miles; and Long's Canyon Trail, 1.25 miles, which leads to Long's Canyon Watchable Wildlife Area, traversing riparian and woodland habitats (wildlife-viewing blinds, 0.75-mile roundtrip). The hike's most unique feature is the view of the K-T Boundary, a thin layer of quartz and iridium that was deposited from an asteroid (possibly killing 75 percent of life including dinosaurs), considered one of the country's best examples (0.25 mile roundtrip). There's also Sunset Point, 2 miles, accessed via South Shore Park Entrance, wheelchair-accessible, with picnic area and overlook. (You can also pick up the Long's Canyon Trail from here.)

A visit to Emick Ranch during tarantula mating season with Greg Emick, who stands by dinosaur tracks located on his land. Photo by the author.

Tarantulas

The only critter to get its own entry, these tarantulas known as the Texas or Oklahoma browns are the primary reason I visited southeastern Colorado in mid-September, during mating season. The males emerge from their burrows for a "walkabout" in search of a mate—roughly late August to mid-September—so they're easier to spot (especially just before sunset). Mislabeled a "migration," fall is a great time to visit tarantula hotspots such as the Lamar, Springfield (47 miles south of Lamar), and Comanche National Grassland areas. (See "Comanche National Grassland" entry.) I was lucky to see them at Emick Ranch (about 20 miles south of Lamar), owned by the family for more than 100 years, on a private tour with owner Greg Emick. I also saw dinosaur tracks, leaf fossils, tepee circles, and restored homesteads. Call Greg directly for details, 719.691.5955.

The scenic Trinidad Lake State Park offers a semi-desert climate, making it a good option for year-round recreation. Photo by the author.

Glossary

BLM. An agency within the United States Department of the Interior, the Bureau of Land Management administers federal lands for a variety of uses such as energy development, livestock grazing, recreation, and timber.

Certified Creative District. Hubs of economic activity that enhance an area's appeal to live and travel, attracting artists and creative entrepreneurs. Colorado's 26 Certified Creative Districts (including my hometown, Longmont) are a huge tourism draw.

Continental Divide. The boundary that separates a continent's rivers systems into a distinct body of water, it separates water flowing into the Atlantic Ocean and Pacific Ocean. Since it's part of Colorado's mountains, it's mentioned often throughout this book, offering some of the state's most stunning wilderness.

Gold Medal waters. Defined by the Colorado Wildlife Commission as waters that produce a minimum of 60 pounds and 14 inches of trout per acre, these are basically the most coveted fishing waters for anglers. Of more than 9,000 miles of trout streams in Colorado, only 168 miles are designated as Gold Medal.

Mountain pass. A navigable route through a mountain range or over a ridge, typically a saddle point between two higher areas, they tend to offer significant recreation areas and amazing mountain vistas. If they remain open during winter months, passes can often be difficult, even dangerous, to drive.

OHV. Off-highway vehicles such as motorcycles, dirt bikes, three-wheelers, ATVs, and dune buggies, they must be registered with Colorado Parks and Wildlife to operate on the state's public lands or trails. Many recreation areas listed throughout offer OHV areas.

SUP. Stand-up paddleboards or the act of using them, SUPing.

UNESCO. Short for the United Nations Educational, Scientific, and Cultural Organization, it identifies cultural and natural properties worldwide of "outstanding universal value."

Via ferrata. Literally "iron path" in Italian, it's a protected climbing route built into the side of a cliff using wires, rungs, steps, and special equipment, allowing climbers to remain safely connected to the mountainside. From Royal Gorge to Estes Park and Telluride, they're a great way for climbers (and nonclimbers, like myself) to experience jaw-dropping mountain scenery.

Index

Page numbers in *italic* text indicate maps.

About the Author

Heather Mundt was born and raised in Colorado. She received her master's in journalism from the University of Colorado at Boulder in 2002, and she has contributed as a freelance writer and editor for several publications, including *Outdoor Families Magazine*, *TripSavvy*, *Smarter Travel*, *The Denver Post*, 5280.com, *TravelAge West / Family Getaways*, *Colorado Parent* magazine, and Colorado Ski Country USA. She lives in the same city where she was raised, Longmont, with her husband, Michael, two sons, Brody and Colin, and two huskies, Tasha and Boris. Her family-travel stories appear on her personal site, www.momfari.com. *Colorado Family Outdoor Adventure* is her first book.

A photo of the author's family at St. Vrain State Park, near their Longmont home. (L to R): Brody, Tasha, author, Michael, Boris, and Colin. Photo by Elizabeth Fehringer of Elizabeth Jane Photography.

SOUTHWEST ADVENTURE SERIES
Ashley M. Biggers, Series Editor

The Southwest Adventure Series provides practical how-to guidebooks for readers seeking authentic outdoor and cultural excursions that highlight the unique landscapes of the American Southwest. Books in the series feature the best ecotourism adventures, world-class outdoor recreation sites, back-road points of interest, and culturally significant archaeological sites, as well as lead readers to the best sustainable accommodations and farm-to-table restaurants in Arizona, Colorado, Nevada, New Mexico, Utah, and Southern California.

Also available in the Southwest Adventure Series:

New Mexico Family Outdoor Adventure: An All-Ages Guide to Hiking, Camping, and Getting Outside by Christina M. Selby

South Mountain Park and Preserve: A Guide to the Trails, Plants, and Animals in Phoenix's Most Popular City Park by Andrew Lenartz

New Mexico Food Trails: A Road Tripper's Guide to Hot Chile, Cold Brews, and Classic Dishes from the Land of Enchantment by Carolyn Graham

Arizona's Scenic Roads and Hikes: Unforgettable Journeys in the Grand Canyon State by Roger Naylor

Arizona State Parks: A Guide to Amazing Places in the Grand Canyon State by Roger Naylor

Eco-Travel New Mexico: 86 Natural Destinations, Green Hotels, and Sustainable Adventures by Ashley M. Biggers

Skiing New Mexico: A Guide to Snow Sports in the Land of Enchantment by Daniel Gibson